BRITAIN'S SECRET WAR
Tartan Terrorism and the
Anglo-American State

BRITAIN'S SECRET WAR is the extraordinary inside story of 'tartan terrorism' in the 1970s and 1980s.

Since 1968 there have been approximately seventy-nine bombing incidents, forty 'political' bank raids and numerous hoaxes and bomb scares. Letter-bombs have exploded in the offices of senior Conservative Ministers and one group has claimed that Mrs Thatcher only narrowly escaped assassination. Judges at eighteen trials involving 1,095 witnesses have handed out sentences to fifty-two Scottish terrorists, a total of 286 years in jail. The cost to the State in terms of damage has been several million pounds. The cost of police and Special Branch activities is incalculable. The terror trials have created new records in Scottish legal history: the longest trial (1976), the longest jail sentence for a non-capital offence (1972) and the most intensive security operation ever seen at a Scottish High Court (1980).

Scotland's crucial role as 'an aircraft carrier' for NATO and the USA ensures intensive scrutiny of her internal political situation by the CIA and Britain's secret police. In BRITAIN'S SECRET WAR the authors examine the counter-insurgency methods used in Scotland. Thorough investigation into the mysterious death of nationalist Willie McRae also suggests some startling conclusions.

BRITAIN'S SECRET WAR makes compulsive, if at times disturbing, reading for anyone interested in the political future of the United Kingdom.

BRITAIN'S SECRET WAR

TARTAN TERRORISM and the ANGLO-AMERICAN STATE

Andrew Murray Scott
and Iain Macleay

MAINSTREAM
PUBLISHING

For Donald Fraser Sutherland

Copyright © Iain Macleay Sutherland and
Andrew Murray Scott, 1990

First published in Great Britain 1990 by

MAINSTREAM PUBLISHING COMPANY
(EDINBURGH) LTD
7 Albany Street
Edinburgh EH1 3UG

ISBN 1 85158 306 8

British Library Cataloguing in Publication Data
Macleay, Iain
   Britain's secret war : tartan terrorism and the Anglo-
   American state.
   1. Great Britain. Terrorism
   I. Title II. Scott, Andrew Murray
   322-420-941

   ISBN 1-85158-306-8

Typeset by Selectmove Ltd, London
Printed in Great Britain by Martins of Berwick

CONTENTS

ACKNOWLEDGMENTS

The main source of information for this book was the vast archive of newspaper cuttings on the incidents and the various court trials, and we must express our gratitude to the journalists and editors of many newspapers including *The Scotsman*, *Glasgow Herald*, *Daily Record*, *Sunday Mail*, *Evening Times*, *Scottish Daily Express*, *Guardian*, *Observer*, *The Times*, *West Highland Free Press*, *Dumfries and Galloway Standard*, *Oban Times*, the *Morning Star* and the former *Scottish Daily News*.

We must also thank the staffs of the Scottish Information Office, the Registrar-General's Office and MORI for supplying statistical information and the US Consul General to Scotland, Donald Holm, and US Embassy Press Officer, Donald Howger, for setting aside time to discuss some of the themes of the book. Over a considerable period of time we have conducted a large number of interviews and must acknowledge assistance from: Gordon Airs, Donald Anderson, Donnie Blair, Adam Busby, Duncan Campbell, David Coutts, Andrew Currie, David Dinsmore, Rob Edwards, Peter Findlay, Lorraine Mann, Dorothy Messer, Shona McKinnon, Fin McLean, William McRae, Professor Derrick Pounder, Ed

Robertson, Arthur Rogerson, George Rosie, Michael Strathern, Tim Tate, Gerry Whyte, Professor Paul Wilkinson, Gordon Wilson; and many others (including some who preferred not to be named) who have assisted us with material for this book.

PREFACE

"Tartan Terrorism" or "War of Liberation"?

EDINBURGH, the majestic capital city of Scotland, becomes in August and September the centre of the cultural world. Incomers from many continents flood in to enjoy three weeks of the world-famous Festival. The highlight of every Festival is the Military Tattoo held on the Esplanade beneath the Castle ramparts. And the highlight of the Tattoo, the epicentre of the Festival's activities, has come to be symbolised by the lone figure of a bagpiper, silhouetted at midnight on the battlements of the Castle, playing a lament. Cameras click, a galaxy of flashlights twinkle, TV cameras film the event on simultaneous live broadcast, nationwide, worldwide. There is a swelling of pride among the kilted military men. Scotland's role in the forging of the British Empire is proudly on display.

On 30 August 1971, the assembled press men had a different story to report to their incredulous editors. A massive bomb had exploded in the Castle and caused serious damage. The blast, heard

9

all over the city and as far away as Portobello and Liberton, had occurred 25 minutes before the piper was due to appear. Speculation suggested that it had exploded prematurely. Had it not done so the television audience would have been horrified by the spectacle of the certain death of the piper and others.

Two bombs, one large, one small, had exploded simultaneously in the Castle lavatories. They had destroyed the lavatories, a tea-room, a ticket office, damaged relics in nearby State apartments and display rooms and had hurled debris into the crowd of dignitaries and tourists who sat in the rows of raised seating on the Esplanade. The crowd was watching a motor-cycle display and, luckily, the noise of the engines partially masked the sound of the blast. There was no panic among the audience, who cheered the arrival of several fire engines. "If it had not been for the inherent strength of the building, there could have been a massacre . . ." stated Lieutenant-Colonel Runacres, Assistant Provost-Marshall (Scotland). As it was, three persons in the audience sustained injury and three members of the Castle staff were in a state of severe shock. The devices had ripped through a two-foot solid stone vault and two feet of concrete floor, pulverising both. Only 40 feet away, Scotland's "Honours Three" – Crown, Sceptre and Orb – survived undamaged.

Within half an hour, all roads from Edinburgh were sealed off. Most of the city centre was cordoned off. There was a full security alert. Army bomb-disposal men conducted an intensive search of the Castle. The police cordon was to remain in force for seven full days. Meanwhile, speculation mounted as to who had planted the bombs and why.

Next day there was a second incident. A tape-recorded message was received at 8.30 in the morning at the offices of a telephone-answering service in Cumbernauld, claiming that a bomb had been planted in Cumbernauld town centre, timed to explode at twelve noon. Full-scale emergency procedures were instituted by the police and many of the local population were evacuated. Traffic was diverted out of the town centre. After an intensive search of a wide central area of the town, nothing suspicious was found.

In Dundee there was a third incident. Hurried evacuation of showrooms of the North of Scotland Hydro-Electric Board and the Gas Board took place, supervised by police after another anonymous warning was received. It too proved to be a hoax.

Government buildings such as St Andrew's House, seat of the Government's administration in Scotland, all Council Offices, Stirling Castle, Army barracks and local government buildings around the country were put under special security measures. Military police operated "stop and search" procedures at a number of locations. To some, Scotland was under armed guard.

No one has ever been charged with planting the Edinburgh Castle bomb. But this was just the very beginning of the continuing phenomenon known by some as "tartan terrorism", by others as Scotland's "War of Liberation". This book examines this continuing phenomenon and concludes that the number of bomb outrages, explosions, hoaxes, "politically motivated" bank raids and acts of industrial sabotage does amount to a war. It is, however, a clandestine war, fought between political extremists from the remote fringes of the nationalist and republican movements and the assorted forces of the police, Special Branch and the various agencies of the "Anglo-American Security and Intelligence Services".

The book is as much about the methods used by the shadowy forces of the British State as those, sometimes successful, sometimes ludicrously inept, methods of the "tartan terrorist" groups. Infiltration, use of *agents provocateurs* and "supergrasses", "black" propaganda, deliberate suppression of information, the spreading of misinformation, coupled with the freedom of action to detain without trial which the Prevention of Terrorism Act has given to the police have all been extensively used in Scotland. However, the State has not merely been reacting to terrorist incidents. There is considerable evidence that the State has acted systematically in Scotland to undermine even perfectly legal political parties, particularly the Scottish National Party.

Some Scottish nationalists regard "tartan terrorism" as a creature virtually summoned up by the State to discredit political nationalism and the peace movement. To others, the terrorists are simply cranks. But, cranks or not, the sheer scale and number of their activities have cost the State dearly and indicate a phenomenon that is unlikely to disappear overnight.

So who are the "tartan terrorists" and what do they hope to achieve? The phenomenon began in 1968 – at the very height of the SNP's first "surge" when the Scottish National Party took the largest share of the vote at the municipal elections in Scotland in May and most commentators were forecasting a clear majority for the SNP at the next general election – leading to Independence from England. With a very large membership of approximately 130,000, the party's apparently sudden rise amazed and alarmed the British Government. Nothing, it seemed, could turn the SNP tide. At its triumphant June Conference, the party endorsed a defence policy opposed to NATO "in its present form". A Scottish Government would not permit foreign nuclear bases on Scottish soil.

But the "Anglo-American Defence Community" and NATO Chiefs of Staffs believed that an SNP victory would destabilise the West's defences. Scotland is the "aircraft carrier" for NATO, of crucial strategic significance for the defence of millions. Then, too, Special Branch and MI5 operate under a remit to protect the British State, which the SNP were committed to breaking up. There was a head-on conflict of interests . . . should a few hundred thousand Scots be allowed to put the stability of the British Establishment and the safety of the NATO Western Alliance in jeopardy? Undoubtedly, secret decisions were taken to help to prevent this. It is a matter of public record that this has been done elsewhere in Europe by the very same agencies, acting with what they perceived to be the best interests of the West at heart. The particular danger of the nationalist movement to the Western Alliance was that, unlike the Wilson Government, to whom they could easily gain access (and did!) to pressurise the Government, on, for example, Polaris, the nationalists were a vast and inchoate force, whose focus and centre was too diffuse to control and divert easily. It proved impossible to simply influence a few leaders to gain control because the movement had sprung up too suddenly and had little actual hierarchy or structure; all the power was at the grass-roots and the leaders were perhaps only nominally in charge in any real sense.

But within the party there was discord. A tiny, but vocal minority, members of the ultra-nationalist 1320 Club, began to plan a military force for the day when, they believed, Westminster would refuse the Scots' demands for Independence after an SNP election victory. This group became known as the "Army of the Provisional Government", founded by the mysterious Major F. A. C. Boothby, a central figure of "tartan terrorism". Boothby, who was an ex-British Intelligence Officer, actually had links with nearly all of the other individuals who went on to become involved in armed "political" bank raids on behalf of the "Workers' Party of Scotland" or who blew up electricity pylons and oil pipelines for the "Tartan Army" and the "Border Clan". Boothby is now widely believed to have been an *agent provocateur* whose remit was to destabilise and discredit the SNP with the image of violent cranks.

There were also unsuccessful attempts to re-establish the "Scottish Republican Army" but numerous other groups did emerge, such as the "Army For Freeing Scotland", the "Scottish Citizens' Army of the Republic", the "Scottish Civilian Army" and the "Army of the Scottish People" – some of which achieved striking success. In the 1980s, when the SNP was at a low ebb, "Siol Nan Gaidheal" was founded, a mass-membership "direct action" group, some of whose supporters became involved in a "military wing" – "Arm Nan Gaidheal" – and others with the "Scottish National Liberation Army", the most successful and persistent group, who have perpetrated over 50 attacks and have been in existence for ten years. One of the SNLA terrorists, David Dinsmore, is a fugitive from Interpol and his links with Scottish solicitor Willie McRae may provide a clue to the mysterious death in 1985 of McRae – regarded by many Scots as a murder by the agents of the British State.

It cannot be argued, however, that all of the terrorist groups were cranks or inspired by *agents provocateurs* for the phenomenon is a baffling and complex one. In part, of course, it arises from a deep feeling of political frustration and powerlessness.

Britain's Secret War chronicles the events and personalities involved and gives an insight into the clandestine world of the "tartan terrorist" and his equally shadowy opponent in the secret police.

1   A STRATEGIC OBJECTIVE

Scotland is where the action is. Those who will do the work are here, or are arriving. Those who will make the decisions are here, or have their representatives on hand. It is towards Scotland that the forces that will determine the outcome are converging. The stakes are high, and the responsibility heavy.

US Consul to Scotland, Mr Richard Funkhauser, 1976

SCOTLAND, one of the oldest nations in Europe, has very little control over her own destiny. Factories, even entire industries, can shut down overnight with the Scots – even when united in protest – virtually helpless to do anything about it. This powerless state of affairs is endemic but it has not come about by accident. When a handful of corrupt aristocrats sold Scotland to England in 1707 or before, they gave away the right of her people to make decisions for the future. The Scots are an institutional minority at Westminster and their powerlessness is simply a normal feature of the system itself. International capitalism has compounded the problem. Who owns Scotland now? It is difficult to tell. But not the Scots themselves – that is for sure.

Scottish political history since 1707 has largely been the story of the Scots' attempts – often thwarted – to attain unity and some measure of self-control over their destiny. In 1707 there were riots in the streets in many Scots towns against the Act of Union, and the three Jacobite Risings of 1689, 1715 and 1745 pandered at least in part to nationalist sentiment. There was a rather inept armed rebellion in 1820, defeated partly because of infiltration by government agents and the Land Raids on Skye in the 1880s achieved little. Twenty-two Home Rule Bills have been raised on the floor of the House of Commons since 1893 and two million adult Scots signed the Scottish Covenant Association's self-government petition in 1950. The modern vehicle for Scotland's national aspirations is the Scottish National Party. There was a great upsurge in nationalist feeling in the 1960s which propelled the SNP to a position in 1968 where they looked capable of securing a majority of the Scottish seats to win Independence. It is in 1968 that the events of this book begin.

The SNP's official policy on the mechanism for achieving a transition from a British to a Scottish government was quite clear. An SNP Policy Statement in 1967 outlined party strategy:

When a majority of the Scottish Parliamentary seats (*at that time 36 out of 71 as a minimum*) is held by SNP MPs, they will ask the UK Parliament to set up a Scottish Legislature with full control over all the affairs of Scotland. Failing such agreement in London, the SNP MPs and any other Scottish MPs who care to join them will form a Provisional Scottish Government loyal to the Crown. The first Provisional Government will submit a Constitution to the Scottish people for approval and a General Election will be held promptly.

This policy of withdrawing from Westminster, which remains in force today, originated from the example of Sinn Fein in Ireland. In the General Election of 1918, 73 out of the 105 Irish parliamentary seats were won by Sinn Fein candidates. These 73 MPs refused to take their seats in the House of Commons and met instead in Dublin a month after the election to convene the Dail Eireann as an independent Constituent Assembly of the Irish nation. The English resisted the legitimacy of the Irish Parliament and their

16

attempts to suppress it led to the war of Irish Independence. Like Sinn Fein in Ireland, the SNP were and are committed to set up a rival centre of power to the existing British State. The existence of a Scottish Parliament in Edinburgh would challenge the cherished sovereignty of the Westminster Parliament over the whole of the United Kingdom. Advocates of the supremacy of the British Parliament would not be able to tolerate a system of sharing power with a Scottish Parliament. Sooner or later a showdown would occur and if the Irish example were followed an attempt would be made to suppress the Scottish Parliament – or bring it under Westminster's authority. At this point, Scots who wished to defend their Parliament would have the choice of surrendering their nation-state's aspirations – either directly or by some staging post of "further discussion on constitutional structures" or some weak and unworkable form of devolution – or resisting outright British interference.

Worried about the dangers of such a showdown scaring away potential SNP voters, the leaders of the SNP played down the significance of this scenario. Perhaps rather naïvely, given the sheer volume of documentary information available on the experiences of previous colonial peoples who have struggled against the British Empire, the SNP leadership did their best to foster the notion of peaceful negotiation. Some constitutional settlement would be effected, they felt, long before any possibility of violence. Privately, SNP leaders like Arthur Donaldson were not so sure. Donaldson, Party Chairman, confessed that "in other nationalist movements throughout history the violent element did not become important until there was unreasonable obstruction from the government concerned". In public, however, the SNP chose to ignore the possibilities of such obstruction.

The sudden upsurge in SNP support was parallelled by the rise of the "peace" movement, whose main vehicle was the Campaign for Nuclear Disarmament. CND was highly popular in Scotland where there were close links with the SNP and considerable overlapping of membership. The SNP declared at its June 1968 Conference that an independent Scotland could not remain a member of NATO "in its present form", and would demand the removal of all foreign military bases from Scotland. Earlier, in 1960, the campaign against the siting of submarine-launched Polaris nuclear missiles at the Holy Loch gained considerable popular support in Scotland. Protestors from the Kilmun Peace Camp blockaded the USS *Proteus* and attempted to board a nuclear submarine. An anti-nuclear frogman scratched his initials on the hull of a depot ship and large demonstrations took place. The campaign was a serious irritation to the American overseas forces. Many Scots town councils joined the protests and popular opinion was galvanised. A bill was raised in Parliament to "ban" Polaris and such was the extent of the protests that the USA did actually consider the unthinkable – pulling out of Scotland.

The Scots had not been consulted on the question of Polaris coming to the Holy Loch. This was an advantage to the Americans because the other European countries which they had asked had refused to have Polaris on their soil! In its powerless state, Scotland was ideal and ideally situated for siting the US and NATO nuclear frontier forces and the Americans committed themselves to staying. Since then, Scotland has become the iron fortress or the "aircraft carrier" for NATO – of crucial strategic significance for the Western Alliance – although all the military strategies reveal the expendable nature of the country and her entire population. For Scotland is a premier target – Holy Loch is the overall number one target in the UK – and only 60 days' use at the maximum is expected from Scotland in the event of nuclear war. Although the Scots continue to express their opposition to nuclear weapons in all opinion polls (the most recent opinion poll, by MORI, on 26–28 February 1990, showed that only 36 per cent of Scots supported an independent British nuclear capability, while 59 per cent were against) their protests have subsided into futility. Few now even question the US presence, the number of installations and personnel involved (18 installations with approximately 3,000 US personnel) or what precisely these personnel do. Even major leaks of radioactive material have gone largely unreported and there have been at least two serious riots by US personnel at Dunoon, including a race riot aboard USS *Hunley*, a nuclear warhead-carrying submarine. The Americans have an interest in keeping Scotland's political situation stable and in keeping their own enormous presence – described by some as "an invasion" – low-key. In these aims they have a willing ally in the British State.

In 1974, a secret treaty linked the CIA and the British SIS (Security Intelligence Services) in a "special relationship", the closeness of which was "a core element" in the military partnership

18

between Britain and the USA. Before that date, of course, the agencies had been almost as close. Duncan Campbell has shown that "British security and intelligence services have been ready to participate alongside the CIA in political operations within the UK". However, there is scope within Scotland for other agencies; DIA (Defence Intelligence Agency), the NRO (US Airforce National Reconnaissance Office) and even the FBI. Add to this sinister alphabet soup the UK agencies: SIS, which includes MI5 (now called DI5) and MI6 (now, similarly, DI6) which is mainly involved outwith the UK. The "Special Branch" utilise the resources of the CID and even the uniformed police and are based regionally in police stations. There is a special police force attached to the United Kingdom Atomic Energy Authority to guard all UK nuclear installations. This force was 682 strong in 1973 and its units are empowered to carry machine-guns and arrest on suspicion. Under the AEA (Special Constables Act) 1976, their remit includes a 15-mile radius of AEA property (including storage depots and convoys in transit). This "constitutionally-unique armed force" was described by one lawyer as "conflicting with all our traditions of civilian and politically accountable policy". Then there is the MOD Police (15,000 strong in 1976) and Commanchio, a 100-strong section of marines with specialist anti-terrorist training based at the Condor base near Arbroath, whose remit includes defence of oil installations and Faslane and Coulport. Perhaps most alarming of all is the presence, at Machrihanish, of one of the only two units of the US Naval Special Warfare Units (the other is in the Phillipines). These units, which deal in clandestine and unconventional warfare, train for covert infiltration and demolition by air, sea or submarine in the Highlands around the Mull of Kintyre. Some part of their training must take place within "enemy" territory – in urban areas – and it is almost certain that these highly trained personnel are on exercise throughout Scotland undertaking training missions, posing perhaps as civilians or tourists. The Army's expert marksmen, Section D11 and the Technical Support Branch, are on standby to deal with terrorist incidents and the Army's Bomb Disposal Squad collaborates with the police. These army units are more like a "military wing" of the police and mostly work in a civilian context.

Then there are the private, or mercenary, organisations. Most of these are small – some are one-man outfits – and they generally involve ex-service personnel. Some, such as Argen Security Services, whose office is near Smith Square, London (although no address is listed anywhere), operate in theatres of war around the world, and others only take on specific tasks within the UK. Zeus Security Consultants, for example, "provide security services of all kinds to Government and other authorities", according to the former military intelligence officer, Peter Hamilton, who is the director. Most are only known to the security and intelligence communities that hire them and remain highly secretive. The use of such operators by the Nuclear Industry during the Sizewell B Inquiry in 1983 was revealed when it was discovered they had been hired to investigate the background of protestors, infiltrate the anti-nuclear movement and harass, beat-up and threaten protestors and those giving evidence against BNFL. In the battle against NIREX at Fulbeck in Lincolnshire in 1986 there was further violence, intimidation, theft and burglary against protestors. There are considerable benefits in using private operators for those who hire them, not least since links can rarely be traced back to the official organisation which has done the hiring. If there is any trouble, the operators can be dismissed as liars, lunatics or fanatics (which, of course, many of them are!).

Nigel West's *A Matter of Trust* examines in detail the work of MI6 between 1945 and 1972. Between 1945 and 1969 Britain was involved in no fewer than 53 small wars – all but two of these counter-revolutionary-type operations. Major-General Frank Kitson's *Low Intensity Operations* published in 1971 was ostensibly a manual for army use overseas but another aim of the book was to provide an outline of the Army's role in suppressing and dealing with internal dissent within Britain, and some of its theories were tested in Ireland and in Scotland. "The Army has acquired a sophisticated and probably unrivalled expertise in coping with the problems of terrorism in a Western democratic society," according to Professor Paul Wilkinson of the Department of International Relations at St Andrews' University. He attributes this to their "extremely high standard of specialist training".

The mysterious case of Colin Wallace, an army Press Officer who apparently fell foul of MI5 and claimed to be "framed" for murder, and the "Stalker Affair" – "an honourable man [who] asked the wrong sort of questions" – show up Britain's security services in a bad light. "One might have more sympathy with the intelligence services if their underhand methods were shown to get results," wrote Richard Ingrams in the *Observer* in May 1989. The testimony of ex-MI5 officer Cathy Massiter, the Starrit Report into the activities of the Special Branch following the death of paid informer Kenneth Lennon in 1974, the affair of Kenneth Littlejohn, a bank robber recruited by MI6 to work in Ireland, and the drugs prosecution trial of Howard Marks, a one-time MI6 agent, have all provided valuable insights into the *modus operandi* of the British secret police. Of course, such revelations are likely to be the last. The new Official Secrets Act which came into force in 1989 makes it an offence for any member *or former member* of the security services to reveal *anything at all* about the services – *ever!* The question of what is or is not a secret, or what is to be kept secret in the national interest will no longer arise because *everything* is a secret. The press are rightly concerned at this infringement on the freedom of speech of the individual and the freedom of the press itself. The *Scotsman* newspaper has been the first to test the legitimacy of this draconian law in the context of the memoirs of Anthony Cavendish, a former MI6 officer.

Many books have been written about the CIA by ex-CIA operatives and the role of the CIA in most regions of the world is a matter of public record. The CIA deposed the Iranian Premier and installed the Shah in 1953. The CIA caused the General Strike in British Guyana which ousted the left-wing government. The CIA spent $10 million bribing politicians in Italy – a total of over $65 million spent there in 20 years – and has been increasingly active in Central and Southern America. In Africa and the Middle East too, the CIA and British SIS "appear to have worked on the principle that the right to have the government of their choice installed in other nations is an Anglo-American birthright". The Pike Report to a House of Representatives Select Committee in 1976 concluded that "whether such subsidies have been used directly to interfere in British elections must remain a matter of conjecture". Logic and common sense insists that they have, and are.

From their base on the third floor of the American Embassy in Grosvenor Square, London, CIA agents collate information and data on all known supporters of the peace and anti-nuclear movements, socialists, communists, nationalists, trade unionists and anyone whose views diverge in any way, or at any time, from unqualified, unthinking support of the US military interest.

Despite the closeness of the CIA and SIS, the CIA does not always share its information with its ally, or with NATO, for the CIA is the master in the partnership, with a huge payroll. SIS is useful to the CIA partly as a cover for the extent of its own operations in the UK and partly because of its superior network in Commonwealth countries. Both organisations operate to all intents and purposes as one, and it is hard to define where one begins and the other ends. This is a historical closeness, too, for SIS operatives were involved alongside the CIA in Vietnam – although the UK was never at war – and one even got a Silver Star for his services.

The sheer proliferation of these agencies within the UK has engendered a unique problem of endemic rivalry. Most have considerable autonomy and, quite apart from their almost complete freedom from any sort of accountability, do not always co-operate amicably and sometimes refuse point-blank to share their information.

Despite this, these agencies are well entrenched within Britain and have gathered considerable amounts of information on "subversives". In 1976, as reported in *The Times* on 19 May, a lecturer at Edinburgh University was approached about the personal background of a former student who was applying for a Civil Service post. The lecturer was told that the "areas of interest" which he was to report on included "communists, members of the SNP and homosexuals". Such were subversives. The establishment view of a subversive has shifted from Lord Denning's definition in 1963 of someone "who would contemplate the overthrow of the Government by unlawful means". In 1978, for example, the Labour Home Secretary, Merlyn Rees, admitted that the "Special Branch used its powers to collect information on people I think are causing a problem for the State". The Council of Europe found MI5 guilty of a breach of human rights in its monitoring of two leading members of the National Council of Civil Liberties, Patricia Hewitt and Harriet Harman, whom they had classified as "subversives". The case, ending in April 1990, is the first ever ruling against MI5 but during the proceedings it was noted that Britain had been in breach of the Human Rights Convention more than any other European State. From armed revolutionaries to those merely causing discomfort by their political views, the net has widened to include those who have never broken or contemplated breaking any laws whatsoever. It is clear that the emotive word "subversive" has included supporters of Scottish nationalism and even members of the SNP itself since at least the 1960s. But is the remit of the CIA and the SIS simply surveillance and intelligence-gathering – or do they involve themselves in "dirty tricks" and provocation amongst political movements? It is an area where there has been an almost sinister lack of investigative journalism. Few questions have been asked about the clandestine and entirely unaccountable activities of these agencies within Scotland and the subject is considered in more detail in Chapter 14. It is clear however that the activities of the "tartan terrorists" have provided a superb training ground for such intervention. The very public manifestation of "tartan terrorist" incidents has provided pretexts for a variety of "counter-insurgency" manoeuvres under the blanket of official secrecy and with the subsidiary aim of discrediting the SNP. Who can doubt that such intervention takes place and has had an effect on Scottish politics?

There have, of course, been public anti-terrorist activities conducted in Scotland by the State. Exercises by the Territorial Army in Scotland in the mid-1970s included scenarios for deployment against militant Scottish nationalists who had supposedly risen in armed rebellion and this was highly amusing to the many SNP supporters and members in the Territorial Army taking part in these exercises. A large exercise involving 45 Commando Group in a major NATO exercise in 1975 deployed men on oil rigs to train in preparation for regaining the rigs in the event of infiltration by terrorists amongst the oil rig crews, and led to the formation of the Commanchio section. In 1977, Royal Marines used pupils from "List D" schools in Helensburgh to stage a mock attack on the Faslane Submarine base and the teenagers were told to shout "English Go Home" and to sing *Flower of Scotland* in an attempt to make the action "more realistic". The Army School of Intelligence in Ashford, Kent, held courses with simulated exercises based on contingency plans for a nationalist uprising in Scotland. In 1978, large-scale police/military exercises were held at Edinburgh Airport with men from 22 SAS Regiment providing commando units inside the airport with other army units, including armoured columns, deployed on the perimeter. SAS exercises also occurred in Aberdeenshire, Glasgow and Perthshire and a week before the Devolution Referendum in February 1979 in Perthshire. Numerous military manuals have considered methods of dealing with civil unrest and nationalist disturbances. Major-General Kitson's counter-insurgency manual has led to the establishment of crack élite units in most of Scotland's main centres of population ready to deal with politically motivated disorder. 22 SAS Regiment – a specialist anti-terrorist squad – wear plain-clothes and use Range Rovers or Rover estate cars and are on three-minute standby.

The BBC Programme *War School* in January 1980 confirmed the British Army view that Scottish nationalists had been regarded as potential subversives since at least the early 1950s. This is borne out by the statistics that there has always been a higher per capita level of telephone-tapping and mail interception in Scotland than in England and Wales. On 31 December 1987, there were 27 phone-taps in operation in Scotland and a further 54 were granted over the course of 1988. Over the same period there were three mail interception warrants plus five granted over the year. While this represents a continued increase, it would, in the words of Lord Justice Lloyd, the Commissioner for Interception of Communications, be "prejudicial to national security to give a breakdown of these figures". The official figures do not, incredibly, include warrants issued to any of the SIS Agencies, including MI5, the MOD Police or the AEA Police. Furthermore, these "official" warrants may be "blanket" warrants in which one application is deemed to cover an entire organisation. "This is because the 'one particular person' who must be specified or described in the warrant may be one particular organisation or one particular association or combination of persons. Obviously, an organisation may cover more than one line . . .". Additionally, the Commissioner's "official" figures may only represent "new" applications; their effect may be cumulative even although the "*normal* duration of a warrant is two months".

There is the even more interesting concept of "non-statutory" warrants, referred to in the Commissioner's Report for 1982, which details much higher levels of phone-tapping. The increase was accounted for by "the need to replace all the outstanding non-statutory warrants when the new Act came into force". Clearly, it is necessary to view the official figures for interception of mail and phone-tapping with considerable scepticism.

Scottish police forces have been remarkably coy in revealing the strengths of their Special Branch complements and until recently personnel numbers were not included in annual reports by Chief Constables. Even now, Tayside Police merely list the duties of Special Branch and not the number of officers involved, which is probably about five. Lothian and Borders are, for some unknown reason, "unable to specify" the number of personnel within the Branch. In 1976 the force was 21 strong. In 1989 Grampian had eight officers, Dumfries and Galloway, one, Northern Counties, two, Fife, two, and Central, two. Strathclyde Special Branch is known to be second in size only to the Metropolitan Police Special Branch yet it is officially designated as "a small unit", which in 1978 was 61 of the Scottish total of 128. Now the figures are being withheld: "it is not policy of Strathclyde Police to furnish information on resource deployment". Thus the figures for Special Branch establishment in Scotland can only be assumed to be approximately the same as the 1978 total.

Many Special Branch officers undertake part of their training outwith Scotland despite the fact that the Scottish Detectives' Training Unit at Ayr offers both "initial" and "advanced" courses. What does this extra training involve – and why cannot it be provided in Scotland?

The secret police have access to vast amounts of information on the public from a range of sources, including, by a process known as "free text retrieval", from the computer banks of the Department of Social Security, the Inland Revenue and Department of Employment. Indeed, their files are listed by an individual's National Insurance number! Their own files are enormous. The MI5 computer in Blount Street, Mayfair, has 20 million records – two and a half times the size of the Police Network Computer, the equivalent storage value of 50,000 paperback books. The Special Branch computer, based at New Scotland Yard, contains 1.3 million files. The organisations find it an easy matter to acquire information on political activists and groups by monitoring all political publications, indexing names from petitions, names which have appeared in letters to the press and on membership lists. Attenders at meetings are noted and demonstrations are photographed as a matter of routine. Information is collected by a comprehensive and widely dispersed network of informants within the political groups themselves and throughout industry and tertiary education. Careers advisers at universities are a particular source from which the SIS obtains information both on potential

25

subversives and potential recruits to "The Ministry of Defence" – the acknowledged way of recruiting for MI5, MI6 and other such agencies. Universities are accorded special attention because of the large numbers of politically aware young persons who pass through them. They have long been regarded by the State as "the homes of revolutionary thought".

The network exists and does its work "beneath the threshold of public consciousness and concern". Conjecture based on specific incidents in Scotland and information from public sources outwith Scotland suggests that Scottish public opinion has been manipulated by a large-scale and low-key covert operation organised and financed by the American and British security and intelligence services. This operation has been subtle and finely tuned and the pattern is virtually imperceptible but operatives at all levels and considerable funds and resources have been directed to ensure that Scotland's political climate remains stable. It is within this scenario that "Britain's Secret War" between the "tartan terrorists" and the "secret police" has taken place.

2   ACTION FORCED UPON US

No one in his senses wants warfare but if we are determined to be absolutely independent, it may be and almost certainly will be forced upon us.

Hugh MacDiarmid, President of the 1320 Club, March 1968

THE year 1320 marks the date of the Declaration of Arbroath, a document sent to the Pope reaffirming Scotland's determination to remain independent from England whatever the cost. The declaration has the same significance in Scottish history as the Declaration of Independence to the people of the United States of America. The 1320 Club was set up in June 1967 by a group of prominent nationalists, including Oliver Brown, Dr Ian Taylor, Major Frederick A. C. Boothby, poet Hugh MacDiarmid and novelist Nigel Tranter, with the aim of re-establishing Scottish sovereign independence.

The Club held a press conference in December 1967, one month after Mrs Winifred Ewing's election victory in Hamilton, at which they introduced the first issue of a new political and cultural magazine, *Catalyst*, to the press. The magazine editorial asserted that the 1320 Club was not a political party and would leave the battle for electoral support to the SNP. The Club believed that within a few years Scotland would be independent and forward planning was required. Dr Ian Taylor, Vice-President of the Club, referred to research in depth over a very wide field "so that we may foresee problems and emergencies which are likely to occur along the road to freedom and during the vital months immediately following the event . . . and prepare solutions to meet these crises of the future". The Club set up investigative committees to deal with topics such as Foreign Affairs, the Constitution, Scotland's Natural Resources, and Defence. Several articles in *Catalyst* examined what was likely to happen in a transition period between the old British and a new Scottish state. The common assumption was that the English would not willingly allow the Scots to set up their own government despite a democratic mandate for the SNP at the polls. It was felt that delaying or blocking tactics would be used which could only be countered by immediate SNP action in withdrawing from the Union and unilaterally setting up a Parliament in Edinburgh. This solution was not new. It was in fact the Sinn Fein policy already held by the SNP. However, the 1320 Club rejected the SNP idea of a Scottish general election being called immediately after the Declaration of Independence. The Club instead advocated a period of at least six months of "Provisional Government", headed by a Scottish Cabinet and Council of the Realm which would take full responsibility for administering Scotland in the "interregnum". This dictatorial directorate was to be filled with hand-picked men and women of "vision, courage, ability and determination" who were "prepared if necessary to spend the next ten years in jail for doing what they steadfastly believed was right".

Since the 1320 Club believed that the British State would resort to the use of force, the first priority of the Council of the Realm was to be defence and the preservation of the Provisional Government of Scotland. At the first sign of repression by British troops, the Provisional Government might go "underground" as in Ireland and continue the struggle by means of civil disobedience or force if necessary. The poet Hugh MacDiarmid, President of the 1320 Club, felt that violence with England was inevitable. Speaking at a Club symposium at Glasgow University in March 1968, MacDiarmid is reported as saying that: "No one in his senses wanted warfare, but if we are determined to be absolutely independent, it may be and almost certainly will be forced upon us". MacDiarmid's motion at the meeting was seconded by Nicholas Fairbairn who is presently the Conservative MP for Perth and Kinross!

The 1320 organisation had the structure of a shadow cabinet. A prime ministerial figure existed in the form of a Co-ordinator of Committees. He presided over a "ministerial" team of conveners each of whom ran a committee with the function of conducting research into a particular subject. The internal business of the 1320 Club was administered by the usual office-bearers. Membership of the Club entailed a severe selection process. There were two kinds of members: associate members who were basically subscribers to *Catalyst* and an élite corps of one hundred full members who alone had the right to vote at Club meetings. Full membership was by invitation only and was extended to those persons who had rendered signal service to Scotland's struggle. The 1320 Club executive was solely responsible for choosing members and only they had access to the membership list which was kept strictly secret from the public and press.

The 1320 Club was obviously preparing to set up its own shadow Scottish Government whether or not Scotland actually voted for Independence. Such a Provisional Government had to have an army to protect it. Consequently, the Club created an Armed Forces Committee whose work consisted of drawing up plans for the type of regular and auxiliary military forces which an independent Scotland would be compelled to maintain. The Convener of this committee was a retired British Army Major, Frederick Alexander Colquhoun Boothby.

In an Interim Report in the summer of 1968, Major Boothby came out in favour of a regular Scottish Army consisting of a Highland Brigade, a Lowland Brigade, a Parachute Battalion and an Armoured Formation as General Headquarters Troops. He wanted a separate Navy but didn't think an independent Air Force necessary. Boothby was attracted to the idea of auxiliary forces on the Swiss pattern. He imagined a Scottish Peoples' Militia consisting of small local detachments which would be highly mobile, lightly armed and would have the advantage of knowing their localities intimately. This partisan army would be in a state of constant and immediate readiness and could be rapidly mobilised by a Scottish Government. The Scottish Armed Forces would be led by an élite professional Officer Corps highly trained at a special Forces University. In his capacity as Convener of the Armed Forces Committee, Major Boothby contacted foreign ambassadors, heads of governments and international arms dealers seeking advice on how to purchase weapons and ammunition. He even wrote to Moshe Dayan, Israel's Army Chief and Defence Minister, asking how the General managed to mobilise against the Arabs with such speed.

Boothby soon decided that his scheme for Scottish armed forces need not wait until Scottish Independence. Unknown to the other 1320 Club executive members, he used his position to gather intelligence on like-minded nationalist extremists and eventually recruited the nucleus of a secret army. If those recruits had knowledge of the history and character of their leader they might perhaps have been a little more wary.

Frederick Boothby was born in Dorset in 1910, the son of Captain F. L. M. Boothby CBE, RN, and Lady May Percy, daughter of the third Earl of Limerick. Thus, he was a cousin of the famous Conservative politician Lord Boothby and well connected with both the English and Irish aristocracy. He had the typical English public school education and as a young man spent time ranching in South America. In 1936 he enlisted as a trooper in the London Yeomanry and rose through the ranks to gain a commission in the Royal Armoured Corps during the Second World War. He saw action on many fronts and was commended for bravery during the Western Desert Campaign. In 1945 he was granted war substantive rank of Major and spent a period in Allied Military Government before rejoining the Army until 1953 when he retired with a disability pension of £500 a year. During his Army service he had gained considerable expertise in techniques of guerilla warfare and counter-insurgency. He then lived in England until 1960 and took a variety of temporary jobs, including manager of a private estate, labourer, motor mechanic and a deliverer of caravans. He found civilian life dull and decided to experiment with alternative lifestyles. He built himself a log cabin in a small wood close to the picturesque Wessex village of Sarratt. He decorated the hut with animal skulls. Here, living alone with a huge Dobermann pinscher dog, he set up the headquarters of the innocuous-sounding

South Hertfordshire Folklore Society. This proved to be something more sinister. Rumours circulated in the village about mysterious nocturnal rites, about young boys and girls dancing in the nude, and strange ceremonial rituals in which blood was spilt. This attracted the attentions of the popular press and eventually Boothby was traced to his lair and revealed as the "Mr X" of a witchcraft cult examined in a TV documentary programme. Boothby fled, pursued by the enthusiastic reporters, and with him went Mrs Rosalie Ainsworth, the painter wife of Royal Academician Edgar Ainsworth, soon to become Boothby's third, and last, wife.

Major Boothby surfaced in Edinburgh as a fervent Scottish nationalist. His first job in Scotland was as a full-time SNP organiser in Edinburgh but he soon fell out with the party hierarchy and left his employment and the party. He then became organiser of the Scottish Plebiscite Appeal Fund but that too ended in considerable acrimony. Boothby, the Englishman convert, then decided to set up his own extreme Scottish nationalist broadsheet, *Sgian Dubh*, Gaelic for the traditional Highlander's "black knife". The first few issues were in fact mis-spelt *"Skian"*. This neo-racialist journal attacked the English and the SNP leadership with equal ferocity and began to advocate terrorist methods. The first nine issues contained statements from a mysterious Scottish Liberation Army and gave detailed instructions on terrorist tactics. Boothby even used *Sgian Dubh* to make an appeal for uniforms and military equipment! He advised on techniques for evading tracker dogs and helicopter searches and how to detect *agents provocateurs*.

F. A. C. Boothby's Scottish Liberation Army was at first a figment of his highly wrought imagination but then became a propaganda or publicity device for attracting nationalists interested in using violent methods. In Wales there was the example of the publicity-seeking Free Wales Army which strutted around in fancy uniforms on Welsh hillsides or at Welsh nationalist demonstrations. They claimed much but did little compared to their more formidable sister organisation Mucliad Armddiffyn Cymru (MAC) who were to create two real martyrs, Alwyn Jones and George Taylor, when a gelignite bomb they were carrying exploded at Abergele on the night before the Investiture of Prince Charles as Prince of Wales. Major Boothby had an honorary commission in the Free Wales Army. The so-called Scottish Liberation Army returned the compliment and awarded Cayo Evans, Commandant of the West Wales column of the Free Wales Army, the rank of Honorary Captain. The Welsh claimed that they received a consignment of sawn-off shotguns from the SLA and certainly there is evidence that a group of Scots with an SLA banner attended the Irish Republican march commemorating the 50th anniversary of the Easter Rising in Dublin in 1966. Nevertheless, apart from some hoax bomb calls and the occasional brick hurled through Labour and Tory Party Committee Room windows with notes claiming an SLA connection, there was no serious terrorist violence in Scotland during the 1960s.

Major Boothby's activities soon attracted the attention of the leadership of the SNP. Party Chairman Arthur Donaldson rightly noted that Boothby had consistently advocated the formation of a Scottish Liberation Army and he accused the 1320 Club of being in league with this idea. William Wolfe, SNP Policy Vice-Chairman, practically accused Boothby of being an *agent provocateur* and declared that his "jaundiced views and provocative writings over the past six years have done more harm than good for the cause of Scottish Independence". The SNP Executive became convinced that the 1320 Club was trying to infiltrate its members into senior positions within the party and denounced the Club as an élitist, self-appointed secret society. An expulsion motion was tabled at the National Council held on 2 March 1968 and supported by an overwhelming majority of the delegates. Membership of the SNP and the 1320 Club became incompatible.

The Club attempted to maintain an independent existence and *Catalyst* continued but membership went into a steep decline and when the SNP gained only 11% of the popular vote in the June 1970 General Election, the embittered members of the 1320 Club felt that some kind of a symbolic stunt was needed to awaken the Scots.

Action occurred in the early hours of Christmas Day 1970 when Scottish police were informed by an anonymous telephone caller that the real Stone of Destiny had been deposited outside Parliament House, Edinburgh, as a "Christmas present" to the people of Scotland. Since the stone under the Coronation Chair in Westminster Abbey appeared secure in its place, the Metropolitan Police and the Dean of Westminster discounted this "Edinburgh stone" as a fake. Bailie Robert Gray who owned a monumental sculptor's business in Glasgow had made several copies of the original Stone of Destiny, stolen from Westminster on Christmas Eve 1950 by four Scottish students. It had remained in various hiding places in Scotland for over four months, and Bailie Gray was not now sure which was the real stone but he was able to say that one of the stones was missing from his yard in Sauchiehall Street. This "Edinburgh stone" was returned to him and he released it into the custody of Hugh MacDiarmid and the 1320 Club. It was transferred for safe keeping to St Columba's Church in Dundee and the care of a sympathiser, the Reverend J. Mackay-Nimmo. Nimmo later became the Chaplain of the Sovereign Military Order of the Knights Templar and the stone remains in their possession, although it has been moved to another location.

But Boothby and the others were dissatisfied with this prank and wanted to take more dramatic action. Boothby had a visitor at his cottage in late autumn 1970 with a proposal which he hoped would stimulate the Scots to action. William Murray, a quantity surveyor from Garelochhead and a fellow-member of the 1320 Club, wished to consult Boothby on a scheme to seize and hold a small Scottish town for 24 hours in order to spark off a national uprising. West Coast ports such as Oban, Fort William or Ullapool were considered. A symbolic occupation of Glen Coe was also considered. Once the uprising was in progress, supporters would post proclamations in prominent places throughout the country calling for support. These proclamations would be in the name of the "Provisional Government of Scotland" and the rising would be carried out by the Army of the Provisional Government or APG. With opinion poll ratings for the SNP on the rise again – up to 36 per cent – the plan appealed to Boothby and others because of its bold simplicity. Boothby agreed to help Murray draft the proclamations and also discussed the possible financial costs of such an action. Boothby agreed to be "Defence Minister" in the Provisional Government; the question of how funds could be acquired was left open.

The APG had now seceded from the 1320 Club. Boothby and Murray began to recruit members for the APG and succeeded in building up a list of approximately one hundred, organised in cells or "schiltroms", the term used to describe the tight formation of Scottish spearmen in the Wars of Independence. Considerable attention was paid to constructing tight security

enabling independent existence of the cells in the event of penetration by agents of the British Intelligence Services, but this proved
to be in vain.

Murray resolved to raise funds by bank robbery and took two of
his volunteers into his confidence – John Gillian, a photographer
in his mid-thirties, and John Stewart, a 19-year-old bank clerk
in Biggar who was a former lay preacher with the Plymouth
Brethren, and had first met Murray in the Gorbals by-election
in October 1970. Gillian in particular believed that "sooner or
later the Scots would have to get the guns out", but it was
Stewart who first suggested a target. Stewart had worked as a
holiday-relief bank clerk in the Royal Bank of Scotland branch at
Penicuik in Midlothian and knew the security systems and layout.
Another raid was planned on a Glasgow bank. However, there was
a lapse of security which led Murray to suspect that there was an
informer in their midst. He was right. The police were already
aware of the details of both planned raids and had "staked-out"
both locations. Murray's contact in the Glasgow underworld –
necessary for obtaining weapons – had let him down. The police
knew the names of the APG men and kept Stewart, Gillian and
Murray under constant surveillance. Murray detected this police
interest and called off the bank raids. He decided instead to rob
a bank in England and chose the Lytham Road Branch of the
National Westminster Bank in Blackpool as the new target. He
picked 1 April 1971 as the date for the raid.

Murray, Gillian and Stewart travelled down to England by car,
checked into a small hotel in Morecambe in Lancashire and went
over their plans for the raid. In the car Murray had an armoury
of weapons including sawn-off shotguns, air pistols and knives.
Thinking that his house in Garelochhead might be searched by
the police he had taken everything with him including his APG
documents, membership list and plans for the raids. But Murray
and his men were about to become April Fools, for in the early
hours of the morning, acting on a tip-off from Scotland's Regional
Crime Squad, English detectives surrounded their hotel and advised
the APG men to surrender. They did so and the police took them
and all their weapons and papers into custody. The rebellion was
over – even before funds had been acquired to organise it!

The three men were charged with conspiracy and carrying
firearms with criminal intent and their trial took place before an

English jury at Lancaster Assizes at the end of June. The verdict was never in doubt. The police had acted swiftly on the detailed evidence of the unnamed informer. While Justice O'Connor accepted that the bank raid was not intended for personal gain, but for idealistic political aims, he sentenced Murray to five years in jail, Gillian, four years, and Stewart, three years. The three stood expressionless in the dock as the sentences were read out but as they were handed down, John Stewart made a clenched fist salute to the public gallery, turned to face the judge and shouted out: "*agus Alba Gu Brath!*", "Scotland for Ever" in Gaelic.

William Wolfe, Chairman of the SNP, denounced the affair as "romantic rubbish" but the 1320 Club and the Scottish Patriots began a campaign to have the men transferred to Scottish prisons. Murray was soon transferred to Perth Prison where he shared a cell with a man called Matt Lygate and taught himself to speak Gaelic. Lygate was also a "political bank-robber" and the two made attempts to recruit new members into the ranks of "tartan terrorism". Murray gained a recruit in Tony Tunilla, a young Glaswegian petty criminal. Murray wrote to Boothby asking him to contact Scottish actor Sean Connery in Las Vegas where he was making the latest Bond movie, *Diamonds Are Forever*. Connery was a keen Scottish nationalist and had sponsored many projects to assist the Scottish economy. He had been considered as an SNP candidate at one time and Murray thought that he might assist the wives and families of the prisoners. He did not. The 1320 Club's Scottish Patriotic Prisoners' Dependents Fund raised only £440 in two years.

Murray and Boothby remained in close contact although many others now held grave suspicions against the Major. During the trial there was clear evidence of the presence of one or more *agents provocateurs* or informers. Some 1320 Club executive members believed that Boothby was one of them. Hugh MacDiarmid wrote to *Catalyst* editor, Ronald MacDonald Douglas, in April 1972 that "if Boothby is playing a double game, he must be exposed and got rid of". MacDiarmid promised support if some kind of action were taken against the Major. Boothby had also tried to get SNP Chairman William Wolfe implicated with the APG by writing a letter to him which seems to suggest that he, Boothby, was ready to take action against oil pipelines if Wolfe would give him the word. It seemed to be a clear case of intended entrapment. MacDonald

Douglas in fact maintained until his death in 1982 that Major Boothby was a police agent. He was not the only one who thought so. In January 1973, Boothby received a letter containing a death threat. He had only five days to flee Scotland. The letter ended "Yours for Scotland, the Scottish Liberation Army". But Boothby was spared assassination. In the event, however, he decided, given the suspicion with which he was regarded, that his position in the 1320 Club was untenable. His resignation was accepted without argument.

At the close of the trial, Scottish Patriot leader, Miss Wendy Wood, declared: "This is not the end of it. Do not think that the English can frighten us off like this. There will be others." Wendy Wood's statement was prophetic. Many APG cells survived and one of the most active centred on the granite city of Aberdeen.

3 FOR A SCOTTISH WORKERS' REPUBLIC!

Matt Lygate: "In the future a day will come when the roles of this court will be reversed, when the workers will sit on the bench and those people who have judged me now will be judged themselves."

Lord Dunpark: "I don't look forward to those days with any longing I must say."

From the transcript of Matt Lygate's trial, March 1972,
High Court, Glasgow

FOR those persons intent on educating themselves on Marxist ideology, a small bookshop in Paisley Road West, Glasgow, was a mecca from early 1970 onwards. There one could find tracts emanating from the national liberation movements throughout the world and read the studies of all the great communists and socialists in history. The bookshop was also the headquarters of a small but tightly organised Marxist-Leninist political party – the Workers'

Party of Scotland, formed in 1966, and from it emanated a plethora of pamphlets and the regular periodical *Scottish Vanguard*. Many of the publications were densely typed on almost every inch of small, stapled booklets and the masthead *Scottish Vanguard – Journal of the Workers' Party of Scotland (Marxist-Leninist) – For A Workers' Republic of Scotland* was nearly always in red ink, with a drawing of William Wallace's sword intertwined with the letters.

Matt Lygate, a tailor's cutter in his early twenties, had been one of the founders of the party. He had led a varied and interesting life since his birth in a "single end" in Govan. His parents were committed communists, his grandparents were Irish, and the young Lygate planned to become a priest, regarding the world as evil and rotten with greed. He emigrated to New Zealand rather than face National Service – which was against his principles. In New Zealand he became embroiled in a feud with the Communist Party, founded his own rival newspaper *Te Tao* (Maori for "The Spear") and led many demonstrations and campaigns. Then he travelled widely – Australia, Hong Kong, Trinidad, Mexico – and became interested in the teachings of Chairman Mao. On his return to Scotland, he was critical of the Communist Party of Great Britain's "British Road To Socialism" and joined Michael McCreery's "Committee To Defeat Revisionism For Communist Unity" after its foundation in November 1963. McCreery wrote a pamphlet on *The National Question In Britain* and called for new Communist parties to be set up in England, Scotland and Wales. The CDRCU's paper was *Vanguard* so, when Lygate and another ex-Communist, Tom Murray, a former member of the International Brigade in Spain, set up, with other Scottish members of the CDRCU, the Workers' Party of Scotland, they took the title *Scottish Vanguard* for their journal. That had also been the title of John Maclean's journal in the 1920s. There were in fact seven ex-members of the Communist Party who met in Edinburgh on 15 May 1966 to set up the party and its first conference was held at 14 Coates Gardens, Edinburgh, on 25 September, when the journal was launched.

Until 1970, the party operated from a bookshop in Morrison Street, Edinburgh – with a short period in The Bookstore in the West Port – and for some time afterwards the party had two bookshops operating simultaneously, one in Glasgow, the other in Edinburgh. The party grew rapidly but since they were a "revolutionary élite" they insisted on building up a cadre of suitable members. Unlike other political groups, you could not just join and do nothing. There was a "candidate membership" period of a minimum of six months, followed by an interview by two delegated members of the party, and an application could still even then be rejected by the Central Committee. If accepted into membership, a "vanguard fighter of the proletariat" was expected to pay a portion of his earnings to party funds, to immerse himself in constant study of Marx, Engels, Lenin, Stalin and Mao Tse Tung as well as the life and work of John Maclean and to participate in all party activity. The party was looking for persons who could develop "the qualities of class-consciousness, ideological clarity, hard work, initiative, sound judgement and fearless self-sacrifice" and who were able to endure "self and mutual criticism without rancour". Only when a candidate could prove him or herself to have read and *understood* the prescribed reading course, would he or she be proposed to the Central Committee for membership of the party.

The party was puritanical, ideological, tightly controlled and therefore highly effective. Their literature was of a high standard, concise and undoubtedly appealing to many socialists in the nationalist movement and to many communists who felt that the British Communist and Labour parties had misinterpreted Marxism on the national question. The WPS provided a direct link between John Maclean's radical programme, the Maoist Communist International, the emerging Irish situation and the Scottish Labour movement's historic involvement in the Spanish Civil War. It was "buoyed-up" by the growth of nationalism. The party contested the Gorbals by-election in 1969, with Matt Lygate as the candidate, but spurned the idea of electoral politics and stood purely to gain publicity. WPS members helped to set up the John Maclean Society in 1968 and the Scotland-China Association. Soon two biographies of John Maclean appeared, largely because of the new interest in him sponsored by the WPS. Hugh MacDiarmid noted this in an article on Maclean titled "The Conspiracy of Silence" in *Scottish Vanguard* (July 1968). The WPS organised a commemoration for Thomas Muir, one of the early Scottish republicans, in High Street, Glasgow, which was attended by Naomi Mitchison, Douglas Young, numerous councillors and political activists from many groups. MacDiarmid sent a text which was read at the ceremony.

The Workers' Party of Scotland by 1970 was expanding and had attracted a number of articulate members. Colin Lawson, Val Houlison, Val Sutherland, Tom Murray and Alex Watt were on the Central Committee. *Scottish Vanguard* and the party were becoming increasingly influential amongst members of other parties and the trade union movement. Moreover, it was a credible alternative for young Scottish socialists to the two "British" Trotskyite groups, the International Socialists and the International Marxist Group, which had just arrived in Scotland.

The Workers' Party of Scotland maintained a great interest in national liberation struggles in all parts of the world and participated in the Vietnam Solidarity Campaign and the protest over the invasion of Czechoslovakia. In 1970 the party received a telegram from Prince Sihanouk of Cambodia thanking them for their support. Matt Lygate stated at his trial: "I have associates in many parts of the world involved in guerilla activity on behalf of the working-class." In the *Scottish Vanguard* of September 1968, a statement read: "The Workers' Party of Scotland holds the view strongly ... that a much greater emphasis must henceforth be placed on the most far-reaching and unrestricted forms of action in Scotland."

As the party moved to the new bookshop in Glasgow, Matt Lygate's influence continued to dominate and he began another term as Chairman of the party. Tom Murray, the veteran of the International Brigade and a highly respected figure in Scottish socialism, had been the editor of the paper but Lygate began to build a strong West of Scotland group. Among new members at the time was William McPherson, an unemployed 30-year-old man who had served in the Royal Highland Fusiliers. He soon became Vice-Chairman of the party. Colin Lawson, a close associate of Lygate's, became Treasurer. Gradually, the power in the party shifted to Glasgow. As it did so, methods and attitudes began to change. The political situation in the early 1970s was chaotic; industrial unrest, riots in Paris, London, America. But other strange things were happening too. There was the major explosion at Edinburgh Castle during the military tattoo in 1971 and suspicion fell upon the WPS. The party had not previously been accused of seeking power by the use of violence.

As the new decade began, it seemed as if the old order was changing and the new young members of the WPS longed to "speed up" this change. One of the main problems of the WPS was funds. Funds were not keeping pace with the new level of activity which the party's Glasgow cadre required. It was decided that new means must be found of raising money to continue the political programme of agitation, education, organisation. In particular, they wished to improve the appearance of *Scottish Vanguard*, to afford better printing facilities so that the paper could compete with the professional-looking newspapers of the "Trots", which were printed in London.

According to one member of the WPS, it was Lygate who first suggested that money be raised by illegal means. Several members, including ex-soldier William McPherson, began to plan a series of armed raids. They recruited a non-member, Ian Doran, to help. The first attack was dramatic, violent and successful. On Friday, 7 May 1971, three armed men sprang out at a British Rail wages van in Maxwell Road, Pollokshields, sprayed ammonia in the faces of the driver and his guard, struck them with a jemmy and menaced two other employees with a shotgun. They made their getaway. They had netted £5,493.

The second target was the Bank of Scotland branch in Kildroston Street in Pollokshields. For Lygate at least, who took no part in the raids, there was no question that the attack on the bank was symbolic. It was merely a quick and easy method of obtaining funds for the organisation. At 10 a.m. on 17 June, customers in the small Bank of Scotland branch were terrified when two gunmen burst in, wearing black-and-white hoods over their faces. One man fired a shot at the ceiling, the other struck down a male employee and blasted open the door to the tellers. While one man brandished a shotgun at the customers and staff, the other jumped over the counter and began to fill a bag with money from the open cash box. Then they made their getaway. This time, their haul amounted to over £3,000.

On 21 October, they struck again. They burst into the Clydesdale Bank in Aikenhead Road, Govanhill, menaced staff with a shotgun, forcing them to lie on the floor and escaped with £5,142. Eight days later the gang struck once more, at the premises of Smith of Maddiston, a haulage contractors in London Road, Dalmarnock. Four men and three women were menaced by men armed with a pistol and a knife and forced to lie on the floor. One of the employees was assaulted as the gang escaped with £3,240. A fifth attack, at the Savings Bank of Glasgow in Albert Drive, Pollokshields, on 19 November, netted £3,963.

The sixth and most dangerous incident occurred on 17 December – in the vicinity of the Vanguard Bookshop itself! This time the target was the Savings Bank of Glasgow branch at Paisley Road, West Kinning Park, and the haul amounted to £6,673. In this raid, a male bank employee was shot in the head but survived. The raids had been meticulously planned and efficiently – if violently – carried out.

The Workers' Party of Scotland funds were now, in theory, over £31,000 richer. However, there were two problems. Firstly, those conducting the raids had seen how easy it was to accumulate large amounts of money and wanted to continue, although the organisation had more than enough money than it needed and, secondly, inevitably perhaps, they began to consider that they should take a share of the proceeds for themselves. The germ of this idea was possibly sown by the raider Doran who was not a member of the party. Lygate was eventually forced to suggest that the raiders should contribute to the party only what they wished. One of the raiders, the party's organiser in Dundee, 23-year-old Alex Watt, offered his entire share but Lygate persuaded him to keep £100. Watt was an idealistic youth who had studied Political Economy at St Andrew's University where he had joined the Young Communist League – and failed his finals – as a result of his commitment. Lygate, Watt claimed, regarded himself as a latter-day Lenin or a tartan Che Guevara and it was he, Watt later testified, who had suggested the raids to raise funds.

Of course, it was inconceivable that such an organisation as the Workers' Party of Scotland would escape police surveillance and the Vanguard Bookshop had been watched for several months. The police also had an "inside man" in the party, Steven Niven, who had given them the initial information. It was only a matter of time before they were all arrested.

The secret police were involved throughout the UK, but particularly in Scotland, in investigations into left-wing groups partly as a result of the Angry Brigade bombs and the IRA's bombing of Aldershot barracks. An anonymous call was made to Govan CID, to Detective-Superintendent Thomas Valentine who had been leading the inquiries into the raids. The police moved in.

On 20 December, at dawn, police raided a number of houses and arrested Lygate, McPherson, Lawson and Doran. Twenty-four-year-old Doran was found to have a Luger pistol and several magazines of bullets at his house in Cathcart Road. At Lygate's house the police found two black-and-white hoods, masks and a packet containing £1,510. After a search of the bookshop, the police emerged with two sawn-off double-barrelled shotguns, a sawn-off rifle, ammunition and a shoe box containing £5,000. All four men were taken to Govan police station and charged and remanded in custody.

The trial began at the High Court, Glasgow, on Monday, 7 March 1972. The prosecution outlined its case. They charged Lygate with three of the robberies and Doran and McPherson with four. In addition, they were aware that at least one other person had been involved. Lawson was not involved in the robberies. He had met Lygate in 1967 and had been at that time more interested in Christian ideology. He had refused to participate in the raids on principle.

A large number of witnesses to the raids gave their testimony in front of Lord Dunpark and the jury on the first nine days of the trial. There was little doubt from the beginning that convictions would be secured by the police, particularly since Lygate said, on the ninth day, that he had "kept guns and money from bank raids carried out in the city by political associates engaged in guerrilla tactics on behalf of the workers. These associates," he said, "were engaged in bank robberies such as happen in Ulster and Glasgow today. There was a movement in Scotland doing similar work here and elsewhere." Lygate maintained throughout the trial that he had played no part in the robberies but he admitted he had been responsible for them.

On the tenth day of the trial, Lygate dismissed his counsel, Nicholas Fairbairn, his junior counsel Edgar Prais and Joseph Beltrami, the instructing solicitor, to conduct his own defence. He was heading for martyrdom. While McPherson was described as the "mastermind" of the raids and the non-political Doran had been the "strong-arm man", Lygate was the unrepentant rebel whom the State wished to break. His final speech to the court undoubtedly played a part in the sentence he was to receive: "My Lord, I would like to say a few words in mitigation on my own behalf on the charges that have brought me before this court. I have been charged with bank robbery. I would like to state that in my life I have no criminal convictions whatsoever. What has brought me along the path into the court has been in actual fact violence – the violence which I have opposed and constantly opposed in this country, the violence which throws 150,000 men unemployed in the country, the violence which throws 1,000 children a year into Balvidie Hospital through bad housing conditions, the violence which has inflicted on the children of this country rickets. As stated by Dr Naismith recently rickets has reappeared in children because milk has been taken from the children of this country and this is violence."

At this point, Lord Dunpark interrupted him to say, "Mr Lygate, this has no relevance at all to the sentence I shall pass on you."

"I am trying to explain the reason why I have taken action. My reason is similar to a surgeon who technically commits violence by cutting open a patient's body but he does this to change the patient, to help the patient, not to kill him. If I am technically in violation of the laws here, if I am technically accused of violence – and that I deny – my violence can be nothing to the millions of people in this country, millions who have suffered at the hands of a few parasitical members of society. I have been three months in Barlinnie and these three months have shown me suffering– young men, sons of mothers whose hearts are breaking because they have nothing to live for. They can't speak for themselves, to come before the court and they are mystified by the procedure here because they do not understand, they do not know. I am not handicapped in speaking for myself and I wish to do that. I am not a youth. I have seen them coming to Barlinnie, and they have trodden the path – the only one available today in the society we have – and the only answer is for them to join the Army and fight in Ulster and murder Irish men and women . . .".

"Mr Lygate, I have given you a good deal of licence. If you have nothing which I regard as relevant to say, it won't make any difference. I am not having a political speech."

"I am not trying to make a political speech. I am trying to clear my conscience here. I am not only here on trial before the court. I am on trial before the people of Scotland."

"Well, violence in Ireland has nothing whatever to do with the sentence I am to impose."

"Very well. It is given to men to live and I have lived for the finest cause in life, the liberation of men. I must clear my conscience and if I have to spend the next 40 years in prison I will never feel I have disgraced my name in this country. I have stood by what I have believed in. Children are branded as criminals because they can't afford to buy the goods produced through the labours of the working-class. This is because of those in this country at the present time that have no social conscience and don't think of anyone else but themselves. I don't do this. I have always thought of other people – everyone who asked me for help I have tried to give it. I believe an ideology must be based on scientific . . ."

"Mr Lygate, I'll give you two more minutes to say something relevant."

"I am trying my best to say what is relevant here. What I am saying is relevant to the working-class."

"Well it isn't relevant to me and it is me you are addressing now, it is only me who has any power over you now."

"Yes I see that. In Glasgow, as you know, slums are abundant in this fair city – slums which children are forced to live and breed in. Am I as an ordinary and understanding human being to stand by and allow that to continue?"

"What has this to do with your conviction for bank robbery?"

"It has this, that my association, my sympathy with people who are involved in bank robbery has been to alleviate pain and discomfort of the people of this country."

"By relieving them of their money from the bank?"

"By getting money from banks which has been stolen from the working-class in this country, people here . . ."

"Sixty seconds . . ."

"Right, I am nearly finished now. I would like to say that in the future a day will come when the roles of this court will be reversed, when the workers will sit on the bench and those people who have judged me now will be judged then themselves."

"I don't look forward to those days with any longing I must say," concluded Lord Dunpark.

On the day the sentences were handed out, there was a large police presence. Security precautions were stringent. Lord Dunpark told the accused that the series of raids which they had executed were serious enough but taken together formed a frightening pattern of criminal conduct which might have continued had someone not given information to the police. Then he read out the sentences: William McPherson, 26 years; Ian Doran, 25 years;

45

Colin Lawson, six years; Matt Lygate, 24 years. There were gasps of amazement in the court room at the severity of the terms. They were the longest ever given out in a Scottish court, on a par with those of the Great Train Robbers and more than twice the average term given to convicted murderers. But Lygate and McPherson smiled and as they were taken down the steps they both yelled: "Long Live The Workers Of Scotland!" Answering shouts from the public gallery, "Up The Workers!", came from a small band who cheered and gave clenched fist salutes. McPherson's shout of "Traitors. They are all traitors!" was the last sound heard as the men were removed from the court.

But one of the raiders was still at large. Alex Watt, the 23-year-old ex-student, had fled the country prior to the arrests, having become disillusioned when the others had decided to share up the spoils. He lived for a while in Dublin where he tried unsuccessfully to make contact with the Provisional IRA, then hitch-hiked his way around Europe and settled down in Holland where he managed to get a job. But Watt was an idealist and his experiences would not let him live at peace with himself. He was tortured by guilt that he had escaped while the others were in jail. Shortly after he was befriended by a small religious sect, the Children of God, he underwent a conversion to Christianity and decided to give himself up. He turned himself in to the British Consul General in Amsterdam on 24 November 1972, was brought back to Glasgow and stood trial in January 1973. His solicitor told the court that his was "a story with a moral which may serve as a warning to others who attempt to play with the fire of political revolution". The Judge, Lord Cameron, said that it was "to his credit that he made up his mind to come back and face the consequences". Because of this and his obvious renouncing of his part in the raids, Watt was given only three years imprisonment.

By contrast, McPherson, described as one of the most dangerous men in Scotland, who spent much of his time in Porterfield Prison, Inverness, studying the writings of Stalin, Lenin, Marx and Mao, had his sentence increased by six years after taking part with three other men in a jailbreak which involved assault and attempted murder of prison officers. His original sentence had been reduced on appeal to 24 years.

The Matt Lygate case was to become a *cause célèbre* in Scotland over the next 12 years and many political groups championed the fight against the "political sentence" which had been given him. Several Labour MPs publicly stated that they believed Lygate was a "victim of class justice". His father hired a private detective to attempt to find evidence to have the sentence reduced, but died in 1976. Lygate was allowed, under heavy guard, to attend his funeral. His mother appealed to the European Court of Human Rights in Strasbourg in 1981 but the court refused to take up the case. Two appeals to the parole board were also unsuccessful. Lygate organised a food strike in Peterhead jail and campaigned for political rights for prisoners. He barricaded himself in his cell in an attempt to prevent his transfer to Craiginches. There, he was eventually recategorised as a "medium risk" prisoner and given a clerical job in the office. He also took up painting and was described as a natural artist. For some time, at Perth Prison, he shared a cell with convicted APG man, William Murray. He was reclassified low risk in 1982 and on 19 September 1985 walked out of the front gates of Edinburgh's Saughton Prison for the last time. He had decided not to eat the porridge on his last morning, he said, because "if you eat it on your last morning you'll be back for more". Quoting Robert Burns before a dozen banner-waving Republicans who had come to greet him he said: "Liberty is a magnificent feast." Although he had pledged not to indulge in criminal activity he had come out his own man, his political zeal undiminished. He was a folk hero for Scottish republican socialists, the "wee political man" in his Lenin cap and denims.

After the jailing of Lygate and the others the Workers' Party of Scotland, largely under the guidance of Tom Murray, Alan Wylie and Duncan Toms, had struggled to retain credibility. They had disowned the bank robberies but campaigned against the severity of the sentences and co-operated in the Matt Lygate Defence Group. When Murray died in 1983, however, the party died with him. Maoism had become distinctly unpopular. Lygate's attempts to re-form the Workers' Party in 1986 have so far met with little success.

4 BAIT FOR BIGGER FISH

General Idi Amin, President of Uganda, broadcast on Uganda Radio in support of the Provisional Government of Scotland and pledged that he would submit a case for Scottish independence to the United Nations in New York.

The Scotsman *coverage of APG trial, May 1975*

SERGEANT William Gibson Anderson had served in the Royal Engineers from 1959 to 1970 and his specialist skill was the use of explosives in combat and for demolition. He was a Dunfermline man but on discharge from the Army moved to Aberdeen where he worked as a roustabout on an oil rig. A short, stocky figure with prominent sideburns and a broad, weather-beaten face, he soon became a familiar figure in nationalist circles.

The "Granite City" and its hinterland was an exciting locale for a nationalist in the early 1970s. Grampian Region was just beginning to feel the impact of the North Sea Oil boom and people were very receptive to the SNP's "It's Scotland's Oil" campaign. In the 1974 General Election, the SNP won Moray and Nairn, Banffshire and Aberdeenshire East. Aberdeen North and South constituencies also had small but enthusiastic electoral teams bolstered by students from Aberdeen University and local colleges. After a hard evening's campaigning, the nationalists would return to their rooms in Hutcheon Street or repair to the "Elite" or the "Tappit Hen" for a pint or two. As well as discussion of campaign tactics and the post-Independence situation, a few, buoyed up by the singing of patriotic songs, discussed other acts which might bring good publicity. The Federation of Student Nationalists ran a crofting scheme on Skye and some of the students had spent the summer months working on the scheme. Other schemes included fly-postering campaigns around Aberdeen. Near closing time William Anderson would sound out potential recruits for a mysterious organisation by asking supporters "Would you die for Scotland?" If candidates answered in the affirmative they were in, if not, they faced the wrath of the belligerent Anderson. Many took the easy way out and joined. The discussion would continue after closing time in the graveyard opposite the "Tappit Hen" when Anderson and his comrades discussed the possibilities of bombing attacks on England. The targets were to include defence establishments at Aldershot, Devizes, Maidstone, Sandhurst and Catterick – all of which Anderson knew well. But it was just pub talk. Or was it?

One of the young men who took part in the discussion was Colin Boyd of Inverbervie and he soon discovered that Anderson's bravado was backed up with 109 sticks of gelignite and 50 detonators because Anderson asked him to store these for him. Boyd had become embroiled after a discussion with Jim McGugan, the SNP parliamentary candidate for Aberdeen North who had attended Boyd's mother's funeral. At that time Boyd had expressed strong sentiments about what he regarded as the ineffectual nature of the SNP and his anger at the oil being taken from Scotland. He wanted to join the "Scottish Republican Army". "Don't be daft, man!" said McGugan. "There is no such thing." Pressed further by Boyd, McGugan agreed that there were people prepared to take strong action and Boyd said that he wanted to join such an organisation. McGugan told him to put this in writing and he would pass the letter on. Two weeks after sending the letter, Boyd received a reply from Major Boothby and was then introduced to William Anderson and a man called William Bell of Inverness. All three discussed the organisation – the Army of the Provisional Government – in a pub and a trip to Inverness was planned when 80 lbs of explosive would be collected which Boyd was to store. He was given a copy of a Declaration of the Aims of the APG. Then the talk turned to possible targets. Boyd thought that it had been decided that oil pipelines were to be the target but Anderson and Bell had other ideas, including blowing up the statue of the Duke of Sutherland at Golspie and the Aberdeen Labour Exchange. Boyd argued that such a target might cause injury to people – which he was against. A few days later, Boyd had become so alarmed that he contemplated throwing the gelignite into the North Sea but imagined that it would probably be simply washed up on the beach. He telephoned the police and told them of his predicament. The police were highly sympathetic!

Boyd wanted to make a deal and discussed how he could provide the police with information about the conspiracy without having to implicate himself. He told the two detectives about the planned trip to Inverness and was provided with expenses and enrolled as a police agent. The police also gave him money to hire a car to take Anderson to Inverness. On 10 February, Boyd drove the hired car to pick up Anderson at the city's Wallace Monument and there was another man also, introduced simply as Gordon. This man stated that "for £10 he would kill anybody". He was not interested in the organisation. He was simply a thug. They set out for Inverness, with the police tailing the car by road and also by helicopter. In Inverness they picked up William Bell and drove out of the town to a lay-by near a wood. As they searched in the wood for the explosives, the helicopter passed overhead at which point they all hid under the trees. No one except Boyd knew why the helicopter was there, or even suspected that they were under surveillance. They found a rucksack with the explosives and detonators and Boyd took these into his possession. There were 51 sticks of gelignite, some detonators and four rolls of wire. Later, Boyd had a rendezvous with the police and handed them over.

But the police did not make any arrests. Instead, they handed the case over to the Scottish Crime Squad to control enquiries on "a wider basis" after advice from the very highest levels of Government. The matter was raised in Cabinet. A general election was imminent and the Conservative Secretary of State for Scotland,

Gordon Campbell, who was facing a strong SNP challenge in his Moray and Nairn constituency, did not want to create martyrs or any publicity which might swell the SNP vote. Instead, a clandestine combined operation was launched involving officers from nearly every force in Scotland and controlled by senior Special Branch officers. In total there were to be almost 16 months of it, 13,000 man-hours of close police surveillance at an enormous cost to the taxpayer.

Colin Boyd, acting on Special Branch instructions, infiltrated deeper into the APG and became a kind of secretary of the organisation. The Special Branch were playing a waiting game to see who else could be persuaded to join the conspiracy. They wanted to entrap some "bigger fish", preferably someone senior in the SNP. Although Boyd had told them of his contact with McGugan, there really was no evidence that McGugan had wittingly involved him in the APG. McGugan believed, in common with many other SNP activists, that Boothby was "a safety valve" who was capable of talking hot-heads out of any terrorist action. The Special Branch officers spent an inordinate amount of time on surveillance of Anderson's home in Springhill Crescent, Aberdeen, and were pleased to discover that Anderson met William Murray in a city centre pub on the latter's release from prison. Then there was a meeting in Aberdeen between Alistair Smith and Jeanette Carpenter of the Scottish Republican Clubs. Smith and Carpenter hoped to form an SRC in Aberdeen but Murray and Anderson wanted to enrol them in their group. The meeting ended in loud and angry argument and was aborted. However, to the Special Branch, it seemed as if the conspiracy was taking off.

By this time the organisation had acquired some other recruits. Anderson, code number "68", was a Captain of the APG and Major Boothby was "01". Boyd himself was "73". William Murray became a Liaison Officer with the "political wing". Another man called Francis Kelly had joined the APG by swearing an oath over a saltire that he would die for his country. A man called William MacKenzie played Strathspey reels on his fiddle at some of the meetings of the conspirators, but was only nominally a member of the APG. Contacts had also been made with a small group in Perth, headed by Michael Fairlie, who had been recruited at the Bannockburn Rally. Fairlie became a Major in the APG and had three men under his command. He went into a Dundee gunshop and purchased a pump-action shotgun. The Aberdeen men planned a raid on a gunshop in Brechin to acquire firearms.

The various sections of the conspiracy generated a considerable number of documents relating to the organisation; concerning discipline, it was suggested that informers be "knee-capped" and "traitors" be shot. Elite "Zero squads" were suggested to enforce discipline. Declarations of the aims and methods were circulated. Lists of targets and detailed instructions for making bombs were produced. Ordnance Survey maps, such as one for Loch Lomond and the Trossachs, were marked with crosses to delineate a line of electricity pylons. Other targets listed in APG documents included power stations at Loch Sloy, Kincardine, Chapelcross, Hunterston, Loch Awe, Ravenscraig, Grangemouth and ITV Glasgow and BBC Scotland. One document outlined a proposal for "swift dashes into isolated townships at dusk with the flag flying from the vehicle and a loudspeaker calling for young men and women". Such an operation, it was proposed, would have a time limit of about 15 minutes. A letter addressed to serving soldiers had been drafted. Nearly all of these documents were simply idle words on paper and indicated the high degree of fantasy involved in the conspiracy. Major Boothby and his men were simply armchair generals with no army. Their organisation had no chance of success. There was tight police surveillance of all its known members and only the complete lack of action and a failure to involve some "bigger fish" delayed a police crack-down.

In the meantime, Anderson attempted to set up an APG cell in Inverness of which William Bell was to be the nucleus. Bell was a 45-year-old architect and kilted "character" who had been expelled from the SNP for fanatical anti-English fervour. He had set up his own party, "Fine Ghaidheil", and stood for Parliament. He also had a history of psychiatric illness and was viewed as being a bit of a crank. However, some "members" were recruited in Inverness and a joint action was planned by the Aberdeen and Inverness schiltroms. They would raid a travelling bank between Grantown-on-Spey and Aviemore. The operation was abandoned at an early stage, as was a plan to blow up power pylons along the Aberdeen to Inverness road.

At the end of August 1974, William Murray joined Anderson in staging a publicity stunt. Two *Daily Record* reporters including Chief Reporter Gordon Airs were invited to a secret meeting at which they were told officers from several "tartan terrorist" groups such as the "Tartan Army" and the "Scottish Liberation Army" were to discuss merging their organisations under the APG banner. Airs and his colleague were picked up at the Bruce Statue at Bannockburn, hustled into the back of a van and driven to a hillside in Stirlingshire beside a ruined castle where several hooded men armed with automatic weapons were waiting. After interviews the pressmen were returned to Stirling. No photographs were allowed. The reporters understood from the interviews that there had previously been a meeting between the groups and that a merger had been agreed. There would be a Scottish Army National Council with a representative from each group on it. The groups which were supposed to have attended this "summit" included representatives from the SLA, the Scottish Republican Army and some potential deserters from the Royal Highland Fusiliers associated with the Scottish Citizens' Army of the Republic, who were on furlough from service in Northern Ireland. The SCAR was a military faction initially associated with the Scottish Workers' Republican Party and the Scottish Republican Socialist Clubs. The reporters were also told that the APG had been offered training facilities by the Provisional IRA but had not yet taken up the offer. Airs had given certain undertakings in connection with this meeting and was later jailed for a night for contempt of court when he refused to break his promise on the grounds of his professional ethics. The story of this meeting was never used by the newspaper.

Possibly the most successful publicity coup by the APG came during the closing months of 1974 when a representative of the Provisional Government of Scotland visited Uganda and was successful in enlisting the aid of Uganda's dictator, President Idi Amin. Amin broadcast on Ugandan Radio in support of the APG and pledged that he would submit a case for Scottish Independence to the United Nations in New York at the next opportunity. He even sent a long, detailed letter to the SNP Chairman, William Wolfe, offering his support, which came as a surprise to Mr Wolfe who promptly and politely declined General Amin's offer. Another letter, even more bizarre and detailed, was received from Kampala, warning Wolfe that he would be in danger if he continued to put his trust in the English. The letters seemed to prove that someone with a detailed knowledge of Scottish politics had briefed the Ugandan dictator. Strangely, the Foreign Office never did discover – or certainly did not reveal – who from the APG had visited Uganda, or how otherwise Amin had received his briefing. By involving themselves in foreign affairs, the APG were becoming a serious irritation to the British State.

The most enthusiastic section of the APG was the Perth schiltrom, some of whose members had taken part in the Bannockburn stunt. Michael Fairlie, Robert Berwick and Alistair Coventry were all musicians in a local pop group and managed to recruit a number of other sympathisers from among their friends and followers in Perth. Fairlie's brother Jim, twice Parliamentary candidate for Dundee West, was a senior SNP figure. Staying with Michael Fairlie over the Christmas and New Year period was Tony Tunilla, a young man who had been recruited to the APG in Perth Prison by William Murray. Tunilla was on the run from the Glasgow police. They were to participate in an APG action which led to the arrest of the entire group.

The leaders of the APG, Murray, Anderson and Boothby, faced the same problem which they had faced in 1971, four years before: lack of funds to buy arms and ammunition. The solution they came up with was the same as before: bank raids. At first it was suggested that the members of the Scottish Citizens' Army of the Republic be used to raid a bank in Glasgow, but they declined, having gained the impression that the APG was riddled with informers. The APG had its own links with the Glasgow underworld through Tony Tunilla and leading members of the Scottish Republican Clubs. However, the SRC members also suspected that the APG was infiltrated by *agents provocateurs* and wisely decided to have nothing to do with the scheme. In the end there was a botch-up.

Fairlie and his team from Perth received instructions to travel to Glasgow on 21 January 1975. Murray had told them to get a van and, little knowing what the true purpose of the van was, they simply went to the nearest van-hire depot and hired one. The legend of the hire company was in a prominent position on the side of the van. They met Murray as arranged in a local pub and he told them the "good news" of their selection as bank robbers. Expecting that they were only to be peripherally involved, the four were not entirely happy but reluctantly agreed and drove to the bank which Murray had selected as a target. Unfortunately it was lunchtime and the bank was closed. They waited in the van for the bank to reopen. Eventually they realised that the bank was not going to reopen and then discovered that the branch had actually closed down several months before! Impatient and angry, they agreed between themselves to rob the first bank they came to and arrived outside a small temporary bank branch. They swung into action and Tunilla grabbed the APG's only available weapon, a single-barrelled 410 shotgun. Just as they were leaving the van, however, a security delivery vehicle parked only yards away from them in a routine call to the bank. The APG men were forced to retreat and look for yet another target.

Eventually they reached the Royal Bank of Scotland branch at Springburn Road. The four men rushed in and found only one woman customer and two bank tellers. Tony Tunilla put the shotgun to the head of the woman customer and ordered the tellers to fill some plastic bags with money. As they did so the tellers managed to slip £1,300 in specially numbered notes with the rest. These were notes kept aside especially for the purpose of tracing the stolen cash in any bank raid. The gang ran from the bank with their haul – over £8,000. Unfortunately they had not parked the van properly and were forced to do a three-point turn in front of the bank to escape.

The policeman in charge of the investigation, Detective Chief Inspector John McVicar, head of the Northern Division of Glasgow CID, realised that the bank raiders were not professionals. They had not worn masks or gloves. They had used a heavy van rather than a fast getaway car. They clearly had not known the area because the van had been seen by a number of locals as it traversed the streets. And, of course, several people had even read the legend on the van's sides. It was undoubtedly one of the most botched bank raids ever carried out! Chief Inspector McVicar stumbled across the Special Branch interest in his subjects and made the connection with the APG. He informed Special Branch of the development and a police observation post was set up outside Michael Fairlie's home at Perth. Fairlie was soon seen to have a meeting with William Murray (at which meeting he had handed over £2,524). There was a larger meeting in the Salutation Hotel in Perth after which there were punch-ups in the car-park between SCAR and APG men. Robert Berwick and Alastair Coventry fled to London with the rest of the money which they spent on a good time. Later they would merely explain that "expenses had been greater than expected".

The Special Branch were forced to call an end to the 16-month surveillance and police arrested Michael Fairlie, Tony Tunilla, Robert Berwick and Alastair Coventry on 31 January, ten days after the bank raid. Only £4,000 of the haul was recovered, including the numbered notes which helped to convict the men. Within seven days the police also arrested ex-soldier Alastair Smith and APG chiefs William Murray and William Anderson. The mysterious "Mr MacKenzie" referred to in evidence as "the Big Fiddler" was also arrested and held in custody for eight weeks after which he was released without charge. His repeated meetings with the accused seemed merely coincidental. Subsequently, although called by both the Crown and the Defence as a witness, Mr MacKenzie was discovered to have disappeared. It seems reasonable to assume that MacKenzie fully co-operated with the police. MacKenzie had met with both William Anderson and William Murray shortly before their arrest. Within minutes of that meeting Murray's car was stopped by police and documents which formed a substantial part of the Crown case of conspiracy were found in the car. There were allegations that these had been planted. Among the papers were references to a Scottish lawyer, apparently involved with the APG. Speculation suggests that this might have been Willie McRae, at the time a Vice-Chairman of the SNP. Another witness whom the police were unable to trace despite the fact that he had been cited by the Crown was David Leadbetter of the Scottish Republican Clubs. Although the homes of William Bell in Inverness and Frederick Boothby in Broughton by Biggar were searched thoroughly in February, it wasn't until 1 April that they were detained and arrested along with ex-policeman John Carlyle. While all the accused were charged with conspiracy, Alastair Smith was granted bail and managed, in the interim, to gain employment with a security firm! He was charged only with possessing pamphlets in contravention of the Official Secrets Act and the other charges against him were dropped as were all the charges against John Carlyle, who left the court a free man.

During the month of May 1975 there were two "tartan terrorist" trials. Colin Boyd was the star witness in both. At the end of them, after four weeks in court and the evidence of 242 witnesses, Michael Fairlie and Tony Tunilla were each sentenced to 12 years for the armed bank robbery. William Anderson got ten years and Alastair Coventry and Robert Berwick were jailed for nine years each. William Murray got another eight years (less than a year after completing four years in jail). Major Boothby was sentenced to three years and William Bell got one year. Boothby served only a few months in jail and was released on grounds of ill-health. In the six or so years of its existence the APG had succeeded only in staging one bungled bank raid and in condemning its members to a total of 76 years of imprisonment.

The hierarchy of the APG had hoped to bring together a coalition of all the nationalist groups which would have been prepared to resist any attempt to suppress by force a democratically expressed demand for Scottish Independence. Their actions had been precipitated by desperation when the SNP failed to gain a majority of Scottish seats in the 1970s. They believed that their actions were based on some sort of popular mandate and would act as a catalyst to force the pace of change by a dramatic gesture. In the event, however, SNP support declined and while the other parties produced their own limited measures of devolution to appease the voters, the SNP failed to make the breakthrough they had anticipated. Nor did the APG succeed in gaining more than the incredulity of the Scottish people and the anger of the very nationalist movement which they had sought to assist. By the systematic use of *agents provocateurs* and informers the British Intelligence community had effectively used the group to create a climate of outrage and suspicion within the nationalist movement and had spread disinformation within the SNP. However, their attempt to entrap the leaders of the SNP by using the APG had largely failed. The APG had been so inept that that had not been possible and, in the end, Special Branch had to content themselves with their minor haul of the APG men and their sympathisers – mere tiddlers to the catch which they had hoped to haul in.

5   PYLONS AND PIPELINES

When the black rain falls, Scotland will rise.

Prophecy of the Brahan Seer

WITH Matt Lygate and his accomplices jailed for their armed raids and the men of the Army of the Provisional Government charged with bank robbery it became clear that a number of incidents remained unsolved. The perpetrators of the massive explosion at Edinburgh Castle during the Festival of 1971 have never been discovered. There had been numerous other explosions and politically motivated acts of theft since that first big bang. There now seemed to be a plethora of "tartan terror" groups: the "Scottish Legion", the "Jacobites", the "Border Clan", the "100 Organisation" and the "Tartan Army". Whether these were all connected, or were indeed the same persons operating under different names, the press tended to lump them all together under the name of the "Tartan Army". This group or groups were responsible for a number of incidents from 1 January 1972 to

31 May 1976 for which 14 persons were eventually charged in a trial that was to make Scottish legal history. At the end of the trial, one man was jailed for five years, another for one year, a third was put on probation for two years and the rest were cleared of all charges. Given the amount of publicity which the "Tartan Army" activities achieved, the embarrassment which they caused to the Scottish National Party, the hysteria engendered amongst Government and NATO security chiefs, it was an unsatisfactory end, as far as the Special Branch were concerned, to one of the most spectacular eras of "tartan terrorism".

The Scottish police had been concerned in 1972 with a number of thefts of detonators and explosives. Most of these incidents remained unpublicised but on Tuesday, 14 March 1972, newspapers carried a police warning subsequent to the theft of detonators from a railway line between Dunfermline and Inverkeithing near Grange Bridge. Then there had been the mystifying disappearance, from the Wallace Monument at Abbeycraig near Stirling on 2 May, of the large two-handed sword of William Wallace. The sword had been removed by nationalists in 1938 but returned. Now, photographs of the six-foot sword pictured against a map of Scotland and a saltire flag, and even on occasion in the hands of men in paramilitary uniform, began to be offered for sale, clandestinely, at nationalist rallies. These thefts were treated seriously by the police, mindful of the Edinburgh Castle incident. But as yet they did not seem to imply an escalation of terrorism.

The failure of the Heath Government to implement its election promises for a Scottish Assembly, given in the so-called "Declaration of Perth" by the Prime Minister, provoked 80-year-old Miss Wendy Wood, a respected figure in Scottish life and leader of the "Scottish Patriots" to announce that she would begin a fast until death to make them carry out their promises. She issued her press statement on 26 November 1972 and the prospect of the life of this elderly woman being entirely in the hands of Prime Minister Heath and Sir Alec Douglas Home appalled the whole Scottish nation. Her fast was given virtually no publicity at its inception and Miss Wood's lone stand, merely to have a promise kept, was universally seen as courageous, though foolhardy. Heath had no real interest in devolution and had merely responded to panic within the Scottish wing of his party. Douglas-Home, however, was actually proud that as a Minister of State in 1951 he had been largely responsible for diverting into futility and oblivion the Scottish Covenant petition containing two million Scots signatures for Home Rule and he was to play an even more questionable role in the 1979 Devolution Referendum. Surely Wendy Wood would die at their hands? Her fast began on 7 December.

The Scots looked on in horror and inertia, but three days after Miss Wood's initial announcement and before the fast itself began there had been three bomb scares. The first was at the Dounreay atomic reactor and led to 2,000 employees being urgently evacuated and the precautionary blowing-up of "two mystery boxes" by experts. The second was at the ICI explosives factory in Ayrshire, and the third was at BP's Grangemouth refinery. All three were claimed by anonymous phone callers to be the work of a group calling themselves "Jacobites". The calls, made to several newspapers, claimed that the "Jacobites" had acquired arms, including mortars and rocket launchers, and had columns in the north – in Argyll and in Perthshire. Although the calls were hoaxes and nothing was found at any of the three locations, it was feared that this was a reaction on the part of some nationalist extremists to the prospect of the inevitable failure of Miss Wood's fast.

Two days into the fast there was an explosion at an electricity pylon near Dumfries. The *Dumfries and Galloway Standard* made it front-page news: "Police and military experts were this week investigating a bomb blast which ripped away one of the supports on the leg of an electricity pylon near Wamphray. The pylon, in a young forestry plantation near Blazehill Farm was not in danger of collapsing, said a police spokesman and the supply was not interrupted."

Approximately ten pounds of explosive had been used and the damage had not been discovered until two days later. That evening an anonymous caller claimed the blast in the name of the "Border Clan" and declared that the action had been carried out "for Wendy Wood and the people of Scotland". A spokesman for Wendy Wood disowned the incident. Miss Wood herself, into the fifth day of her fast, was too weak to comment but the incident raised fears of much greater reaction within Scotland to the prospect of her death – questions had already been asked in the House of Commons by SNP, Labour, Liberal and even Conservative MPs. Pressure was mounting, the Government did not want a martyr on their hands and on the beginning of the fast's seventh day, the Secretary of State for Scotland, Gordon Campbell MP, announced in the House of

Commons that a Green Paper on Devolution would be issued in 1973. A jubilant, though very weak, Miss Wood was able to call off her fast.

The SNP registered protests to the media after newspapers had linked the bomb blast with the party and they obtained apologies. SNP Chairman, Billy Wolfe, in his New Year message on 3 January, warned, without referring to the incident, against "short-cuts". "Frustration", he said, was understandable, but "short-cuts lead to dead-ends". He called for the party to develop greater internal discipline.

Then the Scottish political scene was galvanised with the imminent by-election in Dundee East. A new political party had been born – a splinter from the SNP and destined to exist only long enough to deny a crucial by-election victory in Dundee to the SNP candidate, solicitor Gordon Wilson. George Maclean, an ex-SNP member, standing for the "Labour Party of Scotland" took 1,409 votes and Wilson failed to beat Labour by 1,141. The Labour Party of Scotland was launched in Glasgow in 1971 but the Dundee party of the same name was disowned by them. Neither group was successful. The Dundee LPS attempted to build an organisation and rented rooms. At a special national executive meeting on 24 May 1973, the main body decided to disband so that "the national movement could show a united front". The statement was signed by the Reverend George Wotherspoon, Andrew Gilmour, Neil Gow, John Mackay, Hamish McQueen, John McKechnie and Catriona McKechnie. It passed with only one dissension. Most of the members subsequently rejoined the SNP and some became involved with the pirate radio station, "Radio Free Scotland".

With the run-up to the general election already under way and the SNP highly optimistic about their chances in a number of seats, the last thing they wanted were further bomb incidents. Especially since they faced two unexpected and difficult by-elections, called for the same night, 8 November. The SNP's "It's Scotland's Oil" campaign was rightly acknowledged to be one of the major factors behind the party's dramatic success and the party was greatly embarrassed when an explosion occurred in September at Bridge of Earn, some four miles from Perth, since the target was, for the first time, an oil pipeline. The explosion destroyed a 25-foot, two-ton section of the pipe. No one was in the vicinity but the damage was discovered the next day by the pipe-laying contractors.

The two by-elections were held and while the result achieved by party Chairman William Wolfe at Edinburgh North was relatively poor, Margo MacDonald took almost 42 per cent of the vote to storm home at Govan – a great triumph which brought forth vitriol from opponents. Sir William McEwan Younger, brewery millionaire and Chairman of the Conservatives in Scotland, described the SNP as "the real danger . . . a menace which had to be met aggressively . . . a group of irresponsible mediocrities". A past president of the Liberals described the SNP as "a ragbag of extremists". They were also described publicly as "the polluters of politics", as "the keepers of the nation's inferiority complex". The Shadow Secretary of State, William Ross MP, found the SNP "cheap, shoddy, irrelevant, a disgrace to the name of Scotland". An Aberdeenshire minister went so far as to describe the SNP in a letter to the press as "nascent nazis" because of their anoraks, which seemed to him like a uniform! Such was the tense political situation when the general election was called for February 1974.

There were considerable complaints over the amount of TV time allocated to the SNP and protests over bias towards the "London" parties. The SNP were equally furious, however, when a bomb, estimated at 20 pounds of explosive, damaged the base of a BBC relay station pylon near Falkirk on 3 January. The blast was heard within a five-mile radius. Although BBC staff had been at the station none were injured in the explosion which blew a two-foot hole at the bottom of a wall at the base of the Wester Glen pylon. The attack was claimed by the "Border Clan" in an anonymous phone call to the Glasgow office of the *Scotsman* and the reason given was retribution for the Government's failure to set up an Assembly and the refusal to give sufficient broadcasting time to "nationalist causes". The police believed from the start that the attack was linked to the earlier incident near Dumfries and Detective Superintendent David Pitcaithly, head of Stirling and Clackmannan CID, made a trip to view the pylon at Wamphray. The police announcement that they were to investigate "an extreme group of nationalists" was reported on the front page of the next day's *Scotsman*. They announced a few days later that a definite link between the two cases had been established. The same type of materials had been used in both explosions.

The February general election resulted in the SNP winning 630,000 votes, almost 22 per cent of Scottish votes and gaining seven MPs. However, it soon became apparent that a second election would be called in the autumn. There was little doubt that the SNP would be challenging even more strongly. They were now in second place in 17 seats. The *Scots Independent* of July noted "a flood of interest, support and membership", but also warned that "there is reason to assume that Unionist reaction takes a privy as well as a public form. It is time to be particularly on guard against *agents provocateurs*."

It was a timely reminder, for several weeks later there was another explosion and what was even more annoying for the SNP which had just announced its second Oil Campaign was that the target – for the second time – was an oil pipeline. The explosion occurred in West Lothian near the BP refinery at Grangemouth. Although the explosion had been heard in the Bo'ness area on Sunday, 21 July, it was only after an anonymous telephone call to the *Scotsman* on the following day that police and representatives of the pipe-laying contractors found the damaged section. There was little apparent damage to the 30-inch-diameter steel pipe although police later said that about six feet of the pipe, which was due to link the BP's tank farm at Dalmeny with the Grangemouth refinery, had been destroyed. The caller had said: "Listen carefully, the Tartan Army has blasted the pipeline just beyond Grangemouth about 3 a.m. And another thing, this nonsense about the Scottish Legion. Tell the War Office to call it off – *agents provocateurs* is the usual term."

This phone call announced the apparent emergence of two other groups, hitherto unknown. The attack was denounced by William Wolfe, who did not think he had ever heard of the "Tartan Army" but did not think it was beyond the bounds of possibility that "political opponents of the SNP" were behind the outrage in order to discredit the party. Amusingly, this was the same opinion which the "Tartan Army" caller had expressed with regard to the "Scottish Legion"! This latter group had issued a press release to the *Guardian* newspaper and claimed to be prepared to carry out terrorist attacks on English targets to obtain Independence. According to the press release a group of Scots from business, the professions and the services, including "some well placed in government and other strata of public life", had decided to "inflict serious and sustained attacks on the English and if necessary English commercial and industrial targets and public utilities". A list of primary targets had been compiled and reconnaissance had been completed on each. The group claimed that their organisation could not be infiltrated and that its "command structure" had been carefully planned by a British-trained intelligence officer. The group ended with a statement that "except in special circumstances no communiqué will be issued by the Scottish Legion in respect of its operations". The group were as good as their word: nothing further was ever heard of the "Scottish Legion" – if they had ever existed!

There was now considerable unease in Government circles at the prospect of Scottish extremists' attacks on oil installations and a high-level meeting was convened to consider improved security measures. Professor John Erickson of Edinburgh University's Defence Studies Unit and Professor Alan Thompson of Heriot-Watt University issued a joint report on the problems of North Sea Oil Defence in which they called for six to ten 4,000-ton ships with visible armaments, Sea King helicopters and a paramilitary volunteer reserve unit to patrol pipelines and other onshore installations. They refuted the suggestion that this would be a "Dad's Army" and called for adequate training and payment for the volunteers who would be a back-up force to the existing security forces. This report was considered at a Ministry of Defence seminar in London attended by military representatives from all other NATO countries. The report, 40,000 words in length, analysed the dangers of off-shore protection and raised the question of whether armed security men should be used on oil rigs. The question of NATO forces' involvement in this task was mooted but the responsibility for the security of the 50 or so offshore oil installations remained with the Chief Constable of Grampian Police. There were several conferences on this theme and one was organised by NATO at the Royal Naval College in Greenwich, attended by high-ranking NATO military commanders, civil servants, policemen, MPs and academics. Royal Marines from 45 Commando Group meanwhile took part in an anti-terrorist exercise on oil and gas platforms in the North Sea (and photographs of this exercise later appeared on the front pages of The Times and the Guardian and on page two of the Daily Telegraph). The accompanying articles made it clear that the exercise was conceived to counter possible attacks on the rigs – not from the IRA, but from Scottish terrorists infiltrating the oil rig workforces. The idea was that these crack squads would be the experts in recapturing oil rigs. The "tartan terrorists" were being taken very seriously indeed.

In early September 1974 there was a trial in progress at Glasgow Sheriff Court involving nationalists, which became known as the "Radio Free Scotland" trial. The "pirate" radio station had been operating clandestinely since the mid-'fifties at various by-elections around the country, and they claimed they had built up a following of 60,000 listeners. But in February 1974 they had issued a challenge to the Government and the GPO. "Radio Free Scotland stands ready to provide nationwide coverage . . . to counter . . . the daily poison from the mass media," they claimed in a pamphlet – issued to the very press whom they despised – which gave an address in Glasgow where Radio Free Scotland could be contacted. The "pirate" radio station began broadcasting on 17 February on medium wave, 251 metres, three days each week and on BBC1 each Monday after close-down. The location of their transmitter was soon traced to a house in Hill Street, Garnethill, Glasgow, by an executive engineer of the Scottish Communications Board who had read in the *Scotsman* of the proposed transmissions. With two of his staff, he toured the streets of Glasgow with a locating device and found the maximum strength of the broadcast coming from the top flat at 104 Hill Street after only a couple of hours. Inside the flat, there was panic as the police arrived. Desperate attempts were made to hide the bulky transmitter. It later appeared that both the "lookout men" had been drunk. The police refused to let anyone leave the flat for three hours and brought the press. In the subsequent trial at Glasgow Sheriff Court, Hamish McQueen was charged with illegal broadcasting and fined £40. The Reverend Wotherspoon, like McQueen an ex-member of the Labour Party of Scotland, was accused of lying and being evasive in the court. Wotherspoon admitted that he had told a reporter at his arrest that he was the Director-General of Radio Free Scotland. The Sheriff did not see the joke and suggested that this was a lie. Wotherspoon agreed. "I don't think such a post exists." The Sheriff referred to the "adolescent ineptitude" of the accused. He told them: "You are not in any sense a martyr to your political beliefs. The Scottish martyrs of the past were men of sterner stuff."

As predicted the SNP vote rose to an unprecedented level in the October general election. The party took 11 seats and were in second place in 42 more. Their vote had risen to 839,628, 30.44 per cent of the Scottish vote, and they were only 6.4 per cent behind the Labour

Party. There was actually relief in Westminster that the nationalists had not won the election outright. Few could doubt however that victory was now within the SNP's reach.

Then came another two explosions – this time across the border in England and both claimed by the "Tartan Army". The first of the explosions occurred at Rockliffe in Cumbria on 4 February 1975 when one of the towers of an SSEB pylon which carried electricity from Scotland to England was damaged. There was no interruption to the supply. Then, on 7 February, there was a more serious blast at an electricity pylon in a ploughed field, 100 yards off the A698 Cornhill to Berwick Road, just half a mile inside England. Again, there was no interruption to the supply. Police set up road blocks and cordoned-off the area while experts examined the pylon. Both explosions were later described by a spokesman for Cumberland and Northumbria Police as "unprofessional". The police had been given a "garbled message" received by a girl at a Scottish newspaper office warning of the explosion but the girl failed to note the full details. She did remember that the caller claimed to represent the Tartan Army.

There was a further explosion on 13 September, on the BP oil pipeline, this time at Crook of Devon in Kinross-shire, only yards from the A9097 road, which wrecked electronically controlled safety valves. The valve mounting was encased in a six-foot-square concrete plinth, surrounded by a ten-foot-high wire fence with barbed wire. Police described the blast as "a fair-sized explosion". Bomb disposal experts from Edinburgh concluded that the bomb used was "fairly amateurish". BP were unable to estimate how long the damage would take to repair but were sure that it would not delay the opening of the pipeline by the Queen at a ceremony at Dyce, Aberdeenshire, on 3 November. The pipeline itself was not damaged and would not have leaked even if the oil from the Forties field had been "switched on". The *Scottish Daily News* reported the incident under the front-page banner headline "Find The Bombers!" The "Tartan Army" had not claimed responsibility for the blast, although it was attributed to them. "A spokesman for sources close to the Tartan Army said last night that their reaction amounted to 'mystified pleasure'." In fact, a Tartan Army caller to the *Scotsman* at 8.15 p.m. had telephoned specifically to state that the attack was entirely unconnected with the APG. He also denounced bomb attacks on the Dumbarton railway line and the Clyde Tunnel and described the perpetrators of those attacks as "thugs". On 23 September another valve station was hit – at Kinfauns, only ten miles from the Crook of Devon attack. This 3 a.m. attack, the second within 11 days, was a carbon copy of that earlier attack, but more serious. The steel door of the valve control station was hurled 50 feet on to the nearby dual carriageway and fragments of metal were found 300 yards away in all directions. This device was described as "relatively sophisticated". All newspapers were now giving large amounts of publicity to the Tartan Army and speculation as to its organisational structure.

Gordon Wilson, SNP MP for Dundee East, declared that "the Tartan Army are Scotland's enemies" and another SNP spokesman said: "We share a general puzzled disappointment that the instigators of these explosions have not all been found. We know especially that the last thing on earth that the SNP would do, this side of sanity, would be to prejudice the evident expectation of a peaceful democratic march back to national freedom by using or condoning violence . . . we wish the police would find and produce all the bombers." They also referred to a "deliberate unionist campaign . . . to have the SNP morally outlawed as a violent organisation". This was now a main theme of political attacks on the party; that they were in some way connected with violence and that an SNP victory would only increase the risk of "tartan terrorism".

The SNP were not alone in being mystified at the failure of the police to apprehend the bombers who had proved to be a continuing embarrassment to the Scottish National Party. Cynics within the national movement of course suggested that it was the Special Branch "dirty tricks" department who were themselves causing the explosions. In fact, the investigation into the "Tartan Army" bombers was later described as "one of Scotland's biggest post-war investigations". Strathclyde Police Force, at a strength of 10,000 officers, already the second-largest in the UK, were the first to form a special Bomb Squad of 20 officers, drawn from Special Branch, Serious Crime Squad and divisional CIDs. They were followed by Lothian and Borders Police which formed its own, and then a nationwide structure was co-ordinated after a special conference of police chiefs from all the Scottish forces. The *Glasgow Herald* reported that "it seems they are preparing to go to war against the Tartan Army".

The police estimate of Tartan Army "membership" at this time varied between six and 50. The official membership of the SNP was, at over 130,000, the biggest of any Scottish party in history but they had well over three-quarters of a million voters and not surprisingly there were many "hangers-on" and fringe elements. The police recruited an enormous army of spies to infiltrate these circles and spent many hours on surveillance of the activists whose names were from time to time suggested by their "inside men". They were fairly quickly informed about the photographs of the Wallace sword which began to appear for sale and heard rumours also of a meeting which had been held in the residents' lounge of the Caledonian Hotel off Edinburgh's Princes Street in early 1972 where they believed that a conspiracy had been formed by about two dozen people, but their biggest break came with the arrest of David Sharkey in January 1973. Sharkey was convicted of culpable homicide and jailed for ten years after being found guilty of stabbing a seaman to death at a party. As a result of police questioning over that charge it was realised that Sharkey had been heavily involved in the "Tartan Army" activities. He was offered remission if he would co-operate with the police and he agreed. It was also agreed that he would not be charged for any offences which he had committed as a "member" of the Tartan Army.

Sharkey told the police that he had first become involved after meeting Alexander Swan, an SNP activist in Glasgow who had introduced him to Robert Anderson of Dollar. They had all attended the meeting in the Caledonian Hotel and he testified that it was said at that meeting that all those who did not think they should involve themselves in subversive activities should leave. The meeting, Sharkey claimed, had lasted only 20 minutes but he felt that an organisation had been established. Anderson had later taught him to mix sodium chlorate and sugar and other ingredients and to place these in a container. He had subsequently broken into a building site near the Erskine Bridge and stolen six fire extinguishers. Later he stole two more from a garage forecourt in Govan and these were to be used as bomb containers. All six were dumped among the undergrowth at Sheriffmuir in the Ochil Hills, a remote spot near a stream surrounded by overhanging rocks where he, Anderson and a 42-year-old man named Gerard Joseph McGuigan, of Fort William, had experimented with bombs. The first bomb which Anderson and Sharkey made had shattered a 20-ton boulder. Sharkey then told the police they had taken part in surveys of the power-line route south from Cockenzie. This exercise, he told police, had been organised

by a man called Hamish Henderson, a £7,000 a year Manpower
Services Manager with Clydebank District Council, who had been
SNP Councillor for Glasgow's Craigton Ward between 1968 and
1971. Later, Henderson had driven McGuigan, Anderson, Sharkey
and another man called Donald Currie to the site of the Wamphray
explosion. The bomb there, according to Sharkey, had been placed
in the early afternoon, timed to explode at midnight and they had
returned the next day to see if it had exploded, which it had.
Sharkey was also able to tell the police that he had seen the
Wallace sword – in Anderson's house, lying on the living-room
floor on top of a Scottish saltire. A number of photographs had
been taken by another man and the sword had been returned to
its hiding place beneath the kitchen floor. He had later attended a
meeting in the Golden Lion Hotel in Stirling at which it had been
decided to return the sword and he had himself placed it on a wall
of the County Building.

The police were delighted and as a result of his 16-page statement
made numerous arrests in May 1976. They charged 14 persons on
11 September but the accumulation of evidence and the tracing
of witnesses – eventually 199 witnesses were to be cited and 315
productions lodged at the High Court in Edinburgh – was such
an extensive operation that it threatened to exceed the limitations
of the Criminal Procedure (Scotland) Act which allowed the police
to keep the accused in custody for only 110 days. By the end
of that period the trial had to be concluded and if it was not
then the accused could be freed and exempt from any further
prosecution for the crimes. The police predicament was reported
in the *Scotsman* of 22 September whose front-page article was
headed "Legal Loophole May Free Two Tartan Army Accused"
and noted that two of the five who remained accused could be free if
the trial was not concluded within ten days. Lord Stott also refused
to extend the 110-day period after a three-hour debate and turned
down the Solicitor-General's application.

The two men, Gerard McGuigan, a 42-year-old quantity surveyor from Fort William, and Donald Currie, a 34-year-old main-
tenance electrician from Menstrie, Clackmannanshire, were facing
a total of five charges involving conspiracy, causing explosions and
possession of explosives. Three other men, Ewan MacPherson, of
Clackmannanshire, Hamish Henderson, of Bishopton, and Robert
Anderson faced charges of conspiracy to "further the purposes

of an association of persons by criminal means, namely theft, unlawfully and maliciously causing explosions likely to endanger life and to cause serious injury to property, including electricity pylons, oil pipelines, landlines and installations and premises used for broadcasting and inciting others to commit such thefts and cause such explosions . . . to further the cause of an association of persons known variously as the '100 Organisation', the 'APG', the 'Border Clan' and the 'Tartan Army'."

Nine other persons were named in the conspiracy charge: Sharkey, Swan, Kenneth Taylor, of Arden, Glasgow, Gerald Sweeney, of Saltcoats, Gloria Monaghan, of Stevenston, Ayrshire, Catherine Alston, of Auchinleck, Ayrshire, Iain Paterson, of Stirling, Mrs Lyla Cathie, of Menstrie, and Mrs Jeanette Mackie, of Midlothian.

McGuigan, Currie, Henderson and Anderson were charged with the theft of the Wallace Sword and with the explosion at Wamphray and Westerglen. McGuigan and Currie were charged with the pipeline explosions at Bridge of Earn and West Lothian and Crook of Devon although Ewan McPherson was included in this last charge and in the explosion at Kinfauns. McGuigan and Currie were also charged with attempting to steal arms, ammunition, explosives, detonators, fuses and other articles from various premises in Ayrshire and Renfrewshire over a four-year period. A further charge concerned conspiracy "with each other and with persons unknown" to cause explosions at various places "in Scotland . . . and the north of England". A final charge related to an alleged attempt to bomb the French Consulate in Regent Terrace, Edinburgh, on 31 May 1976. McGuigan was seen with Currie in a car in the vicinity, and seen to go up the steps to the Consulate several times. He claimed he had gone to the rescue of a trapped cat. In the car there was a white substance in an envelope and some wires but this did not in reality constitute a bomb.

All five men pleaded not guilty to all charges. It could be seen from the vague nature of some of the charges that the police were having problems substantiating the testimony of the convicted murderer, David Sharkey. In particular, the conspiracy charge became the subject of ridicule by the defence counsels for the accused.

Various witnesses testified that the meeting in the Caledonian Hotel had been for no other purpose than to inaugurate the Labour

Party of Scotland. Alex Swan stated that at the meeting there had been talk of setting up some kind of community government somewhere in Scotland if Scotland could not secure Independence through the ballot box. Questioned by Mr Hugh Morton QC as to whether this meant UDI, Swan admitted that there had been some theoretical discussion as to what might happen after Independence if England denied Scotland's right to it. The police were unable to corroborate that the meeting in the hotel had been a terrorist conspiracy. Strangely, the chairman of the meeting, Reverend Wotherspoon, was not cited as a witness.

Then began a parade of witnesses – but only 73 were called by the Crown – and these gave evidence mostly on what other persons had said or said they had done. It was all rather vague. But then Ewan McPherson changed his plea to guilty to the two bomb charges he was facing, after his mother appeared, tearfully, in the dock. It was stated that McPherson was "of low intelligence" and easily led. McGuigan had apparently confessed while in custody to the proposed bombing of the French Consulate but claimed it was to be done on behalf of some Breton nationalists held in prison in France without trial and that he had been asked to help by the Celtic League, a claim publicly denied by Alan Heusaff, Secretary of the organisation. The police also produced a letter written by McGuigan concerning "arrangements for our pro-Breton event". A raid on Currie's house had provided the police with some evidence: batteries, two time-switches, two fire extinguishers and other bomb factory material. A charge against McGuigan that he had "possessed a fire extinguisher in suspicious circumstances in his house at Fort William" was dropped. A group called the "Craigton Commandos" was mentioned in court, but this turned out to be merely a singing group. Much of the trial was pure farce.

Incredibly, the Solicitor-General proposed that the two principal accused be freed for the last week of the trial, so that while they attended the trial itself, they could not count each day as part of the 110. This move was opposed by the accused's defence but the Judge, agreeing, refused to set bail. Thus, the pair came and went as they pleased! On the last day of the trial when McGuigan was cautioned and charged at lunchtime, he asked the Sergeant what he was being charged with – and the Sergeant didn't know!

There were some unexpected surprises; an elderly housewife told the court of the night she went on bombing expeditions with some

71

of the accused and acted as "an Auntie" to give the impression of innocence in the event of the car being stopped by the police. Silver-haired 63-year-old Mrs Cathie took part in several visits to the oil pipelines at Crook of Devon and Kinross. A 28-year-old teacher, Gloria Monaghan, told the court how she had acted as lookout at the theft of the Wallace Sword, which she had thought to be a "student prank". She told the court that she had had nervous trouble and insomnia ever since and had been sick at the time, partly out of fear.

Summing up the case on 30 September, the Solicitor-General Mr John McCluskey said that "in a short time the accused had progressed from symbolic theft to dangerous explosions which caused damage estimated at more than £40,000 and endangered life on occasions". He also suggested that the "people in the witness box were just as guilty as the accused". Lionel Daiches QC, defence counsel for Henderson, concluded his case by stating that "unlike the pylon at Wamphray which had only one leg blown off, all the legs of the Crown case have disintegrated"!

On the final day, Lord Stott called for an end to the laughter. He suggested that the Crown case had been quite incompetent. On the evidence there was no Tartan Army, he said, it was merely Currie's predilection for fancy-sounding names. He described the case as "a grim, uncivilised and highly dangerous bombing campaign [which] caused widespread public alarm in Scotland".

The unsatisfactory nature of much of the evidence may have accounted for the fact that while Currie received a five-year sentence, McGuigan one year and McPherson two years' probation, Henderson and Anderson were cleared of all charges. The other nine accused of conspiracy had earlier been released. Sharkey, who had admitted that he had been one of the main perpetrators – indeed, he was described as "the central figure" – was not charged. Many newspapers reported the trial as a defeat for the Crown. The *Scotsman* said: "The Crown has taken a beating . . . the desperate expedients adopted . . . did little to enhance public respect for the law."

Time had been devoted during the trial to analysis of a prophecy of the Brahan Seer: "When the black rain falls, Scotland will rise." Currie had reportedly recited this prophecy to various of his co-conspirators. Was the black rain "oil" and if so, did it require an explosion to "fall"? This was the farcical level of some of the evidence brought to substantiate a conspiracy to overthrow the British State.

6   THE SPIRIT OF INSURRECTION

I can see no likelihood that this fictional serial will establish any kind of pattern for the real future.

Charles Curran, Director-General of the BBC, replying to criticism of the televising of Scotch on the Rocks, *16 May 1973*

IT was perhaps no surprise in view of the dramatic rise of the Scottish National Party that thrillers would be written featuring the scenario of political tension between Scotland and England: where the SNP had gained a majority of Scottish seats but were thwarted by Westminster, leading to armed struggle. What *was* perhaps surprising was that such books should be written by a senior English Conservative MP, Douglas Hurd, at the time Private Secretary to Ted Heath, the Leader of the Opposition, but who later rose to become Home Secretary in Government, while another was written by no less a person than the Press Secretary of Her Majesty the Queen! The thriller which Hurd wrote, in conjunction with Andrew Osmond, former editor of *Private Eye* was *Scotch on the Rocks*. The other novel was *The Dollar Covenant* by Michael Sinclair – the *nom-de-plume* of Michael Shea, the Queen's Press Secretary. His book featured an independent Scotland sliding into anarchy and bankruptcy. He had "cleared it with the Queen and she had no objections" about its blatant political message. *Scotch on the Rocks*, however, was to become much more famous – or notorious . . ..

Scotch on the Rocks first appeared in mass-market paperback in 1971 and sold remarkably well. Hardly surprising, given the political temperature and the paranoia over the rise of nationalism and the nationalists' own suspicions of infiltration by *agents provocateurs*. It was denounced by the SNP as "highly improbable" and there were accusations that the book had been written purely to discredit the movement and to "scare off" potential voters. Tom Nairn, in his essay "Old Nationalism, New Nationalism" in the *Red Paper On Scotland* referred to it as "the supreme chef d'oeuvre of sub-cultural Scotchery . . . holding up our fellow countrymen to the ridicule and contempt of all sane and judicious human beings". The book employs a range of Scottish stereotypes, some of which were rather obviously and unflatteringly based on living nationalist leaders – James Henderson, the canny SNP leader, is a composite of several well-known SNP figures, while the impassioned and cranky Mrs Merrilees is a mocking portrait of Wendy Wood, the leader of the "Scottish Patriots"; then there is the token SNP Socialist (and typically he also turns out to be the leader of the terrorists); a glamorous, and promiscuous, aristocratic blonde, Sukey Dunmayne; and a selection of rude Caledonians, mostly called Hamish, representing a mythical nationalist army, the "Scottish Liberation Army". Perhaps most surprising of all, was the return – after 40 years – of the Glasgow razor gangs, somehow miraculously resurrected from the pages of *No Mean City* (and imbued, apparently with the secret of eternal youth!), to link up with the SLA. Just to ensure that the readers got the message that these were the "baddies" the SLA/razor gangs are later proved to have communist links and to be funded by "Moscow Gold". They are of course defeated by several stiff-upper-lipped heroes conjured from the pages of John Buchan, although, like Sir Walter Scott, the authors took care to make the book's "real" hero, the Special Branch undercover agent, McNair, a Scotsman, and slightly sympathetic to nationalist aspirations.

The mythical activities of the SLA included the burning-down of St Andrew's House, the blowing-up of the Forth Road Bridge tolls and Queen Victoria's statue, the attacking of the Conservative Conference in Blackpool, the assassination (by an error) of the Secretary of State for Scotland and the kidnapping of Lord Thorganby, an anti-nationalist (possibly based on Alec Douglas-Home), who was later "handed back" to the Government unharmed. Eventually, the SLA break out into open rebellion and, for some unknown and barely credible reason, decide to "occupy" the Fort William area, like a latter-day Jacobite rising. One of their number is shot dead and the rest surrender while the Government publicly reveal the SLA's links with the French Communist party and the Breton extremists and simultaneously concede some form of self-government to the Scots.

While the book did not cause more than mild irritation and interest on publication and its reprinting in 1972, it was a different situation when BBC Scotland announced plans to serialise *Scotch on the Rocks* on prime time evening television. Nationalists were furious and many letters began to appear in newspapers complaining of the anti-SNP bias of the BBC. A letter published in the January 1973 issue of the *Scots Independent* newspaper complained that "the powerful medium of television will sow this image of the SNP in the minds of the Scottish people. As the next general election draws near, our anglicised press will rehash their tales of the Party's connections with a mysterious military force and no doubt there will be a few strange explosions."

The protests culminated in an official complaint to the BBC by the Scottish National Party. Gordon Wilson, SNP Vice-Chairman, wrote again a few days after a reply of 26 May from BBC Director-General Charles Curran which had dismissed the serial as "a political fantasy". "I cannot believe," wrote Mr Curran, "that any viewer in Scotland or elsewhere will look upon it as anything but entertainment . . . I am bound to say that I see no likelihood that this fictional serial will establish any kind of pattern for the real future." Mr Wilson wrote back:

Thank you for your letter of 16 May regarding *Scotch on the Rocks*. I note what you say regarding the lack of reaction to the novel but I think you may agree that the TV serial will reach a larger audience and have more impact than the novel.

Having now seen subsequent episodes and having reconsidered the book which the producer of the serial claims to have followed faithfully it seems to me that a second ground of complaint emerges.

Your letter mentions enough realism to achieve that measure of dramatic credibility which is normally described as a suspension of disbelief. The technique is achieved partly by injecting the action in and about the SNP instead of about some mythical political agency in Scotland. Despite some mild disclaimers, the Party is shown to have elements favouring violence for political ends and to have extreme left wing associations.

As is known from the book, the political violence shown in the film is eventually seen to emanate from communist sources. The two references to violence and left wing agitation are completely unfounded and indicate a political slur by the BBC on the Scottish National Party.

And lest you claim ignorance that these allegations exist in fact let me advise you that the Conservative Party has been using this smear for the last five years and that their candidate in the recent Dundee East By-Election employed it once more.

In these circumstances, it would be interesting to enquire why the BBC has adopted a political theme appearing in a book written in part by a Conservative candidate who is personal assistant to the Prime Minister when that theme is currently in use in Scotland by members of the same political party. In short, in five episodes, over 200 minutes, the SNP is pilloried by the BBC.

Mr Wilson concluded his letter by pointing out the very limited rights of reply to which the SNP had recourse.

In an article in the *Radio Times* by Julie Davidson and George Rosie, the first episode of the programme was specifically related to the *real* SNP. The article left no room for doubt and went on to mention "occasional rumours of a secret Scottish army", which "even the extremist 1320 Club denied existed". Hugh MacDiarmid, the 1320 Club's patron, was quoted as saying that "armed action might be forced on the Scots" and the article then went on to interview Gordon Wilson about the possibility of violence ensuing as a result of SNP electoral success. Bob Tait, editor of *Scottish International* suggested that violence would almost certainly be engendered and he found the whole scenario quite plausible. This was quite predictable. *Scottish International* magazine was founded in 1969 and many believed it was heavily funded by the establishment through the Scottish Arts Council to provide an intellectual antidote to the 1320 Club's successful magazine *Catalyst* – and also to give the Arts Council an excuse to avoid giving funds to *Catalyst*. Its role was clearly a political one – anti-nationalist (as its title would imply) – and it went bankrupt in 1973 at the height of the SNP surge. Also interviewed in the article was Conservative MP George Younger, Parliamentary Under-Secretary of State at the Scottish Office, who took the opportunity to remind readers of the SNP's extremist past and the campaign of blowing up pillar-boxes in the 1950s. The connection had been forcibly made for all time: Scottish nationalism equals violence.

Scotch on the Rocks was not mere entertainment. It was a political tract whose crude but highly effective message was a stab at the jugular of the SNP; an attempt to separate the party from its mass electoral success, to forge a link in the minds of the Scottish public between the new generation of highly effective middle-class intellectual leaders of the SNP with communists and mythical terrorists. The SNP had just cause to protest; even although they had little opportunity to make those protests publicly known. They were to protest again, in September 1975, when a BBC mini-series drama *Oil Strike North* portrayed a drunken, rabble-rousing lout – the drama's main "baddie" – wearing an SNP badge and using physical violence to achieve his ends.

But the TV serial of *Scotch on the Rocks* was to produce a quite unexpected reaction in a generation of young Scots. While it may have alarmed, disturbed or merely amused their elders, young Scots in their teens and early twenties found the programmes *inspiring*! A wild spirit of insurrection echoed around the country. The extent of it was quite astounding. It involved hundreds of quite spontaneous and unorganised incidents in nearly every town and city in Scotland over a period of almost three years. In the main, these were escapades committed out of a political bravura, high-jinks rather than acts of terrorism, although there were several more serious incidents. Nationalist grafitti appeared on walls, bridges, shops, banks, hoardings along with fly-posted leaflets demanding "Free Scotland Now" or "Free Matt Lygate" and a whole range of amateurish home-made posters with a hundred political exhortations. Some of these fly-posterers were arrested and charged for criminal damage. This merely acted as an accolade among young nationalists. These were exciting times. Petty acts of vandalism occurred; windows of Government buildings were broken, statues were defaced; Queen Victoria's statue in Dundee was covered in white gloss paint as if it had been bombed by a giant seagull and a photograph and story made the front pages of the Dundee *Evening Telegraph*. A young nationalist, Alasdair Nicholson, was convicted of causing a minor fire at St Andrew's House on New Year's Day, 1973, by breaking a ground-floor window and throwing a petrol bomb through it. Firemen managed to contain the fire to one room and there was little damage. Young nationalists kept watch on military premises, particularly Territorial Army depots and stole explosives. The police were unable to convict anyone for theft of Army equipment from Cultybraggan training camp in Perthshire. At the Scottish Tar Distillers at Lime Road, Camelon, a large amount of gelignite was stolen. Police were alerted and numerous patrol cars were searching local streets within minutes. The search ended with the recovery of all the stolen explosives. Four youngsters *under the age of 16* were later taken into custody. Staff and customers of a post office in Bonnygate, Fife, had to be evacuated when eight packets of plastic explosive were found. A bomb disposal team was called and police were unable to say where the explosives had come from. There were minor fires and vandalism at the offices of Conservative, Labour and Liberal parties and a spate of disappearances of the office plaques, which were simply unscrewed and removed. Union Jacks were stolen so often from public buildings throughout Scotland that many authorities ceased to fly them at all. In Aberdeen for instance the large Union Jack was removed from the City Chambers, together with the key enabling access to the turret from where it was flown and no Union Jacks were flown for almost two years after that. All of this activity was quite spontaneous and widespread and perpetrated by young nationalists who had been inspired by the television serial of *Scotch on the Rocks*.

During the period of this agitation and insurrection, several young Scots from the Dumbarton area experimented with home-made explosives in a disused quarry on the outskirts of town. All were young nationalists and some were keen attenders of chemistry classes at school. It was a bit of a prank – but it ended in the High Court in Glasgow.

Four youths stood in the dock of the High Court during a four-day trial in January 1975 charged with causing at least three explosions between July and September the previous year. The judge, Lord Thompson, pronounced the ring-leader as Raymond Lester, an 18-year-old, and sentenced him to six years in a Young Offenders Institution for his part in constructing and planting all three of the bombs. His accomplice, Robert Maldar, was sentenced to four years. A third youth, 15-year-old Alistair Crawford, was found guilty by a majority verdict of causing an explosion and had his sentence deferred for one year. Crawford and a fourth youth denied that they were members of the "Army For Freeing Scotland".

The first bomb had been placed on 26 June 1975 in the doorway of the Bank of England in St Vincent Place, Glasgow, by Lester and Maldar. This was the biggest device and had been fitted with a booby trap which would have activated the device had anyone opened the hold-all in which it was contained. The bomb contained chemicals in two one-gallon containers and anyone standing over it when it exploded could have been killed, according to a bomb disposal expert at the trial. The second device was intended for Woolworth's in High Street, Dumbarton, but when 15-year-old Crawford refused to accompany Lester to plant the bomb it was decided instead to plant it on the railway line between Bowling and Glasgow.

The fourth youth, James Clubb, a former Chairman of Dumbarton Young Scottish Nationalists, and one of the youths who had attended the experiments at the quarry, testified at the trial that Lester and Crawford had come to his house on the evening of 15 September and asked him to phone British Rail at Dumbarton Station and ask when the next train to Glasgow was. He did so and was told that all trains had been cancelled due to a bomb scare. He said that Lester "seemed to be expecting it". Shortly afterwards there was a bang from the direction of the railway line and Lester said, "That's it." He danced with joy and repeated: "That's it – it's magic!" Then he told Clubb that he had planted a bomb on the line. There had been a bomb scare earlier that day on the same line, between Clydebank and Helensburgh. Helensburgh Station had had to be evacuated. Services had been halted on that part of the line for 15 hours and thousands of commuters had been greatly inconvenienced, having to use buses. BR later admitted they had received *at least* seven bomb hoaxes that day throughout West Central Scotland!

An army bomb disposal expert told the High Court that the bomb was not sufficiently strong to derail a train. He said however that if it had exploded while someone was close to it there was a strong possibility they could have been injured by broken glass or small stones. If it had gone off while someone was defusing it, at best that person would have been badly burned and at worst possibly killed. A police forensic scientist told the court that a mixture of sodium chlorate and sugar in a bottle could cause a high explosion and was "potentially lethal".

The third bomb was planted by Lester and Maldar in the Clyde Tunnel on 21 September. The police received a telephone warning from a young woman at nine p.m. and sealed off the Clyde Tunnel. The bomb exploded in the pedestrian lane as the police were searching for it. It was a "bottle bomb" with a timer, similar to the railway line device. Lester had planned several more bombs in the Glasgow area to take police pressure off the Dumbarton vicinity. He changed his plea to guilty after the trial's first day.

It was clear from the evidence at the trial that no such organisation as the "Army For Freeing Scotland" – also referred to as the "Scottish Freedom Army" – actually existed. Lester and Maldar were workmates and, when discussing Scottish nationalism, Lester simply asked Maldar if he wanted to join the "Scottish Freedom Army" and Maldar agreed. Lester said that the army's main targets were English or Government-owned buildings in Scotland. James Clubb told the court that Lester had asked him to join but had not said what the organisation was to do, "only that the name was self-explanatory. They wanted to free Scotland and explosions would be part of it." Crawford had testified in front of a Sheriff that he had not heard of the AFS and was not a member. Robert Maldar's defence QC stressed, in his summing-up: "There is no question of any organisation and Maldar never had any contact with anyone other than Lester."

Despite the fact that the 15-year-old, Alistair Crawford, was, according to his counsel, merely "an innocent bystander who had acted like a daft laddie", and was not involved in constructing or planting the bomb on the railway line, he was found guilty of causing an explosion. His QC, Mr Donald, complained that "it made a mockery of the law for his client to have had to stand trial . . . he was young and easily led . . .".

Mr John Dowdall QC, defending Raymond Lester, claimed that Lester and Maldar had carried out the explosions out of "juvenile bravado", and added, "in the current political climate there is a danger that this sort of nonsense might receive a penalty which it would not otherwise merit".

Photographs of Lester and Crawford appeared in the *Scotsman* on 8 January and while Lester is clearly an adult, with long, curly hair, Crawford, wearing his school uniform and with short, school-length hair, clearly was not.

In sentencing the three youths, Lord Thompson said he understood that the accused had told the police they had just done it "for kicks" and that the explosions were not done with the deliberate intention of killing people but were committed with "a reckless, criminal disregard for other people's lives". The maximum sentences for the offences were "life" and "20 years". "This," said Lord Thompson, "was how seriously Parliament had regarded these offences. Youths like you seem to think you are big enough and clever enough to act in defiance of the law and to act in such a way as to endanger lives and to put at risk the property of ordinary law-abiding citizens."

This was the most serious of the incidents arising directly out of the televising of *Scotch on the Rocks* which had inspired several hundreds, if not thousands, of young Scots with a spirit of insurrection. Nationalism, when linked, for whatever reason, with the incendiary ingredient of militant resistance to a perceived oppressive and distant authority proved to be a heady brew indeed for the idealistic and easily intoxicated youth of Scotland.

7   GLASGOW PUBS AND REPUBLICAN CLUBS

The Scottish Republican Army are a Socialist army of workers, students and ex-soldiers who want to strike a revolutionary blow for Scotland. They are not connected with the APG, though they had talks in September 1974 at the Perth HQ of the APG.

Anarchist magazine Wildcat, *May 1975*

THE Scottish Republican Army was first formed in 1916 when several veterans of the Scottish Brigade of the IRA who had seen combat in the Irish Civil War returned home. One of the founders was Seamus Reader, who had organised the Scottish Brigade. It was short-lived. Scotland was not ripe for Irish-style revolution. Then, in the late 1930s, the paramilitary Scottish Defence Force had been formed, and the Glasgow Brigade of the SDF, some 80 men, trained on the Campsie Fells. Reader was one of four Commandants. Ronald MacDonald Douglas was another. Then there had been the Fianna na-h-Alba, a quasi-military organisation for working-class boys aged 12 to 15 in Glasgow in the late 1940s and early 1950s. In November 1953, four men, alleged to be members of the SRA, were charged with possession of explosives in a sensational trial. This was the time of the "Great Pillar Box War" when post-boxes were blown up and regalia featuring the EIIR insignia were attacked. Coinciding with an IRA offensive on the Ulster border, it seemed as if the SRA had been reconstituted – but this was not the case. From time to time, a Scottish Republican Army was conjured up by headline-seeking journalists but the truth was that it did not exist. For some Scottish Republicans this was greatly disappointing. There was a yearning, especially towards closing time in pubs, for such an organisation to exist and some people actually convinced themselves that it did.

Glasgow was a city with a large Irish population and many Gaelic-speaking Highlanders; half of the city shared a tribal culture with their Celtic counterparts in Erin. It was a sectarian city. A city of violence, religious fanatics, football loyalty, hard drinking; a city where self-preservation seemed to necessitate membership of a gang or a group. When the Provisional IRA guerilla war in the North of Ireland began in 1969 there were many in Scotland, particularly in Glasgow, who could not condemn them. Scottish nationalism in the West of Scotland tended to have a Republican hue. The city had a heritage of militant socialism, of rent strikes and pacifism prior to the First World War. In 1919 tanks had had to be sent in to subdue the masses. There was a tradition of mass meetings on Glasgow Green, of the "red Clydesiders" such as John Maclean, Willie Gallagher and James Maxton. Glasgow had imbued traditions of working-class loyalty, nationalism and anti-imperialist emotion which had been nurtured by the oral folk traditions of the Scottish folk revival and the anti-Polaris movement. There were many organisations in the West of Scotland with direct links with the "troubles" in Ulster, including the Glasgow Irish Freedom Action Committee and the Republican Bands Alliance. When the IRA Provos began their war they had many supporters in Scotland – and in Wales. In fact, the Official IRA sold all their weapons to the "Free Wales Army" in 1968 and many wondered if the Welsh militancy would spread to Scotland. The rising tide of nationalism and the cultural heritage of republicanism in the West of Scotland made it seem likely that it would. But there were other reasons for the growth of republican sentiment in Scotland.

The Queen came to Stirling University in 1972 and was met by an extraordinary but quite spontaneous demonstration of students, one of whom waved his whisky bottle and shouted *"Slainthe Mhath!"* which in Gaelic means "Cheers!". Fearing aggression, however, the Queen's security men forced her to divert her route. The press exaggerated the incident, the students were denounced, 23 were charged, the President of the Students' Union was "sent down" for one term and some students were eventually expelled. The unfairness of this reaction caused an upsurge in republican feeling and some students formed a Scottish Republican Club. Shortly afterwards students at Strathclyde University formed a second Scottish Republican Club.

The great hero of Scottish republicans is John Maclean, whose role in "red Clydeside" was rather exaggerated by them. Maclean, before his death in 1923, formed the Scottish Workers' Republican Party, which had disbanded in the mid-1930s. The party was briefly re-formed in 1973 in Stirling. Unlike the Workers' Party of Scotland, which was Maoist, the new SWRP was a Trotskyite group. The party split in September 1974, however, after allegations of a bomb plot and rumours of the founding of a military wing to kidnap politicians. This of course was the "Scottish Citizens' Army of the Republic". The party continued for two years and issued many statements opposed to the concept of violence for political ends. There were many tales of what had happened within the SWRP to cause such violent schism and it has been suggested that the party had two factions, a political socialist element and a militant nationalist one. When the nationalists were expelled, the remainder of the party joined – *en masse* – the breakaway Scottish Labour Party.

It was obvious from the very beginning that any republican agitation would be centred in Glasgow and the West of Scotland. There had been a small group known as the Scottish Workers' Republican Club in the Glasgow area prior to the setting-up of the Strathclyde University SRC and some of those expelled from the SWRP were soon members of a new Glasgow Central branch of the SWRC, which soon renamed itself to fit in with the two Scottish Republican Clubs already in existence. Donald Anderson, an ex-soldier, David Leadbetter and Jeanette Carpenter were expelled from the SWRP for trying to set up a "military wing" and for being in contact with a serving soldier in Northern Ireland,

Alistair Smith. Smith was in fact a soldier until January 1975 and later married Carpenter, who had previously been the girlfriend of Bill McPherson (see Chapter 3). These persons, with John Carlyle, who until 1972 had been a policeman and had resigned from the SWRP in protest at the expulsions, soon became the leading lights in this new Glasgow-based "Club".

Part of the reason for the expansion of the "clubs" was the ease with which Student Association funds could be obtained. Each new student club simply had to sign a form and outline in a dozen words the aims of the club and they could obtain perhaps £50 per term. It could be done with two students, and many left-wing groups were up to this trick. It was Student Union money that allowed the proliferation of the IMG, the IS, the RCG, RCT, CPGB, SPGB and numerous other groups throughout the UK. "None of us could be bothered with Donald Anderson's SWRC. We only got you to set it up because we wanted to siphon student funds like the IMG and the IS did," wrote Norman Easton, a continuing member of the SWRP (and soon to be Executive member of the SLP) to a former ally. Thus, new "Clubs" began to be formed and, within two years, there was representation in every major city in Scotland. Despite this, the nexus was always Glagow; where Carlyle was for several years the Secretary of such national co-ordination as the SRCs allowed themselves and Anderson was national organiser. There was considerable resistance to the idea of national co-ordination: each group was to organise and recruit for itself and could do more or less what it liked. Carlyle edited a duplicated newsletter, which soon was retitled *Scottish Breakaway*. In early 1976, the Glasgow Central Branch began to call itself the Scottish Republican Socialist Club, and gradually others began to follow suit.

From the very first, the "Clubs" were clandestine. Necessarily so, because the Special Branch were taking a great interest in Scottish nationalist groups, especially those which were connected with "dangerous" republicanism. This was almost welcomed by some of the SRC leading lights who seemed to want a movement closely allied to violence. One meeting, attended by about 30, including a representative from the Independent Socialist Party of Northern Ireland, was reported in the press. "A warning that force might have to be used for Scotland to gain real freedom from Westminster was given at a meeting of the Scottish Republican Club in Glasgow yesterday. Mr David Leadbetter, Chairman of the Glasgow branch of the Club (*and the missing Crown witness in the APG trial*) said: 'Real freedom has never been achieved without the use of force.'" During an interview, Leadbetter referred to "16 Scottish political prisoners". The close links of the Clubs with convicted "tartan terrorists" was soon noted. Members visited prisons and funded prisoners' aid committees. When the Clubs printed a document giving detailed instructions on how to make bombs they were taking a highly provocative direction. All this was enough to attract the attention of the newly formed Scottish Bomb Squad and the Strathclyde Support Unit (formed to deal with riots and strikes). A ten-page pamphlet of the Glasgow SRSC titled *Special Branch and Security Forces – A Chronicle of Current Events* in 1975 noted that "Scottish police are being sent to England for intensive anti-guerilla warfare training and . . . senior detectives and Scottish crime squad officers have been on courses in the South-East of England to be trained in surveillance techniques". The same article also called attention to the existence of section F4 at the Home Office, which was responsible for dealing with subversive groups. The SRSC founders desperately wanted to be subversives. Cloaks and daggers were part of their daily wear.

A great deal of the activity of the SRSC was conducted in public houses in Glasgow. As pints were sunk and talk of political activity became exhausted, tales would be told of *agents provocateurs*; of dramatic and spectacularly successful military operations against "the Brits". Men would undo their shirt top buttons and reveal a silver phoenix medallion – the supposed "operational medal of the IRA". Events, exaggerated with each new telling, involved quantities of sawn-off shotguns, weed killer and chlorate bombs. Much of the drinking took place in pubs in the "Garngad" – a small area of Dennistoun – or in the Press Bar in Albion Street, in the shadow of the Scottish *Daily Express* (which became the ill-fated *Scottish Daily News*). This was a dingy bar, ill-lit and reportedly favoured by journalists, although it seemed to find favour also with a cross-section of the sub-criminal world and Glasgow low-life in general. The Glasgow republicans always seemed to have close links with the world of the petty criminal, the would-be "hard man", and until the SRSC was forced in 1978 to reorganise (largely by new clubs in Edinburgh, Dundee and Aberdeen) along national lines, the image of republicanism to outsiders was one of poor articulacy, an obsession with the IRA and a lack of organisation and ambition.

In a leaflet headed *Guidelines for Membership and Building Clubs* it states "where one club wishes to start a national campaign round a particular issue, then that Club shall canvass all other clubs and set a date for a meeting and the level of commitment of each club will be left to each club". This again meant that all members got to know what all the groups were doing. And the final sentence states: "No restriction is therefore put on any Club as to the *methods* they wish to adopt to bring about Independence."

The Glasgow SRSC itself seemed extraordinarily devoid of ambition. They were of course a cross-party organisation and some of their members were politically active in the SNP, the SLP, or more active in the John Maclean Society or the 1820 Martyrs Committee or in the Scottish Political Prisoners' Aid Committee. Cynics might feel that this looseness was the best format for *agents provocateurs* to obtain information on persons likely to be enticed into "tartan terrorist" activities without actually having to get involved themselves. Without central control, the Clubs merely acted as a focus for numerous activities occurring outwith their own paid membership. And so nothing happened. The SRSC was almost like an organisation that did not really exist. But the Special Branch were busy and numerous people on the fringes of the Clubs, principally the eight APG men, were arrested, charged and jailed. The ninth, John Carlyle, ex-policeman and SRSC Secretary, was acquitted. The Clubs took care to enjoy "a good relationship with the SNP" by steering clear of any attacks on the SNP – again, a sensible course if the Clubs wished to attract or entice hot-headed nationalists.

The SRSC was a natural clearing-house for all kinds of fantasy and paranoia. Rumours of secret armies abounded. In 1975 there was supposed to have been a well-armed group in Glasgow and another group elsewhere who apparently trained in Moniave in Nithsdale. These apparently had World War Two weapons – Sten guns, Brens, Stirlings . . .. They travelled in a Land Rover from Edinburgh in April or May 1975 and were seen wearing camouflage uniforms but no insignia. Reputedly one of them was an ex-Royal Marines Sergeant-Major. Some people said that their equipment belonged to the British Army and that the men had some continuing connection with the Army – possibly with the Territorials.

In January 1976 it was estimated that ten SRSC members were in prison.

The Queen made what the *Daily Record* described as "A Majestic Mistake" in May 1977 when she specifically condemned the proposals for Scottish devolution: "Perhaps this Silver Jubilee is a time to remind ourselves of the benefits which Union has conferred, at home and in our international dealings, on the inhabitants of all parts of this United Kingdom." It was ill-timed, blatant and attracted fury from many people in Scotland where after all republicanism was in a tiny minority, where even the SNP were monarchists.

The political situation of Scotland was growing increasingly frenetic. It soon became apparent that reorganisation within the SRSC was going to be forced on to the Glasgow hierarchy. New and effective Clubs in Dundee, Edinburgh, Paisley, Aberdeen and Stirling demanded a proper nationally co-ordinated framework. A previous attempt had been made, by Alastair Smith and Jeanette Carpenter, to create a more efficient organisation, but the Scottish Republican Movement which they formed was short-lived. And there was the matter of the "Guidelines" which stated "no national structure exists, but once a year a Convention will be held". No such convention had ever been held. Some of the original members were now dispersed; David Leadbetter, for instance, was now a member of the Stirling Club. Since Donald Anderson had been arrested and remanded in custody, John Carlyle agreed that an AGM be held at Stirling on 24 March 1979.

It was at this time that some persons bent on real acts of "tartan terrorism" came to the fore and in what became known as the "Stanley Green Trial", which began at the High Court in Glasgow in June 1979, the activities of some Glasgow republicans, members of the SRSC and of an organisation known as the "Scottish Citizens' Army of the Republic" (SCAR) were highlighted.

Stanley Green, a 35-year-old typewriter maker who lived in Easterhouse, was no militant. He told the court that he did "not believe in the politics of violence". He had been a member of the SNP when he first joined the Glasgow SRSC but denied that he had taken part in any criminal activity. Green stood in the dock with fellow SRSC members Donald Anderson and Peter Wardlaw accused of an armed raid on Gilshochill sub-post office in Maryhill in January 1979 when £10,060 in money and postal orders was stolen. Wardlaw was accused of taking part in a second, unsuccessful raid in an off-licence in Chancellor Street, Partick, on

23 December 1978. The three men had been arrested after Green looked inside a suitcase he had been given by Anthony Currie, a former flatmate of Peter Wardlaw, who was already serving seven years for the post office raid.

Thinking the case to contain tools, Green was "dumbfounded" to discover three guns, masks, 260 bullets, 51 cartridges and some of the postal orders and money from the raid. He went out to a public house, hoping to find Wardlaw. Instead, he was spotted by Detective-Inspector John Fleming and after the ensuing conversation, the detectives drove him home and found the arms cache. They also found photographs of two masked men with a sword between them and a Scottish flag in the background. Another photograph showed a man in army-type clothing, holding an object and standing near some rocks on which the letters "SLA" were written. These were SRSC publications.

But Green had an alibi for the armed raid – he was at work at the time – and the charge was dropped. He was instead charged with resetting a quantity of postal orders and with having guns and ammunition with intent to endanger life. He was jailed for four years. The case against Wardlaw and Anderson was found not proven. Evidence at the trial was given by Anthony Currie although he denied that he had made a statement implicating the three men in the raid. Currie received very bad treatment at the hands of prison inmates during his sentence because of his supposed reputation as an informer. Lord Stott commented on the men's membership of the SRSC and said that there was "nothing to suggest that the Club had the slightest connection with violence". This seems a little disingenuous, since the idea of violence, even just in prospect and fantasy was an integral part of Glasgow republicanism.

The March meeting of the SRSC had considered several con-stitutional proposals, the result of which was the formation of the Scottish Republican Socialist League. But Donald Anderson returned to the struggle, furious that the SRSC had been taken over in his absence. He issued a bulletin in the name of the now-defunct SRSC and named himself as "Provisional Organiser". He called a meeting to "reaffirm the Clubs". Many members had resented the "bureaucratic manoeuvring" of those who had formed the SRSL and these were annoyed that the full membership had not been consulted and now wished to re-form the Clubs. In the event, very few remained with the Clubs while a new cadre of politically aware and effective organisers came to the fore in the SRSL. These new activists shared a dislike of the clandestinity of the Glasgow Clubs and wished to expand the League so that republican socialism could be taken seriously as a political force. The new League published several periodicals – *Socialist Scotland* and *Scottish Republic* among them – with a much higher quality both of content and appearance than the Glasgow Clubs had ever achieved. Several of the new League activists were from Glasgow and there grew up two entirely separate groups. However, the decision of Peter Wardlaw and his private clique to side with the League rather than the Clubs weakened the Clubs – and sealed the fate of the League.

Wardlaw's private army used the SRSL as a power base but others were using the Clubs for similar reasons. The Clubs were to rumble on in a very low-key way until 1982 when they formed the nucleus of the Scottish Republican Socialist Party, which contested the Queen's Park by-election in that year – putting republican socialism to the electorate – and obtained a resounding *39* votes! Despite all the plotting and the fantasising and all the pints that had been sunk, Scottish republicanism was no further forward and the Scottish Republican Army remained one of the great Celtic myths.

8 COMMANDANT WARDLAW'S WAR

The Scottish Republican Socialist League are the most dangerous terrorist group in Scotland yet – a group with the capacity of killing hundreds. They are the most well-funded, well-equipped and most fanatical terrorist gang the Special Branch has ever unmasked in Scotland. They did not fail for want of trying.

The Scotsman, 15 October 1980

FIRE sub-officer Charles Archibald was the first to arrive at the second-storey flat in Roselea Drive in the Dennistoun area of Glasgow. Minutes earlier, a call to the station had reported a loud explosion followed by a fire. Outside the building, police and firemen were ushering the last of some 30 families to the comparative safety of a car park. The crowd looked up to where a plume of black smoke poured from the open window of the flat towards the sky. It was a Friday afternoon in late June, 1980. Inside the building, officer Archibald was joined by fireman Thomas McIntyre. The two men donned breathing apparatus and, using chemical extinguishers, made short work of the blaze which was largely confined to the sitting-room. As the smoke cleared, their suspicions were confirmed that the fire was not caused by natural means. Among the charred remains of a table they found a watch and two blackened batteries connected by wire – clearly, the timing mechanism of a bomb.

Within a few minutes of this discovery, officers of Strathclyde Police's Special Branch were converging on the flat. The findings surprised even them. Among the debris they unearthed bomb-making equipment, several sawn-off shotguns, a walkie-talkie radio and a printing machine with several charred leaflets headed "Free Scotland". Further examination produced the name of an organisation and a man's passport.

Special Branch officers were soon on the trail of an obscure left-wing group, the Scottish Republican Socialist League, and pursuing the leader of its military wing, self-styled terrorist, Commandant Peter Wardlaw, across Scotland.

The police operation codenamed "Charlie Chaplin" resulted, after a long chase, in the detention of scores of Scottish nationalists under the provisions of the Prevention of Terrorism Act and in the conviction of seven young Scottish Republicans. They were Peter Wardlaw (32), Leonard Reynolds (32), Dominic McGrady (30), Alexander Ramsey (29), David Hunter (24), Thomas Bryan (23) and Ewen Bickerton (20). These men were found guilty of committing various capital crimes including conspiracy to cause acts of terrorism in the United Kingdom to further the aims of the Scottish Republican Socialist League or some other organisation to the prosecutor unknown, armed bank robbery, possession of fire-arms, ammunition and explosives and the making and planting of bombs with intent to cause damage to property and injury to the public. The verdicts came at the end of a 16-day trial which made Scottish legal history both for its intense security and for the fact that the jury were out for more than nine hours before reaching their verdicts. The judge, Lord McDonald, sentenced the seven to a total of 72 years, the heaviest penalty of 16 years falling on their leader, Peter Wardlaw.

The Scottish media in following up what they thought was a good story perpetuated a number of myths about the Scottish Republican Socialist League which obscured both during and after the trial the truth about the origins, aims and methods of that organisation. One distortion concerned the reason for the foundation of the League. The Scottish press put forward the idea that the League was a sinister new terrorist reaction to the failure of the British Government to implement the majority "Yes" result of the 1979 Devolution Referendum. Nothing could be further from the truth. In fact it was mere coincidence that the League appeared to have been set up after the Referendum. There was no new organisation. An existing group, the Scottish Republican Socialist Clubs, had slightly changed its name at an emergency Annual General Meeting held in Stirling University at the end of March 1979. Militant Scottish Republican tradition has in any case little time for schemes of devolution handed down by British governments. They want complete Independence for Scotland not half-way houses. There was not even a sentimental attachment to the one concrete achievement of the Devolution Act, the Scottish Assembly building at Calton Hill, Edinburgh. Indeed, the terrorists who subverted the League underlined their contempt for devolution by attempting to blow up the Assembly building twice.

Another and more serious misconception about the SRSL was that it was founded as a terrorist organisation. This was completely untrue. As a result of a conspiracy by some League members, a separate group was formed calling itself the Army of the Scottish People (ASP). This conspiracy never had a majority within the League or influence over SRSL policy. As late as June 1980 even as the conspirators were being rounded up by the police, the SRSL National Executive issued a statement reaffirming the League's ideological position against acts of individual terrorism. In fact there was a general feeling both during and after the March 1979 conference of the League that the police had done the organisation a favour by arresting Peter Wardlaw, Donald Anderson and Stanley Green. With the possible paramilitaries out of the way the new League National Council thought that the era of "bombski" romanticism was well and truly over. A false sense of security fell over the movement and the necessity to guard against internal subversion was relaxed, while the leadership busied itself with the dull but essential tasks of organising political events and drawing up a new constitution.

The first real challenge to the new League came when Donald Anderson and Peter Wardlaw were released from prison in August

1979. From Anderson the challenge was open, political and legitimate. He wanted to reassert his leadership over Scottish Republican Socialism and re-create the Clubs in their original looser, more democratic, form. The urgency of Anderson's assault tended to obscure the more subtle and sinister plans that Peter Wardlaw had hatched while in prison. Given the results of the subsequent trial and with hindsight it is easy to identify which was the greater threat to the integrity of the Scottish Republican Socialist League but Peter Wardlaw's activities were by their nature secret and those who knew had an interest in not telling. In retrospect, Donald Anderson's rebellion played right into Peter Wardlaw's hands and this coincidence might suggest that both men were aware of each other's plans. After all, they had been in prison for quite some time and evidence from the trial indicated that Peter Wardlaw had made his first recruit, Alex Ramsey, while he was still inside.

As the conflict with Donald Anderson's old guard intensified, the supporters of the League discovered that they could only rely on a hard-core of some 30 activists who could at any one time attend essential meetings. The majority of these League loyalists came from branches outwith Glasgow, principally Aberdeen, Dundee and Edinburgh. The League support and outlook was therefore Scotland-wide and national. The real problem for the League leadership was Glasgow. Here Donald Anderson and his rival "Provisional Committee" had their main base. The League did have the allegiance of some notable Glasgow men such as the SRSL National Organiser John Graham and Executive member Lewis MacDonald, but in a showdown it was just possible that the League might lose a majority vote in its Glasgow branch to Donald Anderson's Provos. Given this delicate balance of political forces, one person's influence could tip the scales. Peter Wardlaw therefore became the key man in Glasgow. Wardlaw and his friends and relatives came down on the side of the League. He did so because he believed that his terrorist purposes could be better served by a political group that was tightly organised and centrally controlled. At the Stirling Conference in the autumn, Donald Anderson's proposal to go back to the original "Clubs" structure was narrowly defeated. He and his friends subsequently re-formed the rival Scottish Republican Socialist Clubs. Peter Wardlaw's part in the victory of the League leadership was rewarded by his election to the Executive post of Minutes Secretary, one of the League's four named national office-bearers. From this moment Wardlaw was in the heart of the organisation. He could now use the League as a base in his projected war with the British State.

Peter Wardlaw was a 32-year-old former TV mechanic and soldier. He had deserted from the British Army rather than be posted to Northern Ireland. Short and balding, with gold-rim spectacles and goatee beard, he liked to compare himself with a notorious Belfast Republican, "Bald Eagle". He was later described by the Special Branch as a "professional revolutionary". Peter Wardlaw's military campaign was organised in four stages. First, he would recruit a nucleus of members; second, an Active Service Unit would acquire the money needed to finance his operations; third, he would provide education and training for his men in the use of explosives and fire-arms; and finally he would launch a wave of bombings and assassinations throughout Scotland.

Recruitment was for the moment to be confined to the League and to Wardlaw's associates. However, using the SRSL as a cover, contacts were made with other Scottish nationalist groups such as the Scottish National Party's newly formed 79 Group and the militant "Sons of Scotland", soon to be renamed Siol Nan Gaidheal, Gaelic for "Seed of the Gael". The League corresponded regularly with, and sent delegations to, the meetings and demonstrations of other Republican organisations operating in the United Kingdom. These included Sinn Fein, the Irish Republican Socialist Party, the Welsh Socialist Republican Movement and Coivin, an extreme Welsh nationalist group led by convicted ex-terrorist John Jenkins. Peter Wardlaw therefore had plenty of opportunities to make contact with the military wings of Welsh and Irish Republicanism such as the IRA and the Irish National Liberation Army. In Scotland Peter Wardlaw concentrated on Siol Nan Gaidheal as a possible future source of recruits. He met their representatives and sent League Executive member Gerry Whyte to their relaunch meeting in the late autumn of 1979. Gerry Whyte later made himself infamous by being photographed wearing full IRA-style paramilitary uniform at the 1980 Bannockburn Rally – which photograph appeared on the front page of the *Sunday Mail*.

Finance was next on Wardlaw's list. The League was not at this time a wealthy organisation. At the National Council meeting held in Glasgow on 7 October 1979 it was noted that their bank account contained less than £35. The position of the Glasgow branch was even worse. They had no money at all. In fact at that meeting they pressed the national body to collect a levy to help them raise money for a second-hand duplicating machine. Peter Wardlaw did point out, however, that Glasgow hoped to solve their money problems in the near future. None of his colleagues would have guessed quite how.

Commandant Wardlaw's Army of the Scottish People struck its first blow on the morning of 24 October 1979. Peter Wardlaw and Alex Ramsay, a 29-year-old taxi driver, both wearing face masks, burst into a post office in Oxford Street in the Gorbals district of Glasgow. Alex Ramsay thrust a twin-barrelled sawn-off shotgun into the face of the postmistress, 25-year-old Patricia Ward, and then ordered her to open the door to the back of the post office. While Ramsay was holding her at gun-point his scarf mask slipped from his face and in the confusion Miss Ward was able to hide a bag containing £1,000. She further thwarted the raiders by jamming the safe with the wrong key. Wardlaw and Ramsay, alarmed that the raid was not going as planned, fled with only £978. The result had been barely worth the risks, but for the ASP a beginning had been made.

Later the same afternoon the terrorists' careers almost came to an end. Wardlaw was interviewed in Easterhouse by Detective-Sergeant Robert McElvenny and another policeman about a stolen car. When they told him they were taking him to Craigie Street police station on the south side of the city, Wardlaw said he supposed they would be trying to do him "for that thing in the Gorbals this morning". This half-admission startled the police because no publicity about the Gorbals raid had been given to the media. When pressed for details Wardlaw blurted out, "Sorry I can't answer that or I'll end up getting done – shot!" This intriguing statement failed to arouse the interest of the police. It ought to have done, for earlier the Special Branch had been tipped off that some political connection with criminal activity was going on in the city and Wardlaw was of course a known Scottish Republican activist. In the event he was held that night and released in the morning. Wardlaw was lucky, the attention of the police was focused elsewhere.

In early November a wave of detentions of Scottish and Irish nationalists occurred throughout West Central Scotland. Some 12 people including League National Organiser John Graham and

Section of pipeline at Bridge of Earn damaged by Tartan Army bomb,
Sept 1973

Scene of the Tartan Army blast at Kinfauns, Sept 1974

Major F. A. C. Boothby with Hugh MacDiarmid, 1975

Spirit of Wallace Republican Band

SNG march at Ayr, 1980: Tom Moore is leading

Scottish Republican drum corp at a rally, c.1980

SÌOL NAN GAÌDHEAL

to act where words go unheeded

JOIN US NOW !

SÌOL NAN GAÌDHEAL, 44 FREDRICK STREET EDINBURGH EH2 1EX

...so long as 100 of us remain alive we will never submit to ENGLISH RULE

síol nan gaídheal
a fraternal organisation

DECLARATION OF ARBROATH 1320

FREE SCOTLAND

MATT LYGATE
(24 Years Political Sentence)

RELEASE SCOTTISH
FREEDOM FIGHTERS **NOW!**

Front-page facsimiles from the Daily Record *and* Scottish Daily·Express

Willie McRae (right) with John Swinney

Peter Wardlaw, photographed at Peterhead Jail, c.1987

various leading members of Siol Nan Gaidheal and Sinn Fein were held under the Prevention of Terrorism Act. Graham and the others were, significantly, forced to take part in an identity parade but despite this no one was arrested. When the League gathered for their reconvened National Conference at Stirling University in mid-November, it was felt that the police action was an intelligence-gathering exercise to find out some information about the newly formed SNG. The rest of the conference dealt mainly with organisational and constitutional matters and at the end of the proceedings the delegates were quite satisfied with the progress made during the first nine months of the League's existence.

The SRSL entered 1980 determined to organise a series of public meetings as the spearhead of a new recruiting campaign. Wardlaw and his "army" comrades had other ideas of bringing in the New Year. They would celebrate the new decade with a bang.

During their trial, Peter Wardlaw's flatmate, Leonard Reynolds, a 36-year-old unemployed bricklayer, gave evidence that Wardlaw made a bomb after Christmas at their flat in Ark Lane, Dennistoun. "Lenny" claimed that Wardlaw said that they had made this up for a protest on the devolution issue. The bomb was nothing big. In Peter Wardlaw's words it was "just a firework". When the incendiary device was assembled, Wardlaw, Reynolds and Alex Ramsay took it by car to Edinburgh on Hogmanay, the last night of the fateful year of 1979. Their intention was to blow up the Scottish Assembly building on Calton Hill – but they were forced to abandon the mission and return to Glasgow.

The failure of the Scottish Assembly attack left the conspirators with an assembled incendiary bomb on their hands. This had to be used and soon. After some thought they came up with another symbolic target. They would burn down the building which housed both the South African Consulate and the Glasgow Stock Exchange. The bomb was duly planted at St George's Place in Glasgow city centre. They put it in a bin in the lane at the back door of the Exchange. The device consisted of a metal box attached to a plastic container with some fluid in it. This assembly attracted the attention of the 75-year-old caretaker James Dunn and his friend, 60-year-old James Brown. Mr Brown decided to remove the box and as he picked it up he tilted it on to its side. As he did so, there was a hissing noise and flames shot out with a whoosh. Both men ran for their lives.

As the conspiracy spread to other leading members of the SRSL, those not party to it noticed a sizeable downturn in the "normal" political activity of the League. There was an understandable resistance to an attempt by the National Organiser to compile a master-list of members and meetings and demonstrations became less well attended. It was almost a classic illustration of the old Marxist-Leninist view quoted in the League's first internal bulletin that "the necessary emphasis on the strictest security and clandestine action inevitably forces the terrorist to abandon meaningful agitational and organisational work in the working-class". A rot had set in from which the League would not recover. Meanwhile, Peter Wardlaw's activity in Glasgow provoked the usual police reaction. A number of Scottish Republican suspects were rounded up in mid-January but, fortunately for the terrorists, suspicion fell mainly upon Siol Nan Gaidheal's Drumchapel stronghold. Nevertheless, Peter Wardlaw took the hint. It was to be some time before the "Army of the Scottish People" struck again – but when they did it was to pull off their most spectacular success.

Wardlaw planned his next action down to the last detail. Four men were involved. Wardlaw himself, Alex Ramsay, Dominic McGrady and Ewen Bickerton. Their target was the early morning post van which daily took more than £100,000 in banknotes and postal orders from Gorbals Post Office to distribute to other offices around Glasgow. The hijack took place on 10 April 1980. The van, with a driver and assistant inside, had just left Gorbals Post Office and was reversing into a cul-de-sac to turn, when the masked raiders, armed with a pistol and sawn-off shotguns, pounced. They bundled the driver and his assistant into the back of the van and tied their hands behind their backs. The van was then driven to a link-up point where two getaway cars were waiting. After unloading the money and postal orders into black plastic bags the raiders tried the back door of the van – and found it locked! Panic almost set in until they realised that the rear door of the van automatically locked when the alarm system was triggered off. The driver had to be freed in order to go to his cab and press the button that unlocked the alarm device. From then on it was an easy matter to transfer the 17 sacks of money into the two cars and make good their escape. Wardlaw's luck had held. His organisation was now

£100,000 richer. Phase One – the acquisition of funds – had been successfully completed.

Flushed with his success as an armed robber, Commandant Wardlaw turned his attention to the problem of training his men and supplying them with the materials of war. For this task he came up with an operation which had the twin aims of netting hundreds of pounds of explosives and demonstrating to the Provisional IRA that the Army of the Scottish People was a serious terrorist group worthy of fraternal support and co-operation. The scheme was a daring one – a raid on the giant explosives depot at Gartloch Road, Hogganfield, on the outskirts of Glasgow. The firm, Explosives and Chemical Products Ltd, was housed in the grounds of an old farm and had storage facilities for more than 58,000 lbs of explosives. If Wardlaw's men could steal even a fraction of this, they would have something tangible to trade off with the IRA in exchange for training and weaponry.

The first part of the operation was to eavesdrop on what went on inside the depot. This was initiated on the morning of 16 May, when they succeeded in clipping on to the firm's telephone system a sophisticated electronic device containing a tiny transmitter. But they had made a serious mistake. The device only worked when two clips were attached to the telephone cable. The ASP men had, by error, connected only one. This had the disastrous effect of "knocking out" every phone in the building. Post Office engineers were called in and one of them discovered the bug. Even before this, the terrorists' attempts at espionage had degenerated into farce. The Depot Manager, Mr James Brown, observed two men training binoculars on him. He got his own binoculars and started observing the two men – for the best part of the afternoon. Not surprisingly, the operation was aborted.

Despite their setback as spies, the Army of the Scottish People was in buoyant mood. An occasion for celebration presented itself on 22 May. This was the 160th anniversary of the 1820 Martyrs. A march was held through the town of Strathaven followed by a rally in the park at the monument of one of the three hanged radical leaders of the rising, James Wilson. The speakers covered the whole spectrum of the Scottish Republican Movement: John Murphy of the 1820 Society, Lenny Reynolds of the Scottish Martyrs Committee, Duncan Toms of the Workers' Party of Scotland, David Hunter of the Scottish Republican Socialist League,

Gerry Whyte of Siol Nan Gaidheal and a representative from Sinn Fein. All these groups had contingents on the march but the SRSL's section was the most splendid. By making a show, however, Peter Wardlaw almost gave the game away. Using the proceeds of the robbery he spent money on a luxury coach, a flute band and drum corps to lead the march. On the bus home he acted like some latter-day mafia Godfather, showering money on his friends and the "organisation". David Hunter, the League's Treasurer, was handed a bag containing £1,500 to buy printing equipment. Others, including Hunter, were promised the resources and accommodation required to enable them to work as full-time officials of the SRSL. Wardlaw was now outflanking the elected leadership of the League. His conspiracy was in full gear.

The Army of the Scottish People now had a well-organised and fanatical following. It had high explosives, automatic fire-arms, a number of prepared safe houses scattered throughout Scotland. Getaway cars were waiting ready for use in a Glasgow garage bought as an operational quartermasters. Who could now doubt that success would attend the final phase of their operations, a terrorist campaign to shock Scotland out of the Union with England? They believed that they were ready.

Symbolism again dictated the target and the time of the attack. The Scottish Assembly building in Edinburgh would be blown up – demolished – on the eve of the anniversary of the Battle of Bannockburn. The expedition set out on the evening of 19 June. Earlier, David Hunter, Treasurer of the League, a computer programmer from Edinburgh, had been asked to join the bomb-planting team of Wardlaw, Ramsay, Thomas Bryan and Ewen Bickerton at their flat in Roselea Drive, Dennistoun. Hunter became worried when he was informed of the purpose of their mission and the additional fact that he was to be one of the drivers for the two getaway cars, despite the fact that he had not driven for years! In Edinburgh, the Cortina was parked at the top of Calton Hill. The other car, an Alfasud, was left as close as possible to the Scottish Assembly building at the bottom of the hill. While Thomas Bryan stayed in that car, Wardlaw, Ramsay and Hunter got out and took three plastic bags from their hiding place under the back seat of the car. These contained guns and ammunition. Meanwhile, at the top of the hill, Bickerton extricated the bomb from the black tool box in the Cortina's boot and began to carry it towards the

Assembly building, a distance of several hundred yards. At this point a "wild-looking man" began to take an unusual interest in the Cortina and began peering into it. It was later suggested that this man was "an amorous homosexual". Then a bus party of tourists appeared, intent on visiting the nearby observatory. Wardlaw and the rest of the ASP squad had walked up the Calton Hill steps and had reached Bickerton. Ramsay fiddled about in one of the bags looking for ammunition for their revolvers – and didn't find any. He panicked. Without any "ammo" the guns were useless, then there was the man beside the car and the tourists . . .. This was too much for Commandant Wardlaw. He called off the mission.

The next day the bomb intended for the Scottish Assembly building blew up in the terrorist hide-out at Roselea Drive, Glasgow. Shattered by the incompetence of this "own goal", the self-styled Army of the Scottish People disintegrated. Its "soldiers" scattered and Peter Wardlaw went into hiding. Blissfully unaware of the above events, the remaining "political" members of the League leafleted the 1980 Bannockburn Rally of the Scottish National Party. The following day they held a National Council meeting in Edinburgh. As late as this the Scottish Republican Socialist League was amending its constitution and membership rules in anticipation of a successful recruitment drive. Some of those who attended this last representative meeting of the League were soon to be arrested.

The police acted in the early morning of Tuesday, 24 June. At dawn they raided houses in Glasgow, Paisley, East Kilbride and Edinburgh. The Special Branch detained eight persons under the provisions of the Prevention of Terrorism Act. Their methods on this occasion have been widely criticised. One incident involved about 20 uniformed and plain-clothed officers who burst into the Horseshoe Bar in the centre of Glasgow. They brandished guns and ordered the arrest of League Executive members John Graham and Lewis MacDonald. In the confusion, an innocent man who happened to be drinking with the two republicans was also arrested. It took 48 hours for the police to establish that the only "cause" which this man supported was Glasgow Rangers Football Club! John Graham's house was also raided and in the early hours of the morning his two young children were brutally tipped out of bed during the police search. Police told his wife he would get at least 20 years. He was in fact released two days later.

101

The most serious incident occurred in England. Detectives, believing that they had tracked relatives of Peter Wardlaw to a house in Cleveland, instructed armed uniformed officers to raid the premises. They kicked in the door and terrified a completely innocent man and his wife. The man was so frightened that he jumped through a plate-glass door. The woman became hysterical and required medical treatment. Some time later, due to pressure from their Member of Parliament, the couple got a full apology from their local Chief Constable. As "Operation Charlie Chaplin" progressed, scores of Scottish nationalists and republicans were detained and questioned as detectives searched for the leaders of the conspiracy. For a week, Peter Wardlaw and his lieutenants eluded them.

Detective Chief Superintendent David Fotheringham, head of Tayside Central Crime Area, had set up a police observation post overlooking Siol Nan Gaidheal member, Gerry Whyte's house in Benvie Road, Dundee. On Sunday, 29 June, Fotheringham learned that a caravanette van which had been parked at the tenement close had left, heading towards the city centre. Immediately the police set up road-blocks around Dundee. Taking a calculated risk, they pounced on the terrorists in the Marketgait area of the city centre. A marked police car drove out behind the van and while it was in traffic a squad of unarmed police led by Detective-Inspector Fotheringham, bravely stopped the vehicle and detained Alex Ramsay, Ewen Bickerton and Thomas Bryan under the provisions of the Prevention of Terrorism Act. The police met no resistance from the ASP men despite the fact that the terrorists were in possession of three shotguns, six rifles and 260 rounds of ammunition.

Most of Wardlaw's army was now caught and his "soldiers" were subjected to tough interrogation. Inevitably one of them "broke". Acting on information received, detectives traced Wardlaw to a house in the seaside town of Arbroath.

In the top floor flat in Rossie Street, a quiet cul-de-sac in the Lochlands area of Arbroath, Peter Wardlaw and his girlfriend Bernadette Tunilla were in bed. As they slept, the police hurriedly organised a cordon of the area. At dawn, all was in readiness as senior detectives trained high-powered binoculars on the windows. Two police marksmen wearing bullet-proof flak-jackets and carrying handguns entered the building and edged their way cautiously along a darkened hallway. But just before they reached the inside door of the flat, a frantic radio message from the officers in the street warned them that Peter Wardlaw was standing beside the window with a Luger automatic pistol in his hand.

Keeping well out of the way of Wardlaw's field of fire, the two police marksmen shouted to him to surrender. At this challenge Wardlaw opened the door to the flat, stuck out his head and warned the officers that he was not coming out. His first inclination was to shoot it out with the police – but he wasn't alone. His concern for his girlfriend, Bernadette, was too great. After 15 minutes of tense negotiations Commandant Wardlaw gave up the unequal struggle. The police siege and Wardlaw's campaign for a Free Scotland was over.

The trial commenced at the beginning of October and lasted nearly four weeks. By this time, despite brave talk by some of its remaining political leaders, the Scottish Republican Socialist League was defunct. Membership collapsed and the National Council was reduced to issuing only the irregular statement. Pickets and demonstrations outside the court-house were beyond the capacity of the League. Inside the court the alleged terrorists were held in a vice of steel. One of the accused, Lenny Reynolds, described later the police paranoia over security arrangements. He explained that every day a police bus took him and other prisoners from Barlinnie to Glasgow High Court. One morning the bus, instead of going through the town, came via the motorway. As the coach approached one of the motorway flyovers, a senior police officer made the following remarks: "I told them I didn't want this route. We're too open to rocket launcher attack from overhead bridges."

The police concern with security was so obsessive that even the court staff, hardened to many a criminal trial, refused to enter the building unless the "stop and search" procedure was lifted by Strathclyde Police. Underneath the court buildings, police frogmen hunted through the sewers for suspect materials. This "Northern Ireland"-type security operation was not cheap. The "fortress" was maintained at a cost of well over £100,000.

The trial lasted 17 days, cited 297 witnesses and went through 200 productions. During its course many of the original defendants were released. Among them were Isobel Hunter, a laboratory assistant and wife of David Hunter, Colin Hammond, a burner at Yarrow Shipbuilders, and Lewis MacDonald, a trainee work study officer with Eastwood District Council. Some of the original 27 charges were dropped. They included those charges relating to the first attempt to bomb the Scottish Assembly building in Edinburgh and the Glasgow Stock Exchange incendiary device. Another dropped charge concerned previous "tartan terrorist" armies and a possible link between the League's military wing – the Army of the Scottish People – and the Army of the Provisional Government. The charge of conspiracy to free Tony Tunilla, the brother of Peter Wardlaw's girlfriend and a leading member of the APG currently serving his time in prison, was also dropped. The police had alleged that Wardlaw and an armed gang were intending to free Tunilla by ramming a prison bus with a lorry while Tunilla was being transferred from Glasgow to Perth. There was no hard evidence in the trial that Peter Wardlaw's group were the APG under a different name. One of the accused, Dominic McGrady, escaped the main conspiracy charge but the others were all found guilty.

The sentences on the seven remaining Army of the Scottish People men were handed down on Wednesday 15 October 1980. Branding the men as "cowards", the judge, Lord MacDonald, refused to consider the plot an incompetent one carried out by bungling amateurs. "It was a serious conspiracy entered into by determined and unscrupulous individuals – a menace to the safety and well-being of decent citizens in this country." As he heard the sentences totalling 72 years passed on himself and his comrades, Peter Wardlaw smiled and threw up his arms in a victory salute. An associate later said that Wardlaw and the others were delighted at the heavy sentences. They wanted to be regarded as martyrs by the Scottish people.

In spite of this gesture of defiance from Peter Wardlaw, Lewis MacDonald, who had also been in the dock but who had all the charges against him dropped, stated the "official" view of the remaining League leadership when he said: "Our struggle will go on without violence. The Scottish Republican Socialist League is not a terrorist organisation."

Peter Wardlaw and his self-styled Army of the Scottish People failed in their intention of rousing Scotland from its post-Devolution Referendum apathy. The group did provoke a hysterical reaction from the British State but the hoped-for repression of the Scottish people by the secret police was confined to the terrorists' own political base in the republican movement with the result that one of its most effective organisations – the Scottish Republican Socialist League – was smashed to pieces. Nor did Scotland regard the conspirators as martyrs. The media labelled them as common criminals and their mistakes and errors became subjects of jokes in pubs and clubs throughout Scotland. They did succeed in generating brief notoriety and publicity for the aims of Scottish republicanism but their terrorist methods alienated potential support. The terrorist activities of the Army of the Scottish People were stopped by police action but had it not been for an unlucky self-made mistake the ASP may well have succeeded in its campaign of bombing and assassinations. If nothing else, the trial had proved to the public and the police that terrorism in Scotland is not necessarily sporadic or unco-ordinated – nor is it perpetrated solely by a few bumbling cranks.

9   OPERATION DARK HARVEST

If any person has taken soil from the contaminated island of Gruinard,
off the West Coast of Scotland, it could put the whole country in
danger. If the group [the Scottish Civilian Army] has gone to the
island, it is like someone going to an area infected with rabies, taking
a few animals home with them and then distributing them around the
countryside.

Hamish Gray, Conservative Energy Minister and MP for Ross and
Cromarty, 1981

GRUINARD Island is a rugged, wedge-shaped, heather-clad
and rocky outcrop of the Western Highlands of Scotland, Surrounded on all sides by the white Atlantic breakers of the Minch,
it lies in Gruinard Bay less than a mile from the Ross-shire mainland.
The Western Highlands boasts one of the last wildernesses to be
found in Europe and visitors are very welcome to share the
beauty of this unique countryside with the hospitable native
Highlanders. Welcome everywhere, that is, except on the 520

acres of Gruinard Island. Here, until very recently, the signs that dotted the shore like white sentinels offered only a stark warning: "This Island is Government Property under experiment. The ground is contaminated with Anthrax and Dangerous. Landing is prohibited."

For Gruinard Island has been abandoned by ordinary people since the Second World War. Dark days breed dark deeds. Gruinard Island was the scene of one of Britain's blackest schemes for mega-death. There, in a two-year period from 1941, a team of Porton Down scientists led by the soon-to-be-knighted Doctor Paul Fildes experimented with new forms of biological warfare weapons. These included anthrax bombs which were exploded in the presence of domestic animals to test the effects of biological agents on living tissues. There were 13 field trials involving anthrax conducted on Gruinard during the testing period. In the initial experiment a six-inch-diameter cannister containing a small explosive charge and a brown "soup" of anthrax was suspended from a gantry. When it was detonated, a cloud of spores drifted over sheep which had been tethered at regular intervals around and away from the bomb. The anthrax bacillus soon showed that it was robust enough to survive the effects of the explosion. The sheep began to die the day after the blast. None survived. From these tests, Dr Fildes was able to work out the doses needed to inflict maximum damage on enemy cities. The Gruinard field trials in 1942 and 1943 showed that anthrax worked horrifyingly well. It would be possible to inflict a painful death upon millions of people. During the summer of 1942 Sir Winston Churchill considered using anthrax to bomb Berlin with the intention of making the Capital of Nazi Germany uninhabitable for hundreds of years. Aachen, Frankfurt, Hamburg, Stuttgart and Wilhelmshaven were other famous German cities chosen to be seeded with the agents of death. As the Allies advanced during the closing stages of the war, the anthrax plan was abandoned yet Gruinard Island remained contaminated as a deadly monument to one of the more evil thoughts of Britain's greatest wartime Prime Minister.

Anthrax has many "attractions" as a biological weapon. As it is a highly infectious disease of cattle and sheep as well as human beings, it is effective against economic targets. A potential enemy's agriculture would face permanent contamination for anthrax spores are virtually indestructible and can lie dormant in the soil for decades before multiplying in animal tissues to kill the carrier. In humans, anthrax usually affects the skin with boils but the more severe and fatal form experimented with on Gruinard attacks the gastro-intestinal tract and lungs causing severe breathing difficulties. Fortunately for human beings, the usual form of anthrax can be treated with penicillin and is not infectious from one person to another, but as soil is an ideal carrier, anthrax would be difficult to contain if an infection was deliberately spread throughout the countryside.

For years, the anthrax island in Gruinard Bay had been almost forgotten by the British Government and an apathetic public. On Friday, 9 October 1981, close to the 40th anniversary of the contamination of Gruinard, that changed. A group, later identifying itself as the "Scottish Civilian Army", sent a three-page document entitled *Operation Dark Harvest* to the *Scotsman* newspaper in Edinburgh. The language was dramatic, almost biblical. The reaction to the statement ensured that Gruinard Island would no longer be ignored with the same indifference as before. The document began with a history of the deliberate pollution by the British Government of Gruinard and ended with the following nasty sting in its tail.

> We effected a landing on Gruinard Island last week and collected a large number of soil samples with a total weight of 300 lbs. By the time you read this statement the campaign (*Operation Dark Harvest*) will have started in earnest. The first delivery will have been made. And where better to send our seeds of death than to the place from whence they came? Porton Down has just received a gift from Gruinard Island, the first of many.

The group went on to claim that Operation Dark Harvest had been carried out by a team of microbiologists from two unnamed universities, aided by members of the local population. They accused the authorities of "total indifference" to the problem of Gruinard.

This statement from the Scottish Civilian Army indicated that their first target was to be Porton Down Biological Defence Establishment. After obtaining the contents of the terrorist SCA document on the Friday, the Ministry of Defence carried out a major search of Porton Down. Initially, nothing was found.

However a Ministry spokesman later the same day revealed that the authorities were indeed very worried about the deadly potential of Operation Dark Harvest. He tried to calm public fears by saying that there was a strong possibility that the Dark Harvest statement was a hoax and added that if this was the case, then it was highly irresponsible. He continued that it would be even more irresponsible for anyone to take the soil samples from Gruinard as the effect of this would be "colossal".

The situation at Porton Down was evidently serious enough to warrant a second search. This time the authorities found a small sample of soil in a plastic bucket outside Porton Down's perimeter fence. Urgent tests were carried out on the soil and these indicated that the level of the active anthrax agent – "bacillus anthracis" – was higher than would be expected in ordinary soil samples. Porton Down was forced to admit that the soil left on their doorstep was consistent with soil from Gruinard Island. In a statement issued along with this confirmation that the soil *was* potentially infectious, the scientists of Porton Down issued a strong warning that any meddling with anthrax would endanger public health. The police were ordered to initiate a full investigation.

The police operation started with a general alert being issued to all local forces. The original "Dark Harvest" document was taken from the *Scotsman* office by Special Branch detectives who subjected it to a series of forensic tests in an attempt to trace those behind the so-called "Scottish Civilian Army". Security was increased on and around Gruinard Island by the Minstry of Defence and police CID men began to question the locals about the activities of strangers. While MOD officials, including the Director of Porton Down, Dr Keith Watson, were forbidden to discuss Gruinard, the Northern Constabulary, which had set up a special task force in Inverness to track down the Dark Harvest group, announced that they had found a possible lead. On the seashore at Udrigle, directly south of Gruinard, a diver's face mask was found by the searching security forces. Local people confirmed that three or four skin divers had been seen in the area around about mid-September. This lead proved to be false, but the James Bond image created by this wild-goose chase led to the Scottish press christening the group the Dark Harvest Commandos.

Reaction to the Scottish Civilian Army threat to contaminate the mainland with anthrax ranged from outright disbelief to absolute horror at the suggestion. At first, before the findings of the tests on the dumped soil samples were known, some experts and even politicians expressed a restrained admiration at the audacity of the group. Professor Steven Rose, a biologist with the Open University and a member of the Bertrand Russell Committee Against Chemical Weapons, was reported to have said that "if the operation was a hoax it would be an extraordinarily effective way of drawing attention to the hazards of chemical and biological weapons". Even Mr Hamish Gray, Conservative Energy Minister and Member of Parliament for the Ross and Cromarty constituency which included Gruinard, said, according to the press, that if the package was a hoax he would see it as a perfectly legitimate way of focusing attention on the problem. This, as the Scottish quality newspaper, the *Glasgow Herald*, said in an editorial, was "a fairly open-minded statement by a Conservative Minister". When it was discovered that the soil *did* contain anthrax, the tone of the public announcements changed. Hamish Gray said that the group's action was "like someone going to an area affected with rabies, taking a few animals home with them and distributing them around the countryside". He warned that the whole country was in danger because of this "act of gross irresponsibility". The Defence Minister, Mr John Nott, announced the concern of his department and reassured the public that his Ministry was being kept abreast of any further development. The Ministry of Agriculture said that experts would be called in to deal with any possible outbreaks of anthrax among livestock. If this did happen animals would have to be destroyed and their carcasses burnt.

Just after 11 a.m. on Wednesday, 14 October 1981, a painter working 390 feet up on that most English of national monuments, the Blackpool Tower, made a very curious discovery. In the lift wheelhouse, behind a locked door, he found a linen bag. Suspecting a bomb, he called the police. They examined the package and discovered that it contained a sealed tin wrapped in a knotted polythene bag. Suspicious that the tin contained a biological hazard to the public, the police called in advisers from the Ministry of Agriculture and Fisheries office at Preston. Finally, the package was removed and taken to Porton Down for analysis. The find was not preceded by any warning or claim of responsibility from the Scottish Civilian Army but the site of the dumping of the anthrax-contaminated soil at Blackpool was given symbolic political significance by the presence there of the week-long 1981 Conservative Party Conference at which the British Prime Minister, Mrs Margaret Thatcher, was due to give a keynote speech. The British Government and the police now realised that they were dealing with a sustained terrorist campaign, for 12 days later Department of Health tests at Porton Down confirmed that this second package of soil almost certainly came from Gruinard Island, although they claimed that this particular sample did not contain anthrax spores. This may well have been the case for as an article on Gruinard Island in *Nature* magazine explained, it was clear from the findings of a survey of the island made in 1979 that only the parts of the island where the Second World War experiments were carried out were still heavily infected by anthrax. In addition to this area there were also certain "hot spots". These "hot spots" were the patches of ground where animals that had contracted the disease had died. Not all of Gruinard was covered in anthrax spores but had the soil samples planted on the mainland been taken from the hot spots, the scare that followed the actions of the Dark Harvest group would have been very real indeed.

While British Government ministries and the police braced themselves for the discovery of another biological time-bomb, the leaders of the Scottish Civilian Army changed their tactics and struck at the heart of the British administration in Edinburgh. A typewritten message headed "Operation Dark Harvest" was found pinned to a wooden board fastened to the doors of St Andrew's House. This communiqué was discovered early on the Monday morning of 7 December 1981. At first, the worried civil servants breathed a sigh of relief at the announcement that "no more parcels of soil will be dumped on the mainland". However, a more careful reading revealed a last sting in the tail of Operation Dark Harvest, for the signed Scottish Civilian Army document claimed that the anthrax-containing soil dumped at Porton Down was not in fact from Gruinard Island at all – but from the nearby mainland of Scotland! They were saying that mainland contamination by anthrax spores from Gruinard had been proved by Porton Down itself! The message continued with a claim that the protest had achieved its ends. But Operation Dark Harvest was not quite over. The statement concluded with a threat that "further reminders in the form of an annual event would be given to ensure that the island remained very much a part of British life".

In the event, this message was to be the last communication from the Scottish Civilian Army. Despite a thorough investigation by the Northern Constabulary and the Scottish Office, no trace was ever found of the group. While it is believed that "dissident" Scottish academics, possibly connected with the nationalist or peace movements were behind the operation, speculation has also added the name of veteran Scottish nationalist and Glasgow solicitor Willie McRae as one of the operation's "masterminds".

At first, in the wake of the publicity which Operation Dark Harvest received, little was done by the authorities to satisfy the demands made by the Scottish Civilian Army. However, to guard against the possibility of another terrorist threat, the Ministry of Defence did review the various methods of decontaminating Gruinard Island. After a suitable delay to allay any allegations that the Government might be "caving in to terrorism", a committee of six scientists, headed by Professor W. D. P. Stewart of Dundee University, was set up in late 1985 to report on the best and cheapest method of cleaning up Gruinard. This committee suggested that the hot spots still contaminated with anthrax should be treated with a solution of formaldehyde and seawater in order to kill off the spores and sterilise the area. By the summer of 1986, the work of decontaminating Gruinard was put out to private tender and, with a blaze of publicity, the Ministry of Defence announced that Gruinard Island would soon be safe. Somewhere in Scotland someone raised a glass. It was about time.

10   PARAMILITARY CLANSMEN

... all peaceful means have failed and will continue to fail, while we
face an aggressive imperial enemy such as England.

*Concluding paragraph of statement delivered to the Falkirk offices
of* Firinn Albannach, *the official magazine of Siol Nan Gaidheal,*
Spring 1983

IN the same letter as the above, which was a Declaration of War
against England, Arm Nan Gaidheal, the Gaelic name for the self-
styled "Army of the Gael", claimed in a period between November
1982 and March 1983 to have carried out six "acts of war against our
English oppressors and their colonial lackeys in Scotland". These
attacks were made using incendiary bombs placed in or close to
empty buildings in an area that stretched across the central belt
of Scotland from Glasgow to Edinburgh and from Dundee in the
north to Galashiels on the border.

The main targets of Arm Nan Gaidheal's bombing campaign
were the "colonial lackeys" of the British Labour and Conservative

Parties. Labour Party Headquarters in Glasgow and Dundee were seriously damaged. Conservative Party premises in Glasgow and the Assembly Rooms in Edinburgh were attacked, the latter occurring as a protest against the use of the Assembly Rooms to house a reception in honour of British Prime Minister, Margaret Thatcher. In the south, a factory in Galashiels, the Laidlaw and Fairgrieve Spinning Mill, was fire-bombed because, Arm Nan Gaidheal claimed, "this firm recently paid off Scots workers but kept on the English". Lastly, the terrorists said that they had set fire to the "English Army Stores" in Edinburgh.

Whatever the truth of the above bombing claims, the date of the start of Arm Nan Gaidheal's military campaign in November 1982 is significant for in that month an organisation with a similar-sounding name "Siol Nan Gaidheal" was finally expelled from the Scottish National Party. The SNP decided at its June 1982 Annual Conference to eject all organised political factions such as the militant Siol Nan Gaidheal and the Republican Socialist 79 Group. A tremendous amount of personal and political bitterness had been generated in a party whose democratic and strongly anti-terrorist stance had previously been respected by all sections. The expulsion of Siol Nan Gaidheal led to all restraints being removed from a militant faction within the SNG, which for years had advocated a military solution to the problem of how to attain Independence for Scotland. As far as the newly expelled Siol Nan Gaidheal were concerned, if the SNP leadership were embarrassed by the activities of Arm Nan Gaidheal, so much the better.

Siol Nan Gaidheal's relationship with the SNP had not always been so bad. At first, the SNG soothed the SNP leadership into a false sense of security by declaring their organisation to be a fraternal and cultural movement. They seemed like a latter-day Scottish nationalist equivalent of the Masonic Order and indeed many of their prominent founding members were associated with a group called the Grand Priory in Scotland of the Order of the Temple of Jerusalem. There are a number of more or less secret societies which claim the disputed mantle of the Knights Templar. However, the organisation most likely to have helped in the foundation of Siol Nan Gaidheal is the Sovereign Military Order of the Temple of Jerusalem in Scotland or possibly an offshoot from this society caused by an attempted takeover or faction fight within the Templars. The Sovereign Military Order claims direct descent from the mediaeval Order of the Temple set up in Jerusalem in 1119. Although suppressed by the Pope and many of the European monarchies in 1307, the Knights Templar were never banned in the Kingdom of Scotland because King Robert the Bruce had been excommunicated from the Roman Catholic Church for the murder of the Red Comyn before the high altar of Greyfriars Church in Dumfries. The Templars fought for Scotland with Bruce against the English at the Battle of Bannockburn and maintained a shadowy existence throughout the period of the independent Scottish Kingdom. The Scottish Templars emerged once again to support the Stuart cause during the Jacobite Risings and Charles Edward Stuart, the Bonnie Prince Charlie of historical romance, was invested in Edinburgh as Grand Prior of the Scottish Priory of the Temple of Jerusalem.

The present company of Scottish Knights was formed in 1972 with a definite Scottish nationalist stance. One of the aims of the Order is to secure the recognition of Scotland's place as one of the nations of the world. Another is to protect and promote the national culture and heritage of Scotland. The Order claim to have been specially entrusted with the keeping of the sacred relics of the ancient Scottish Kingdom. They have in their possession what they claim is the genuine Stone of Destiny "stolen" from its resting place beneath the British monarch's Coronation Chair in Westminster Abbey by four Scottish nationalist students on Christmas Eve, 1950. They assert that the stone which was returned to the authorities in 1951 was merely a clever fake and that therefore the present Queen has no right to rule Scotland because she was crowned over a fake Stone of Scone in 1953. The Sovereign Military Order of the Templars also claim to have had in their possession the six-foot-long, two-handed sword which once belonged to William Wallace, Guardian of Scotland. The Wallace Sword was in fact stolen by the "Tartan Army" terrorist group in 1972 from its resting place in the Wallace Tower at Abbeycraig near Stirling and disappeared completely for many years. Photographs of the sword in the hands of a uniformed "Tartan Army" soldier were sold at nationalist gatherings to raise funds for the "Tartan Army" and other extremist organisations. The Templars say that they were responsible for bringing the Sword of Wallace back from its hiding place so that it could once more provide an inspiration to the Scottish public. Whatever the truth of their role in the

Wallace Sword episode, the Templars seem to be very familiar with the world of militant Scottish nationalism. They were also well placed to forge another sword to fight for Scotland, the Highland Claymore of Siol Nan Gaidheal.

The Grand Priory of the Sovereign Military Order of the Temple of Jerusalem are and were Jacobites. In the summer of 1979 they were organising support for a Belgian fraudster who called himself Prince Michael James Stuart and who claimed to be the direct heir of Bonnie Prince Charlie and therefore the rightful King of Scotland and England. In order to press the claims of the Pretender Prince Michael, the Templars set up a more openly political nationalist grouping called the "Sons of Scotland". This grouping's Templar origins were revealed by their use of their early logo which consisted of a silhouetted mounted Templar Knight and by their strong advocacy of the Jacobite Pretender Prince Michael. In fact, the first public statement of the "Sons of Scotland" announced a national campaign to restore the Scottish monarchy. Towards the end of 1979 a Gaelic name "Siol Nan Gaidheal" – literally meaning "seed of the Gael" – appeared on the political literature of the "Sons of Scotland" and within a short time the new name replaced "Sons of Scotland" entirely. Throughout this transition, the name of Tom Moore, National Secretary, and a contact address in Prestwick appeared on most of the printed propaganda material.

While the Knights Templar maintained close connections with Siol Nan Gaidheal personnel and encouraged the early development of the organisation, they quickly realised that Siol Nan Gaidheal was outgrowing its function as a propaganda vehicle for the restoration of the Stuart monarchy and was becoming difficult to control. They decided to set up a new and more modest monarchist group – the "Scottish Movement" – which quickly faded after Prince Michael's claims to the Scottish throne were proved fraudulent.

Tom Moore from Prestwick and Gordon Walker from Kilmarnock, influenced by the Knights Templar, set up the prototype Siol Nan Gaidheal, the Sons of Scotland, in 1978, Moore, a charismatic figure in his early twenties, said that he became a fervent Scottish nationalist when he returned to Scotland after 12 years of schooling in New York. He found "the Scottish spirit sadly lacking and the SNP mealy-mouthed". He wanted an organisation whose "aim was to inspire nationalism without inhibition or restraint". Certainly, Tom Moore proved himself to be an unrestrained faction fighter and two early challengers to his rule, early Siol Nan Gaidheal chairmen, Gordon Walker and Norman MacLeod, were quickly dispatched, thus allowing him to maintain his undisputed command over the political destiny of the Siol.

Moore had the exiled Scot's sense of nationhood. He perceived within the Highland Gaelic myths of the Celtic Twilight the power of legend to transform the real world and regenerate Scotland and the Scottish people. Moore's idea was the classic revolutionary nationalist conception of using the past to forge the future. Self-confidence was the key for Moore. Scots should be conscious, proud and unashamed of their own identity. Siol Nan Gaidheal members were urged to wear Highland dress and on "public parade" this meant that the traditional Gaelic weapons, the Sgian Dhu, dirk and claymore must be worn regardless of "English" laws such as the 1936 Public Order Act. As a sign of a renewed Scottish Renaissance, a golden symbol of the rising sun of Gaelic Scotland was emblazoned on the white banners of the new Siol Nan Gaidheal. The day of the paramilitary clansmen had dawned.

During the early part of the decade of the 1980s, Scottish National Party marches and demonstrations were joined by a distinct and separate Siol Nan Gaidheal presence. The SNG contingents were awe-inspiring and visually stunning. They marched as a disciplined body of men, military style, in columns of two with ample space between each member. On parade, every member wore the full Highland dress of kilt, plaid and leather jerkin. Their regalia was adorned with the ancient weapons of the Sgian Dhu, knife, dirk and the basket-hilted broadsword. The SNG men marched boldly behind a Celtic colour party of their yellow and gold banners, each of which hung down from a nazi-style crossbar which proclaimed the Gaelic word for freedom – "Saorsa". The march swung in time to the beat of a military drum corps dressed in the black paramilitary garb of the Provisional IRA. Whenever the SNG appeared, a shiver of excitement and tense expectation spread through the ranks of the more traditionally minded SNP marchers. The SNG presented an emotional force that was difficult to ignore.

The SNG were superb morale builders. Their ceilidhs, folk nights and social functions provided the best entertainment whenever the nationalists were in town. Rousing music, comradeship and a really good time put some spirit back into what it meant to be a Scottish nationalist. Patriotic Scots could shout and sing and even jump on stage, fired with the enthusiasm of born again nationalism. It was like the best of the old times from the past surges of Scottish nationalism – Hamilton and Govan and Govan again. Younger members of the SNP flocked to the SNG in their hundreds, forsaking the rival British youth culture of punk rock and the new Mods. It seemed for a while that Siol Nan Gaidheal's aggressive combination of militant activism and Jacobite romanticism had hit on a formula of hope for the nationalist movement. If Tom Moore and the SNG had been content to remain a cultural and fraternal organisation and had distanced themselves from the faction fighting in which the SNP was now immersed, their group could well have provided a positive focus for the rebuilding of a national identity. Instead, the SNG became a target for the internecine hatred between the left and right wings of the SNP and ultimately destroyed itself as a response to the intensity of the crossfire in which it became enmeshed.

Tom Moore decided to dabble in the politics of the Scottish National Party. Perhaps influenced by his upbringing in the United States, he began to introduce a distinct anti-communist flavour into Siol Nan Gaidheal's political propaganda. One pamphlet, for example, declared the SNG to be completely against foreign political parties with their irrelevant foreign ideologies. This anti-communist stance was picked up by the traditionalist leadership of the SNP who were smarting from attacks on their competence by an increasingly organised republican socialist left wing. Given the atmosphere of intense faction fighting at the time, the emergence of a new political pressure group within the SNP opened up possibilities for a centre-right alliance against the militant left.

When Siol Nan Gaidheal organised their major relaunch meeting in Edinburgh in November 1979, there was a surprisingly large contingent of members of the National Executive Committee of the SNP at the gathering. Winifred Ewing, the heroine of Hamilton and newly elected Euro MP for the Highlands and Islands constituency, was one of the prominent figures in attendance. Mrs Ewing regarded herself as a guardian of certain fundamental nationalist ideas and values which she believed required to be upheld if the SNP was to attract majority public support. Fundamentalists like

Winifred Ewing were strong supporters of the slogan "Independence–Nothing Less" and tended to regard the SNP as a single-issue campaign which should project a neutral or slightly left-of-centre stance so that potential support from all sides of the political spectrum would not be alienated. The fundamentalists believed that a left-wing takeover of the SNP would be a disaster and should be resisted at all costs. At the Siol Nan Gaidheal meeting, Mrs Ewing found many kindred spirits within Siol Nan Gaidheal and was to maintain friendly relations with the organisation right up to its expulsion from the SNP. She was always willing to be a principal speaker at SNG rallies and commemorations.

The motives of the other SNP National Executive members who attended the meeting were less political. Indeed, William Wolfe, former SNP Chairman and his life-long friend, Willie McRae, were so impressed by the emotionally charged atmosphere of the meeting that they decided to join the SNG. Wolfe at that time was a bitterly disappointed man, having been leader of the party during the period of its dramatic upsurge during the 1970s. He now felt that he was somehow responsible for the fact that the upsurge had not led to the breakthrough to Independence. It was characteristic of the man that he was quite prepared to stand aside in order to give new people a chance to lead the party along more adventurous lines. Wolfe decided to use his remaining influence to support schemes to further the national heritage of Scotland. He was attracted to Siol Nan Gaidheal because of its cultural claims. Eventually he resigned from the SNG, in May 1980, after he was elected SNP President. He had also grown sceptical about the group's activities.

Willie McRae, a Glasgow solicitor and a former SNP Vice-Chairman, was attracted to the uncompromisingly nationalist aims of Siol Nan Gaidheal, especially their resolution to "publicise the desperate need for Scottish independence, and to expand Scotland's knowledge of her own culture". He liked the emphasis on youth and admired SNG's pledge to "take direct action where words go unheeded". Willie McRae was not afraid to use his position on the SNP National Executive Committee to help the SNG. Indeed, he told one Executive meeting of the party: "I am a fully paid-up member of Siol Nan Gaidheal and proud to be so." He went on, "I think that by and large these people are doing a good job. They are the kind of young people the SNP ought to be fostering and looking after. The SNG were struggling for a way to help

Scotland and getting very little help from the SNP." For McRae, the SNG made an attractive alternative to the SNP "who were in the doldrums and had no leadership worthy of the name". McRae was to assist the Siol by advising them on legal matters and succeeded in persuading them to discontinue their wearing of broadswords and dirks on public parades because this contravened the 1936 Public Order Act and made their wearers open to arrest on sight. Willie McRae was the one SNP leader whom the SNG listened to and respected. He assisted many SNG members who had been arrested and his insistence on having them medically examined prior to leaving custody provoked more than one serious altercation with Special Branch officers.

As a lawyer, McRae had also assisted the SNP campaign against the Atomic Energy Authority's proposals to dump nuclear waste in Scotland and represented the party at the Mullwharchar Inquiry (see Chapter 12). He was probably influential in shaping Siol Nan Gaidheal's militant anti-nuclear stance and urged the SNG to participate in an SNP rally against nuclear dumping in February 1980 in Ayr.

At the rally, more than 500 SNG men marched in Highland dress with their soon-to-be-infamous banners, dirks and broadswords. The march, in Tom Moore's home town, was a spectacular success. The SNG had forced their way on to the consciousness of the whole nationalist movement. Of course, there were many who were critical of the sudden appearance of a large body of uniformed men, and there were complaints that some of the contingent had been heard to sing the nazi song *Motherland, Oh Motherland*. The well-organised left wing of the SNP soon recognised the potential threat of the anti-socialist SNG combining with the traditional SNP "fundamentalists". They branded the Siol's militant trappings as "fascist" and the savage infighting resulting from such allegations soon attracted the attention of the largely anti-nationalist Scottish press. Soon stories began to appear in which the SNG was likened to a Scottish equivalent of the National Front and questions were raised as to whether the Siol wore paramilitary uniforms and drilled in secret. They were suspected of having access to fire-arms, hard hats and riot shields.

While Tom Moore and the other Siol leaders may have found these vague allegations – aimed to discredit the SNG— rather amusing, at least two SNP Constituency Associations took them seriously. Clackmannan and East Stirling CA and Paisley CA protested to SNP HQ in Edinburgh. There were more serious complaints of hooliganism and rowdy behaviour at the SNP's Annual Rally at Bannockburn where an SNG column had marched separately as a distinct group despite instructions to the contrary by the SNP stewards. This led to a five-member SNP Committee of investigation into the nature of Siol Nan Gaidheal. The committee was chaired by journalist and broadcaster Colin Bell and included the ex-MPs Andrew Welsh and George Thompson. The Committee met over several months and collected a body of vague and contradictory evidence. The most damaging allegations were provided by two disgruntled ex-Chairmen of the SNG. These two men were Gordon Walker, who had co-founded the SNG with Tom Moore, and Norman MacLeod, who had just resigned his chairmanship after a bitter feud with Moore. MacLeod provided evidence that the SNG had allowed into its ranks two men who had stood trial as members of a terrorist group and had faced charges of conspiracy to cause explosions. These men had been expelled from the SNP and were still proscribed from membership. Tom Moore did not deny that the SNG had at least two ex-terrorists as members. Indeed, he made a virtue of the fact and defended the men in a manner that was hardly calculated to conciliate the Committee of Investigation. He declared in his usual forthright manner, "We are delighted to have them. We are proud to have them. If there were a thousand others like them Scotland would be free." The Committee seized on these revelations and postulated the view that because Siol Nan Gaidheal did not limit its membership to members of the SNP it was impossible for the SNP to use its disciplinary procedures to prevent any member of the Siol from engaging in activities which might politically damage the SNP. This was confirmed by the numerous reports of undiminished rowdyism by SNG supporters towards SNP stewards at nationalist rallies and marches when the SNP refused the SNG the right to march. The conclusions of the Committee's investigations were reported to the National Executive Committee, who endorsed the Committee's recommendation that Siol Nan Gaidheal be expelled forthwith because their activities were no longer compatible with those of the Scottish National Party. The recommendation thus went forward to the party's policy-making body, the National Council, which met in Arbroath in December 1980.

121

At the National Council meeting, one of the foremost advocates of the expulsion of Siol Nan Gaidheal was the party's Vice-Chairman for Policy, Jim Fairlie. Fairlie was respected in the party as an uncompromising fundamental nationalist and he spoke for many moderate SNP members who were confused by the emergence of pressure groups within the party. Of course, Fairlie had personal experience of the deadly attractions of extremism for his own younger brother, Michael, had been jailed for his activities in the APG trial in 1975. Fairlie articulated a vague feeling that the loyalty of the faction fighters was suspect and indeed that they might become unwitting pawns of *agents provocateurs* who wished to break up the party and consign it into political oblivion. He was not only concerned with the militant tendencies of Siol Nan Gaidheal. He also pointed a finger of suspicion at the articulate left-wing 79 Group, named after the year when Scottish democracy "died".

The 79 Group openly advocated a campaign of civil disobedience under the slogan "Join The Scottish Resistance". However, evidence to allow Fairlie and others to call for the banning of the 79 Group did not exist. Although Republicans, with some overlap in membership with other groups, the 79 Group were against terrorist tactics. In addition, membership was restricted to SNP members, unlike membership of the Siol. They made no secret of wanting to take over the party and persuade the party to adopt their three principles of Independence, Socialism and Republicanism as its official policy. Moreover, they were also highly successful within the party and by May 1981, at the Annual Conference in Aberdeen, the 79 Group succeeded in imposing most of their programme of civil disobedience on the party as a whole and also got a conference commitment to withdraw an Independent Scotland from NATO.

The 79 Group and Siol Nan Gaidheal, in many ways politically incompatible, found themselves in a temporary marriage of convenience during the closing months of 1980. The SNG were already facing expulsion at the Arbroath National Council in December. Now the 79 Group found themselves the victims of a fundamentalist move to ban them. Tayport Branch had tabled a motion of expulsion which would come before the National Council at the same meeting. The 79 Group initiated a letter-writing campaign in the press, circulated all their members and drafted a pamphlet for the delegates. Tom Moore for Siol Nan Gaidheal declared: "We have now until December 6th to convince people that we [SNG] are not what we have been painted. We will have a wee campaign to see if we can do that." Moore's "wee campaign" took him and his lieutenants throughout the length and breadth of Scotland. He spoke to SNP branches and gatherings up and down the country and mobilised a groundswell of opinion against the expulsion motion. The meeting in Arbroath was a "feast of factionalism". The move to ban the 79 Group was thrown out and the National Executive Committee's expulsion motion was so watered down that it was to be almost two more years before the Siol was to be effectively banned from the party. Tom Moore's "wee campaign" was a remarkable exhibition of the potential power of radical nationalism and it marked the high-water mark of Siol Nan Gaidheal's influence within the SNP. The SNG had won the first round in their political battle with the nationalist "old guard". Unfortunately, they refused to learn the lessons of the conflict and failed to "clean up their act". The rhetoric and glamour of extreme activity proved irresistible.

Glen Etive, in the Western Highlands was listed as a potential site for the dumping of nuclear waste. Scientists from the Government-sponsored Institute of Geological Science were due to carry out tests in the area and one of the main activities of Siol Nan Gaidheal from July 1980 was to monitor and hinder the IGS activities. The SNG set up a caravan in Glen Etive and manned it permanently for 18 months until the nuclear dumping threat was lifted. This venture, which had originally been suggested by veteran anti-nuclear campaigner Willie McRae, found great support also among the grass-roots of the SNP who readily contributed money to the collecting cans of the SNG. The Glen Etive caravan was to provide a focal point for a number of enthusiastic young unemployed members of Siol Nan Gaidheal. The co-ordinator of the caravan project was Bob Anderson, an ex-"Tartan Army" sympathiser, who was given the remit to run the project entirely on his own initiative. Hugh Brogan and Alistair Tennant were among the live-in activists at the caravan. On most weekends several other activists would arrive and one of the most enthusiastic was David Dinsmore who soon joined the caravan on a permanent basis. Dinsmore became the National Organiser of Siol Nan Gaidheal.

The Glen Etive caravan, near Ben Trilleachan, was a sort of nursery school for "tartan terrorists". While most of the "training" consisted of yarns told around the camp-fire, there were on occasions more practical demonstrations in the woods. One such occurred in the late summer of 1980 when a man dressed in paramilitary uniform burnt a Union Jack and issued a statement to David Leadbetter which was printed in the *Lochaber Free Press*: "Nuclear waste will not be dumped in Glen Etive or in any part of this land – only over the geologists' dead bodies. Any landowners who allow drilling to take place will be dealt with." Most of the landowners, who had been made aware by the SNG group of the leaked documents which Willie McRae had obtained, were hostile in any case to the idea of test drilling – and most were irritated at the secrecy with which the IGS were to have carried it out.

Within the SNG ranks however there was a police "plant" and considerable and mysterious efforts were made to undermine their presence. A public telephone box, the group's only contact with the outside world, was smashed. A cabin cruiser which belonged to one of the group was smashed and sunk. The group were blamed by an anonymous caller to the *Oban Times* for vandalism at a local social work hostel for mentally handicapped children. The frequent police raids only occurred when few members were at the caravan. The group did however cause inconvenience to the IGS scientists and insisted on conducting physical searches of "dubious" visitors to the Glen. Scientists were discovered in the guise of hillwalkers, as "students" in University mini-buses, officials of the Red Deer Commission, the Natural Environmental Research Council – the body deputed to locate suitable waste sites – even the Ordnance Survey, who sent a party of four *by helicopter* to check a "trig point"! They were unable to proceed as freely as they had hoped.

Eventually the Glen Etive campaign petered out, mainly due to the Mullwharchar Inquiry decision which effectively ended the idea of nuclear dumping in Scotland until the late 1980s. However the legacy of the caravan project was a group of young nationalists who were ideologically prepared to countenance the use of violent methods to achieve political ends.

By the summer of 1981, Tom Moore and the leaders of Siol Nan Gaidheal did not appear to care whether they remained in the Scottish National Party or not. The SNG's open association with another extreme Scottish nationalist organisation, the 1320 Club, finally put the Siol beyond the pale.

The 1320 Club had increasingly come to depend on one man, the Honorary President, Ronald MacDonald Douglas, who, by the early 1980s, was well into his eighties. Douglas had just failed in a last attempt to unite the extreme nationalist groups into a Scottish Republican movement which he claimed would offer a more powerful political alternative to the SNP itself. Unfortunately for Douglas, only Siol Nan Gaidheal were interested in his scheme for unity and, as a result of talks, it was resolved to merge the 1320 Club with Siol Nan Gaidheal. Douglas felt that the Club's militant traditions would survive incorporation within Siol Nan Gaidheal. He declared that the Club's aim of "total independence from England through violent means if necessary" would be carried on. Of course, when Tom Moore negotiated the merger with the 1320 Club he incorporated that group's expulsion from the SNP, so the Siol's days within the party were clearly numbered.

In May 1981 at Aberdeen the SNP mainstream, urged on by Siol Nan Gaidheal and the 79 Group, had adopted a campaign of non-violent civil disobedience against English rule in Scotland and had elected an NEC to carry it out. At last the SNP had seized the radical initiative from Siol Nan Gaidheal. From now on, the SNG role seemed less relevant and the group failed to attract new recruits from the SNP. Siol Nan Gaidheal had become in a sense the victim of its own success.

The SNP's own civil disobedience campaign came to a head on 10 October 1981 when an attempt was made by the SNP to occupy the old Royal High School building on Calton Hill. This building was highly symbolic as it had been meant to house the devolved Scottish Assembly and it had been rebuilt internally to fulfil this function. Six SNP members, including Policy Vice-Chairman Jim Sillars, were arrested after they had broken into the building in Regent Road. They had intended to read out in the Debating Chamber, the Declaration of Calton Hill, an SNP document protesting at the high level of unemployment in Scotland and drawing attention to the Government's contempt for the Scots, whose Referendum majority in favour of the Devolution (Scotland) Bill had been ignored. It was obvious, however, that something further was planned for some of the nationalists had brought sleeping bags and food with them. In the event, the protest was squashed by security guards and the police.

If Sillars and the other SNP members had been successful in leading an occupation of the Assembly building, they would have given added symbolism to an official SNP demonstration against unemployment scheduled for a week later outside the same building. Many SNP members turned up for that second rally prepared and expecting to use non-violent civil disobedience methods to beseige and occupy the building. Expectation was high as a result of Jim Sillars' example and Tom Moore announced that Siol Nan Gaidheal "would not stand idly by". The Siol could have been expected to have led the nationalists into the building in a wave of enthusiasm. It was not to be. Neither Siol Nan Gaidheal nor any part of the large SNP crowd attempted to gain access. There were, of course, a large number of police, some of whom had dogs. If the nationalists had come expecting a Bannockburn, they got a Culloden. SNP President Billy Wolfe led 71 volunteers with 71 little Scottish flags representing the constituencies of Scotland up the hill to the gates of the building where their request to enter the site was turned down. They then sat down in the road for a two-minutes silence in protest. After this embarrassingly timid demonstration, the crowd obeyed the leadership's appeal to leave peaceably. The SNP's "Scottish Resistance" campaign of civil disobedience dissolved with the crowd that day, and it was partly that spirit of disappointment that helped to swing the mainstream SNP against both Siol Nan Gaidheal and the 79 Group at the stormy May 1982 Annual Conference at Ayr, which finally threw out both groups.

By May 1982, the political climate had altered drastically. An atmosphere of British jingoism was evident as a result of the Falklands War and the Social Democratic Party had arrived on the scene in alliance with a rejuvenated Liberal Party and challenged the SNP as the champions of "Home Rule". The General Election was barely a year away but the SNP found itself in a deep slump. The time for radical experiment was over. Siol Nan Gaidheal could not adapt to the new political situation. Tom Moore stood down as leader and quickly dropped out of any nationalist activity. The only real energy left in the SNG came from a hard-core group of militants who had been associated with the Glen Etive campaign who wished to prepare SNG for its new existence independent of the SNP. Thus a national headquarters was maintained in Falkirk and a quarterly newspaper *Firinn Albannach* (Gaelic for "Scottish Truth") produced. Publicity was generated through a series of spectacular raids on the symbols of Anglo-American imperialism. In one, a camp was organised outside the United States nuclear submarine base at Coulport on the Holy Loch. The SNG marched up to the gates of the building, ceremonially burnt a Union Jack and hurled it over the perimeter fence. In November, 80 kilted SNG men marched through St Andrews to the Castle where they refused to pay admission fees and simply barged through the gate. On the Castle battlements, watched by police, they burned a Union Jack to symbolise "the coming end of English rule". In another event, Siol Nan Gaidheal activists "redecorated" the town of Berwick upon Tweed with "Free Scotland" posters and slogans painted on walls – and on a large model of the aircraft carrier HMS *Hermes*, part of a recruiting display – during the town's 500th anniversary of "English rule".

Celtic romantics to the last, the SNG militants decided on an even more melodramatic gesture. They set up a military wing and declared war against the British State. Arm Nan Gaidheal was born. Siol Nan Gaidheal was now openly condoning the practice of terrorist violence as a tactic and Arm Nan Gaidheal's communiqués were reported to *Firinn Albannach* whose editorials claimed to "understand the reasons for their [Arm Nan Gaidheal] existence". Soon, however, Siol Nan Gaidheal's rhetoric of violence had crossed over the line into real violence. Fortunately Arm Nan Gaidheal's attempt to use force generated only farce.

The Arm Nan Gaidheal's communiqués in *Firinn Albannach* mentioned six incendiary bomb attacks on "English Army Stores" in Edinburgh, Labour and Conservative Party headquarters in Glasgow and Dundee, a spinning mill at Galashiels and a fire-bomb attack on the Assembly Rooms in Edinburgh. It does not seem probable that Arm Nan Gaidheal were involved in all of these attacks, and responsibility for some of them was claimed by other organisations, but they were undoubtedly involved in some of the incidents.

The first claimed attack occurred in the early hours of the morning of 17 July 1982 when Army security police discovered a fire at Redford Barracks in Edinburgh. The blaze had started in two empty rooms in the Barracks and had only been discovered subsequent to a phone call to Scottish newspapers by a caller claiming to represent the "Scottish Independence Army". The caller said that incendiary devices had been placed at Barracks in the Edinburgh area. As a result of the call, police and the Army security police checked Edinburgh Castle, Scottish Army HQ at Craigiehall, Glencorse and Dreghorn Barracks as well as Redford.

Nothing was found in the initial search. Later the Army indicated that they didn't believe there was a connection between the warning and the fire. The police announced that they had found no evidence to suggest that the fire began as a result of any device.

Whatever – or whoever – had caused the fire, the fact remains that a new terrorist "organisation" had been announced. The caller had taken pains to disassociate his group from the "Scottish National Liberation Army" which had gained notoriety from a series of letter-bomb attacks on prominent public figures. Given the claim in *Firinn Albannach* that the attack on Redford Barracks was carried out by the "Scottish Independence Army" it is possible that this was the beginning of a distinct terrorist group which later called itself "Arm Nan Gaidheal" but which, in the summer of 1982, did not wish to be too closely associated with Siol Nan Gaidheal. After September 1982 when the banning of Siol Nan Gaidheal came into effect, responsibility for a number of fire attacks on offices of "anti-Scottish" political parties was claimed by "Arm Nan Gaidheal". Their methods in these attacks were crude and not very effective. In both the Glasgow cases, where separate attacks were made on a Conservative office and on Labour's Scottish HQ at Keir Hardie House, petrol was poured through the letterbox and a slow fuse was used to ignite it. The Conservative office suffered only minor damage to the door since the fire went out, but the Labour HQ was gutted. The fire brigade arrived and put out the blaze but a large number of leaflets and material had been smoke-damaged. In neither incident was there any danger to life.

The attack on the Dundee offices of the Labour Party, also claimed by Arm Nan Gaidheal, was a more dangerous affair. It followed the same pattern as the other two; an inflammable liquid poured through the letterbox of the second-floor offices in Rattray Street and ignited. The message later received by the police claimed that the fire was an act of revenge for an unprovoked attack upon a nationalist by a Dundee Labour Councillor and other Labour members. It gave warning that attacks on nationalists would be avenged: "Let the Labour Party beware – next time we shall take our revenge in blood."

The attack itself could have had even more dire consequences, for three students lived in the flat immediately above the Labour offices. The fire brigade received a desperate phone call in the early morning of 2 December from them. They were unable to escape from the flat down the dilapidated stone stairs because of dense smoke on the stairway. The students were led to safety by firemen wearing breathing apparatus. Although there was no loss of life, the Labour offices were severely damaged and they were unusable for some time. George Galloway, Secretary of the Dundee Labour Party and soon to be the controversial MP for Glasgow Hillhead, called those responsible "lunatics". He said he knew nothing of either a physical or verbal attack on a nationalist. "It is a preposterous allegation and merely goes to show the extraordinary characters we're dealing with – extraordinarily dangerous characters," he said. Galloway continued by demanding that the SNP leadership condemn "this Scottish nationalist extremism which has become rampant over the last few years". Alan McKinney, SNP National Organiser issued a statement deploring what had happened and angrily pointing out that it had absolutely nothing to do with the SNP which had no extremist members.

Whether Arm Nan Gaidheal actually carried out the Dundee attack, it certainly caused a major embarrassment for the SNP in the city where their leader, Gordon Wilson, was a sitting MP. Another terrorist group, the "Scottish National Liberation Army", later claimed responsibility for the attack. The Labour Party certainly used the event to maximum effect, rushing out a last-minute leaflet in Gordon Wilson's Dundee East constituency, more or less accusing Gordon Wilson of complicity in terrorism. The SNP were furious – and unable to obtain an interim interdict before polling opened. The Labour move proved counter-productive. Gordon Wilson was too respectable – and well respected – for this kind of smear tactic to work and he retained his seat with an increased majority.

The attack on the Assembly Rooms in George Street, Edinburgh, can definitely be linked with Arm Nan Gaidheal, since the details of the attack were revealed in a three-day trial in November 1983. Siol Nan Gaidheal member Ian Paton was convicted of setting fire to the Rooms on 24 November 1982. Paton, a 26-year-old plumber from Port Glasgow, dropped milk cartons filled with petrol through a window at the Assembly Rooms. The resulting blaze set off a fire alarm which alerted the manager of the Assembly Rooms. He found an emergency fire door and wooden panelling alight but was able to douse the flames with a fire extinguisher. It was later on that night that the *Scotsman* newspaper received a message from Arm Nan Gaidheal stating that the attack was a protest against the visit of Prime Minister, Mrs Thatcher, to a function to be held in the Rooms two days later. The attack remained unsolved for two months until another incident occurred. This time the Prime Minister was due to attend a dinner at the Glasgow Holiday Inn to celebrate Glasgow Chamber of Commerce's centenary. Acting on information from an *agent provocateur* within the ranks of Arm Nan Gaidheal, Glasgow police kept watch on the homes of those involved in organising Mrs Thatcher's visit. One observation post was set up close to the home of Matthew Neill, Chief Executive of Glasgow Chamber of Commerce, in Arkleston Road, Paisley.

Shortly before 10 p.m., on Thursday, 28 January 1983, two Siol Nan Gaidheal militants, Ian Paton and Gordon Docherty of Anstruther, Fife, broke into Neill's garage. They forced open the petrol cap of the car, inserted paper into the fuel tank filter pipe and ignited the paper. They then ran off and jumped into a getaway car driven by another nationalist comrade, Peter Stewart. Alerted by the commotion and the coincidental arrival of Matthew Neill in another car, the three police officers in the observation post – an inspector and two constables – dashed into the garage, put out the fire and radioed for assistance. Stewart's car was quickly traced and a car chase began through the Paisley streets.

During the chase, Paton and Docherty got out of the car and escaped up a side street. The police eventually caught Peter Stewart when his car collided with a parked vehicle in Ladyloan Street, Paisley. Stewart was arrested and soon the police were able to arrest Paton, whom they found at his parents' home in Port Glasgow. Eight members of Siol Nan Gaidheal, including Docherty, were rounded up and detained for questioning under the Prevention of Terrorism Act in February 1983. Once arrested, Ian Paton fully co-operated with the police and gave them valuable information about the Arm Nan Gaidheal organisation. Mr Alan Blair, Paton's defence agent, even told the Sheriff, Peter McNeill, that "if the organisation is now dead and buried it is due to a large extent to Ian Paton". Such co-operation gained its reward for, although he was subsequently convicted, with Gordon Docherty, of attempting to set fire to Matthew Neill's car and had already been convicted of the Assembly Rooms fire, Ian Paton was sentenced by Lord Wheatley, Lord Justice Clerk, to only 120 hours of community service. Gordon Docherty was fined £75 and Peter Stewart was fined £80 for three road traffic offences. During the trial, Paton's agent had told the court that there were "far more sinister people in the organisation" than Paton or his co-accused.

After the trial those remaining in the organisation found that they could no longer trust each other. Talk of *agents provocateurs* and police informers dominated the increasingly sparse gatherings of Siol Nan Gaidheal. Eventually the unheroic nature of the Arm Nan Gaidheal activities and the members' behaviour during the trial persuaded even the most die-hard supporters that their cause was doomed.

The SNG claimed in 1985 to have been behind the theft of a priceless Scottish relic from a St Albans church on St Andrew's Day. The relic, a 16th-century brass eagle lectern, originally looted from Holyrood Abbey in 1544 by an English earl, had actually been stolen by another group – the "Scottish National Guardians" – who were able to prove their claim by sending a photograph of the eagle with a current copy of a newspaper propped up on it. The police agreed that the Siol had merely been "jumping on the bandwagon". This ignominious episode was the last public mention of the SNG. The latter-day Jacobite romance was over, the march of the paramilitary clansmen had ended. In 1988 however, a new organization was set up with the name Siol Nan Gaidheal, claiming no links with the previous group and a membership in 1990 of 300.

11 THE "WAR OF LIBERATION"?

The military campaign . . . has been a tremendous success with over fifty attacks in a four-year period, and despite State and media suppression of news of many of the attacks . . . has been widely publicised and . . . has shown itself to be essential to the morale of the Scottish people . . ..

Saorsa, *the newspaper of the Scottish National Liberation Army,*
March/April 1986

OF all the extremist groups in Scotland the shadowy organisation known as the "Scottish National Liberation Army" remains at once the most obscure and the most persistent. The group claim over 50 attacks since their inception in December 1980. Moreover, their activities continue. The SNLA initiated a persistent "letter-bombing" campaign to leading public figures including Margaret Thatcher, Princess Diana, even the Queen, which made them front-page news. And since then their methods appear to have widened to include bombing incidents at other targets.

The question that has to be asked is, does the SNLA actually exist? Does it have an organisational structure or is it merely the activities of one or two terrorists? The history of the organisation is in two distinct phases. The SNLA appears to have been entirely relaunched in 1984 and since then it has had some support from Ireland – not from the IRA, but from an offshoot of the Provisionals, the INLA. The situation is further confused by the emergence of a new political party – the "Scottish Republican Socialist Party" – at roughly the same time that the SNLA's activities began. This led to press analogies with Ireland, where the INLA is the "military wing" of the IRSP. The Scottish Republican Socialist Party, however, has consistently denied any connection with the SNLA. And the "reborn" SNLA has strenuously denied any connection with the "political cowards and opportunists" of the SRSP. Yet the attacks continue. An "SNLA communiqué" claims responsibility for massive bomb damage at the Foster Yeoman Quarry in Glensanda, on the Morvern Peninsula in Argyll, in 1989. So it is obvious that there are still some members active in Scotland.

So who are the SNLA terrorists and what evidence is there of an organisation called the SNLA? Several months after the 1980 trial involving Peter Wardlaw's faction, a high-level police conference was held into the sudden escalation of armed bank raids (there had been more than 20 in the Glasgow and West Central Scotland area within the previous few months). The Special Branch examined the raids for any political motivation and although they discounted the possibility that political extremists were behind the escalation of large-scale robberies, they did not rule out the possibility that a new Scottish extremist group was involved in raising funds. The SNLA claimed that its initial funding came from an Edinburgh publican, now deceased, but that other funds were to be raised by "expropriation" – i.e. robbery. It has also been suggested that the remnants of the "'Scottish Citizens' Army of the Republic" were involved in the founding of the SNLA.

A few weeks later, on 31 December 1981, a front-page story in the *Glasgow Herald* told of the discovery of a huge explosives cache between Newton Mearns and Dumbarton. A country road was sealed off when the 50 lbs of gelignite was discovered hidden in a canvas bag together with detonators and wiring at the edge of a field on the A77 minor road, which links Glasgow with Stranraer and the ferries to Ireland. Strathclyde's special task force was called out and two Army bomb disposal men inspected the gelignite which was removed in an unmarked van. The police attempted to locate the source of the explosive, which they suspected had been stolen from the rundown Pilmair Quarry about half a mile from where the cache was discovered. A blood-stained rag and a quantity of detonators was found separately in the same vicinity. The police did not at this point believe that the discovery had "anything to do with terrorist activity but that cannot be ruled out".

The next source of concern about the existence of a new terrorist group came from the Scottish National Party. An article in the 6 December 1981 issue of the *Sunday Post* reported that a poster circulating in Glasgow, featuring the slogan "Liberty Now" and a picture of a militant young lady with an armalite rifle slung over her shoulder was worrying the SNP: "Definitely not the image the Nats want to project – but the poster also bears the logo of the Scottish Resistance campaign. There's no publisher's name on the poster and attempts to discover who's circulating it have come to nought."

Then, on 1 March 1982, came the first of a series of bomb scares claimed in the name of the "Scottish National Liberation Army". The first caused major traffic disruption in central Edinburgh and proved to be a hoax. The second, on 17 March, was not. A crude letterbomb device was received at the Edinburgh headquarters of the Social Democratic Party in Great Stuart Street. Army bomb disposal officers took the package into nearby gardens in Randolph Crescent and detonated it. Police described it as a "crude incendiary device which would have caused injury had it been opened". A member of the SDP voluntary staff had become suspicious when she noticed that the package bore the same lettering as an anonymous threatening letter received on 25 February. An SDP official telephoned their offices in Glasgow and a second package was discovered. Staff put it into an empty room and called the police. Bomb disposal experts later defused the device at Strathclyde Police HQ. The SDP described the incidents as "a frightening experience for the office staffs". A letter, constructed from cut-up newspaper print, which had accompanied the Edinburgh package was printed on the front page of the *Scotsman* newspaper on 20 March. It read: "The safest place for an English middle-class party is England as you will soon find out." A fourth letterbomb was sent to John Nott, the Conservative Defence Secretary of State, at the House of

Commons. A man telephoned the Glasgow office of the *Scotsman* claiming that it had been sent by the SNLA because of the decision to go ahead with the Trident missile programme.

The next attack was on 24 May at the Scottish Assembly building in Edinburgh. The incendiary bomb was meant to explode during a sitting of the Scottish Grand Committee, but the device was described by Army experts as 'little more than a bunch of wires connected to a box of matches". In addition to this it was actually delivered wrongly, being placed in the letterbox at the part of the old Royal High School building– used not by the Parliamentary Committee, but by the Crown Office. A bomb was placed at the Conservative Party Scottish headquarters in Somerset Place, Glasgow, on 18 June. It was described as "a crude device" by an Army bomb disposal team. There was a "mystery blaze" at Redford Barracks in Edinburgh on 17 July following a telephone claim to newspapers that incendiary devices had been placed at Barracks in the Edinburgh area. Police and Army security police checked Edinburgh Castle, Scottish Army HQ at Craigiehall, Glencorse and Dreghorn Barracks but denied that there was any connection between the warning and the fire. They were, however, unable to explain how the fire had started and the CID said that their "inquiries were continuing". No one was injured. On 29 July Scotland Yard denied any knowledge of any explosive device having been received at Buckingham Palace. The police "denied absolutely" that any attacks had been made on the Queen. Twelve days later, a letterbomb in a 'jiffy bag' received at Conservative Party HQ in Smith Square, London, was pronounced to be a hoax since the bomb "was not in any way viable".

After these first nine or ten 'attacks', mostly hoaxes and betraying a high level of ineptitude, there was a lull until November. A new political party, the Marxist-orientated "Scottish Republican Socialist Party" was launched from the shell of the Scottish Republican Socialist Clubs and included many members of the banned Siol Nan Gaidheal faction and left-wing Republican 79 Group supporters. The basic aim of the party was the foundation of an independent Scottish Socialist Republic. The organiser of the SRSP, Donald Anderson, said that the new party was "more than just a protest against the undemocratic trends within the SNP". He announced that the party would be fielding a candidate at the Queen's Park by-election and cheekily called on the SNP to stand down so as "not to split the nationalist vote". The party's first candidate would be Alistair Tennant, a 21-year-old unemployed graduate and a former SNP 79 Group member. Political observers wondered how much former SNP support the new party might attract, but many SNP veterans felt that the Republican Socialist "fringe" was unlikely to expand or to find normal party political activity conducive. On the day that the date of the Queen's Park by-election was announced, a full-page article appeared in the *Evening Times* titled "The Case of Matt Lygate". Lygate's sentence is described in Chapter 3 but the major article went beyond a rehash of previous press clippings since it published the results of various interviews – one of which was with Alistair Tennant. Lygate's activities and his political credo were thus shown to have been reborn in the SRSP and hope was expressed that Republican Socialists would now work through politics rather than by armed bank robbery.

That not all Republican Socialists wished to do so was made apparent on Saturday 6 November. A fire caused severe damage to the Labour Party's Scottish HQ, Keir Hardie House, in Lynedoch Place; 150,000 copies of a special leaflet had been destroyed, telephone lines and electricity cables cut. The police believed that petrol had been poured through the letterbox and ignited. Helen Liddell, Labour Party Secretary, described the incident as "a major irritation and inconvenience coming at the start of the by-election but it will make us all the more determined". She estimated the damage at £20,000 plus about £4,000 for the leaflets. Two years later it was revealed that the damage repair work after the fire had revealed a considerable number of faults and structural problems and the cost of repairing these was put at around £50,000. Mrs Liddell in 1984 described the situation as "a financial nightmare". Although the fire was attributed to the SNLA, responsibility has been consistently denied by them.

The *Glasgow Herald* on Monday, 8 November, ran the story but also reported another incident: a firebomb at the Conservative headquarters in Somerset Place, Kelvingrove, less than 24 hours after the Labour blaze. This fire destroyed furnishings, carpets, files and office equipment and cut the telephone lines and electricity supply. A Conservative spokeswoman said that the damage "will cost thousands to repair". Police believed that this fire was caused by the same method as the previous incident and concluded that "whoever was responsible did not want serious damage to occur". They considered the possibility that both fires were started by the same person, at a time when the streets were still busy, making early discovery of the fires likely. An anonymous telephone call alerted police to the Conservative blaze but none was received for the Labour fire. The SNLA claimed the Conservative office attack – but not the Labour fire.

The next incident, on 23 November, resulted in the formation of a special police 'task force' to track down the perpetrators of the offences. The incident itself, a letterbomb to Patrick Jenkin, the Industry Minister, was hardly any less inept. The device, which was intercepted by an alert secretary, was later described by the police as unlikely to have killed anyone but "could certainly have caused severe burns". It had apparently been sent in reprisal for 400 redundancies which the British Steel Corporation had recently announced at the Lanarkshire steel works of Craigneuk. The local trades union leaders denounced the action. What interested the police more was a letter received at the Glasgow office of the Press Association the same day purporting to be from the SNLA. This letter, printed in Letraset capitals in long, uneven lines, bore similarities to the writing on the packages sent to John Nott and to Patrick Jenkin. Moreover, it bore the same date and postmark as the Jenkin package. The letter claimed that the SNLA had carried out seven attacks in the past six months; the letterbombs to Mr Nott, the SDP offices in Edinburgh and Glasgow, the Crown Office, Edinburgh, Conservative Headquarters in London and Edinburgh, and Buckingham Palace. If this was to be believed the SNLA were *not* claiming responsibility for the fire at the Labour HQ in Glasgow, the fire at Redford Barracks, or, more importantly, the letterbomb received that day by Patrick Jenkin. In fact, all they were claiming were the letterbomb incidents and the firebomb attack at the Conservative offices which might easily have been the work of one man. Had they laid claim to either of the other incidents, it might be imagined that there was more than a single terrorist operating.

So far, the incidents had been treated as sporadic outbreaks but the letter to the Press Association prompted a major investigation into the SNLA by several police authorities, including Strathclyde, Lothian, Scotland Yard and anti-terrorist squad officers. It would seem however that either the SNLA could not count or there were at least two units operating quite independently. The reference to "avenging" the workers of Craigneuk was actually on the letter which had missed out mention of the Jenkin device.

Police continued to deny that Buckingham Palace had received a letterbomb. The SNLA claimed that the package was sent on 29 July but had been unreported. The other SNLA claims were supported, even although most had previously remained unreported in the press. The letter itself and the SNLA claims were now the subject of considerable press attention. The BBC's *Reporting Scotland* news programme carried an extensive report on the letterbombs, featuring an interview with the journalist who had opened the SNLA letter.

In the *Scotsman* the day after the BBC report, a large article headed "Letter Bomb Campaign Linked To Rise In Republican Activities" specifically produced the analogy of the IRSP and INLA with the SRSP and the SNLA. "Security sources believe the group [SNLA] have modelled themselves on the notorious INLA . . . a copycat shadow of their Irish counterparts . . . but SRSP members last night strenuously denied any connection with the SNLA. But the emergence of the group is a clear indication of a quickening growth in the activities of extremist republicanism in Scotland which is being closely watched . . .". Since the authors of the article could not find any specific evidence of Irish-style links between the SRSP and the SNLA, they reported that the SRSP candidate held his first press conference in a "disused public house once the subject of a bomb attack by Irish-related extremists. On the walls were posters in praise of dead IRA hunger strikers Bobby Sands and Matthew Lygate who is now serving a lengthy prison sentence for bank raids to raise funds for another extreme left-wing group in Scotland . . . the SRSP campaign began with a declaration on self-determination first issued by Sinn Fein's foreign affairs department."

The *Sunday Standard* newspaper reported the aftermath of the letterbombing campaign, in an article titled "A Dose Of The Jitters When The Postman Calls". It was reported that staff at the Scottish Liberal Party headquarters in Clifton Terrace, Edinburgh, had panicked when they received a well-worn "jiffy bag" with wires dangling from it and the address written in "a less than literate hand". They called the police and the package was carefully opened in a place of safety. It was found to contain a copy of the booklet *Police Powers and Politics* which a zealous party member felt ought to be perused by the Liberal Executive! Meanwhile in Glasgow the Labour Party staff were now so wary of packages arriving by mail they called the police to inspect one suspicious package. The police ran their detector equipment over it and it was indeed positive. Police specialists opened it to find that it contained two pairs of tiny gilt feet fashioned into badges – gifts from the Society for the Protection of the Unborn Child for the Labour candidate, Helen McElhone, and Labour Secretary, Helen Liddell!

The Queen's Park by-election was described by the media as one of the dirtiest election campaigns seen in Scotland for years. Since 1967, Scottish by-elections have always been desperate affairs, but after the previous fire at Keir Hardie House, there was a second fire attack at the Labour election rooms in Gorbals Street. A brick was thrown through a window of the Labour Rooms while party workers were still inside and two break-ins occurred at the Labour offices in Allison Street. The Conservative candidate claimed that a 20-year-old party worker had been assaulted by three youths when he was leafleting. Nor did the SNP campaign rooms – or party workers – escape the usual by-election dirty tricks.

The disparity in the number of letterbombs was given a new twist with a front-page leader article in the *Scotsman* on 1 December, the day before polling in the by-election. The article's headline was "Wave Of Letter Bombs Reported; Previously They Had Been Hushed Up". It began: "Whitehall and Westminster staff are on full alert this morning amid fears that more postal fire bombs are on their way to leading politicians. Mrs Thatcher, the leaders of Britain's main political parties and a Home Office Minister were the targets yesterday . . .". The article went on to reveal that Mrs Thatcher, Prince Charles, several Cabinet Ministers and Opposition politicians had been the targets of similar but unreported incendiary devices in recent months.

The package received in Mrs Thatcher's office was opened by Peter Taylor, the office manager at No 10 Downing Street. Less than 40 feet away, in the first-floor study, Mrs Thatcher was holding a meeting when the letterbomb exploded. Luckily, Taylor was wearing spectacles but he received burns to his face and his hair was singed. He had the presence of mind to drop the package and stamp out the fire. Three hours later, in the House of Commons, Mrs Thatcher condemned those who sent letterbombs and warned MPs to be careful. "Letterbombs anywhere are most distressing and we are all vulnerable," she said. "From time to time MPs have received them and we have to be extremely careful." There was to be a review of mail screening procedures. Despite the routine description of the devices as "crude but viable" the astonishing fact was that they had broken through the tight security cordon, despite the sophisticated electronic surveillance equipment. The press were not allowed to photograph the rooms and offices where the devices had exploded or to interview the members of staff who had opened the packages.

The Post Office pointed out that their staff at Westminster had discovered all four letterbombs sent there and that suspect mail was routinely taken to nearby Cannon Row police station for X-ray screening. They also revealed for the first time that several other incendiary devices destined for Prince Charles, No. 10 Downing Street and leading politicians, including Michael Heseltine MP, had already been intercepted by them – in addition to those sent to Patrick Jenkin, the Industry Secretary, in November and John Nott, the Defence Secretary, in March. In order to clear its own record, the Post Office had inadvertently revealed these other incidents, which had been "hushed up" by the police for reasons of their own. The police were forced to admit that they knew of these other devices and that they were all identical in appearance. All were contained in seven-inch by five-and-a-half-inch yellow padded envelopes of the Air Kraft trade mark – similar to the "jiffy bag" in which both the bombs to Mr Jenkin and Mr Nott were contained. The police refused to reveal any more details of the devices or the postmarks that were on the packages. Scotland Yard would not categorically agree that the bombs were the work of the SNLA and mentioned the possibility that they might be the work of extreme animal rights protestors.

It was not only the Government and political parties that were on the alert. The general public too were aware of the tense situation. Bomb scares were frequently reported. One disrupted the start of the CBI Annual Conference in Scotland in 1983. A suspicious package found on a high-speed Aberdeen to London train two days later was blown up by the Army after the train was stopped short of Edinburgh. Later it was revealed that the package had contained nothing suspicious.

There were three more attacks – none of which received any publicity. A "suspicious parcel" was planted at the Glasgow HQ of British Steel – leading to evacuation of all staff. Although police described this as a simple hoax, the SNLA preferred the term "inert device". Two more "inert devices" were placed in pillar-boxes in Glasgow in protest at Mrs Thatcher's visit to the city. There was a destructive fire in a forestry plantation near Perth, claimed by the organisation.

Meanwhile more explosive mail was on its way. A brown padded envelope addressed to Glasgow's Lord Provost, Dr Michael Kelly, burst into flames in Glasgow City Chambers in the hands of the Provost's Secretary, Eric Hamilton, about 9 a.m. on 17 February. The package fell on to the carpet and burned until one of the curators rushed in with an extinguisher and put out the fire. Mr Hamilton required hospital treatment but returned to work later that day for the Royal visit to Glasgow of Princess Diana. Letters were received at the Glasgow offices of the Press Association and BBC Scotland claiming the attack on behalf of the SNLA as a protest at the Princess's visit and warning of more to follow.

While the Lord Provost promised a review of security, Detective-Inspector Bert Walker, heading the inquiry, admitted that "some craft was needed to rig up the trigger which activated the device when the package was opened". The bomb, he said, had been constructed from materials which were readily available and could have been posted anywhere in Glasgow. He described it as "a fairly clever incendiary device". The bombers were getting more efficient and also more daring – bombs were exploding closer to home.

The Royal visit went ahead as planned, with more intense security. Next day's tabloids were triumphant: "Brave Di Shrugs Off The Evil Bombs" was the *Sun*'s headline: "Threats did not ruffle dazzling Di. First she met youngsters in the City's Royal Hospital for Sick Children then the Princess toured Easterhouse, a huge housing estate with some slum property. But Special Branch and uniformed police kept a close watch in case the terrorists tried to strike again . . .".

But the SNLA letterbombing campaign was in full swing. The bombers were receiving instant publicity for each new incident, surely one of the main aims of a terrorist campaign. The question in everyone's mind was not "Will they strike again?" but "Where and when?"

The question was soon answered. Less than a month later, on 16 March, another bomb sent to Mrs Thatcher was safely defused at a postal sorting office in Victoria. Two other bombs had been received the day before, at No 10 Downing Street and at the US Navy's European Headquarters in Mayfair. While the package addressed to the Prime Minister was safely defused, the second exploded and caused injury to a Senior Petty Officer in the US Navy. Government offices throughout the UK were put on alert in the belief that more incendiary devices were in the mail. The police discounted claims that an Argentine terrorist organisation or Ukranian anarchists were behind the devices. Three hours before the Mayfair blast, the Glasgow offices of the Press Association had received a letter from the SNLA claiming that the attacks of 15/16 March were in reprisal for the Craigneuk sackings. The letter had been posted first-class in Glasgow and did not specify targets. The Thatcher letterbomb was of the same type as that sent to Provost Kelly.

The SNLA achieved success with their use of "inert devices" or hoax bombs in May 1983 when SNLA men used a rubber dinghy to cross Loch Long and planted two empty fire extinguishers wrapped in polythene under culverts a mile apart on a road near the Coulport nuclear base. The road was the base's main access, which convoys of nuclear warheads would use, and the entire area was sealed off as part of a major alert as first one then the other device was traced and made safe by controlled explosions. The SNLA claimed that they had had no intention of causing an explosion and merely wished to demonstrate how easy it would have been for dedicated extremists to cause catastrophic damage.

The SNLA claimed responsibility for a letterbomb sent to the Army Careers office in Penge in south-east London. That device was discovered and defused safely by an Army Sergeant. Ten days after that, the Prime Minister was due to address a meeting of Conservative candidates in the Crest Hotel in South Mimms, Hertfordshire. A "jiffy bag", posted in Glasgow, addressed to the Chairman of the Conservative Candidates' Association, Mr Jeremy Hanley, arrived a couple of hours before Mrs Thatcher was due to address the meeting. Hanley's deputy, Mr Robert Key, a 37-year-old Harrow schoolmaster, became suspicious and made a hole in the side of the bag. Then he carried it from the hotel dining-room into the garden and called the police. The Army disposal team who defused the device said that it contained an explosive substance and would have caused "serious injury" if it had been opened. A letter from the SNLA sent to the Fleet Street offices of the Press Association had claimed responsibility for the device, carried out in retaliation for cuts in Scottish industry. But a second bomb attack was claimed by the SNLA within the next 24 hours and not reported. The claim, only publicly revealed on 29 June, was of a much more serious nature.

An anonymous caller telephoned a news agency and claimed that an SNLA unit had planted a six-pound plastic explosive device and sealed it in a veterinary medical chest under Perth City Hall stage. It would be detonated by remote control. The SNLA caller maintained that the bomb had lain undetected for 25 days, discovered only 48 hours before Mrs Thatcher was due to launch the General Election campaign at the Scottish Conservative Conference in Perth City Hall. Surely this could be considered to be a hoax, given that previous SNLA activities had been confined to capsules of lighter fuel attached to matches or crude arson attacks and use of hoax bombs? Or were the SNLA about to step up their activities? Had they indeed obtained plastic explosive? Strangely, Tayside Police refused to confirm or deny the incident: "We cannot comment on this, it is a security matter." They did, however, question at some length the agency news reporter who had received the anonymous call. Several months later, the incident had become confused and a report referred to it as "a bomb hoax" relating to a claim that "three devices hidden in the City Halls were timed to go off at half-hourly intervals". Police had already searched the building but carried out a further search, using sniffer dogs and special equipment without disturbing the conference. It seems fair to assume that there were *two* separate incidents at the conference, with this second one being a definite hoax while the other incident remains shrouded in mystery. Was it too a hoax – or had a bomb actually been planted in the City Hall? And, if so, had Mrs Thatcher been in danger? A claim was made by a BBC news programme in October 1984 that a bomb *had* been planted but that the plot had been discovered by a police undercover agent. Tayside's Assistant Chief Constable, James Cameron, categorically denied that any explosive device had been found. The programme revealed that their evidence had come from a man who claimed to be one of five founding members of the SNLA. The searches had been initiated by Tayside Police after Strathclyde Police had obtained what they regarded as absolutely certain information that a bomb had been planted and that it was radio-controlled. Consequently, there was complete radio silence as the search was made, for it had been known for a police radio to trigger such a device. The SNLA "contact" told the BBC that he had pressed the radio button outside the hall while Mrs Thatcher was speaking – and nothing had happened. Army experts believed that had a six-pound plastic explosive charge exploded, not only would Mrs Thatcher have been killed but quite probably most of the platform party and several hundreds of the audience. The "contact" was then allowed, through BBC reporter David Scott, to give an explanation for such an attack: "It would have been a turning point in British politics. While the first public reaction would have been shock and revulsion, the assassination would have awakened the political conscience of Scotland in the long term. The rest of the world including England would have alienated Scotland and the Scots. We would then be forced to fend for ourselves in a political sense and it would be then that the people would turn to a socialist republic."

This statement was described by the reporter as "both sinister and disturbing". Professor Paul Wilkinson, an expert on international terrorism, was interviewed on the programme and asked whether the SNLA posed a greater threat than the Army of the Provisional Government or the "Tartan Army". Wilkinson did not think so, since the SNLA attacks had not threatened life. He felt that it was the kind of phenomenon which democratic societies had got to learn to cope with and that they were isolated, with no support among the Scottish people and would therefore meet with "as little success as groups have in the past. They are on a hiding to nothing."

There was a lull in SNLA activities until 12 May when another letterbomb was sent to Scone Palace, Perth, the home of the Earl of Mansfield, a Conservative Minister whom Mrs Thatcher was visiting. Fortunately for Lord Mansfield and the Prime Minister, the police were maintaining a scrutiny of all packages posted in Glasgow through the main Glasgow sorting office depot. The package never reached its destination. Nor did any organisation claim responsibility for it. The device consisted as before of two tubes of petrol, a box of matches and a piece of emery paper. The police issued a nationwide alert, believing that Scotland could be hit by "a wave of letterbombs". They had not revealed to whom the package was addressed and gave the impression that the letterbombers were now targeting ordinary people – at random

– and urged *everyone* to check their mail carefully. The alert came hours after a series of swoops on houses in the Falkirk area by Special Branch.

All of this letterbombing activity had provoked a great amount of police surveillance of nationalists known to have extreme or left-wing views, and police had concentrated their efforts on the members of Siol Nan Gaidheal and the Scottish Republican Socialist Party. This had led to numerous interviews from which the police had gleaned much useful general background information on both groups. Since all of the packages had been posted in Glasgow using the same type of "jiffy bags" or padded envelopes, it was also a fairly simple operation for the police to ask each postman to report these envelopes and which post-box they had been collected from. In this way it was established that the bomb addressed to Lord Mansfield had been posted in a box in North Hanover Street in Glasgow city centre. The next day, a man was arrested under the Prevention of Terrorism Act and four others, including two young women, were taken into police headquarters for detailed questioning. The arrested man appeared at Glasgow Sheriff Court on Monday, 16 May 1983. He was 20-year-old David Dinsmore of Midthorn Crescent, Falkirk, and he was charged with posting the package on 12 May addressed to Lord Mansfield and with intent to cause an explosion and injury. He made no plea and was remanded in custody. The application for bail by Dinsmore's solicitor, Hugh McTaggart, was refused by Sheriff Mowat QC.

Dinsmore had been National Organiser of Siol Nan Gaidheal but had soon become National Secretary of the SRSP. Possibly he had felt that the Siol had become moribund, whereas the creation of the SRSP had seemed to generate new activity. The SRSP was busy organising events such as the Matt Lygate rally to Saughton Prison, meetings of the John Maclean Society in Glasgow Trades Council, the 1820 Martyrs rally, a bus to Belfast for the Easter Sunday parades, a major Glasgow rally in support of the Irish Republican movement plus their planned participation in the May Day rally and their own party meetings. They had a more open attitude to co-operation between groups. Dinsmore threw himself into working for the SRSP and almost his first activity was to arrange a joint campaign between the two groups against the hated warrant sales. This was a robust campaign, involving physical fighting. On 15 April, in Paisley, nationalists and republicans had prevented Sheriff Officers from delivering a warrant, and two members claimed to have been beaten up when the police brought in reinforcements. Three days later, SRSP and SNG activists occupied the Glasgow offices of the Sheriff Officers involved while pickets stood on the main gates and distributed hundreds of leaflets. The occupiers remained inside the building for five hours until they were physically removed. Again there were claims of police brutality. It was alleged that three activists were beaten up by Sheriff Officers while police looked on and did nothing. One of the activists was subsequently charged with breach of the peace. The SRSP newsletter of 4 May then reports that, on 22 or 23 April, "the premises of every Sheriff Officer in Glasgow were attacked by unknown persons and many thousands of pounds worth of damage are reported to have been caused. Police throughout Scotland are ordered to guard the premises of Sheriff Officers in every part of the country, Despite this, reports are coming in of attacks in many parts of the country, e.g. Paisley, Greenock and Falkirk."

These claims of damage do not appear to have received much publicity in the national press, but it is plain that Scottish republicans were now on the rampage, active on many fronts. The police had to do something. They arrested Dinsmore. Three of the other four taken into custody were released from Stewart Street police station on 20 May without charge, but one, 46-year-old Don Molloy, from Port Glasgow, was subsequently taken into custody by Lothian and Borders policemen on a warrant from Edinburgh Sheriff Court and charged with the arson attack on Redford Barracks. One of the other released men was a 19-year-old Irishman, Martin Kelly, of Dublin, who left Glasgow immediately to return to Ireland. The Irish Consul stated that his return was voluntary and he could return if and when he chose to do so. The third released man was Donald Anderson, SRSP Organiser, who had been arrested in a Drumchapel pub where he had been invited for a drink. In custody he had been questioned continuously for 52 hours "on the ideology of the SRSP and asked to give names and addresses of members".

There was a dispute between SNG and the SRSP after Dinsmore's arrest. This grew bitter and several satirical publications appeared, one a parody of *Firinn Albannach* subtitled "News and Views of Sod of the Gael" from the fictitious address of 33 Judas

Street, Edinburgh. "It has been a busy time for Sod of the Gael what with grassing each other off to the police, securing our expenses as prosecution witnesses . . .". Others were in the form of leaflets: "Shop a Friend Today Join Siol Nan Gaidheal". The SRSP newsletter of June 1983 was more restrained, reporting that the "militant?" Sol Nan Gaidheal had pulled out of the joint warrant sales campaign. An accompanying letter was copied to the press. It told of David Dinsmore's arrest and attacked the attitude of Siol Nan Gaidheal. "An article appeared in the Sunday Mail on 15th May stating that David had been expelled from Siol Nan Gaidheal for his 'association with the SRSP'. The Siol are trying to claim that they expelled David on the Thursday before his arrest . . . to cover up the fact that certain Siol executive members decided to desert David rather than be publicly associated with him." The SRSP decided to proscribe the SNG and demanded that any of their members who were also SNG members make the choice of remaining in either organisation – but not both.

The SRSP formed a David Dinsmore Defence Committee to publicise his case. Despite days of questioning, Dinsmore was continuing to maintain his innocence of the letterbomb charge. The Defence Committee picketed Stewart Street police station, at which event two members were arrested, one for taking photographs and the other for breach of the peace. There had been four other "effective demonstrations" and the newsletter also reported that ten SRSP members had been arrested within the first two weeks of June. Dinsmore was held in total isolation in Longriggend Remand Centre for three days and all requests for access from friends, family and lawyer were denied. The Defence Committee claimed: "There is a growing realisation that David Dinsmore is being used as a scapegoat. The authorities, unable to catch the perpetrators of the increasing number of terrorist acts . . . have simply picked on one man in order to make an example of him."

The obvious proof of this was that the letterbombing continued, despite Dinsmore's incarceration. "Mail Bomb Terror At Tory HQ" ran the headlines on 3 June as another letterbomb arrived. This one, addressed to Conservative Chairman Cecil Parkinson, failed to explode and ignited harmlessly on the floor. A "girl secretary escaped serious injury". Soon afterwards, an SNLA letter with a Glasgow postmark was delivered to the Press Association, claiming responsibility for the London letterbomb attacks on 3 and

4 June. Scotland Yard awaited a second bomb – which did not arrive. The authorities were now taking all precautions. Candidates and political leaders were under increased security. On a lighter note, the additional police presence outside the Labour Party offices in Glasgow had proved costly for Labour supporters since more parking tickets were now being issued!

With the General Election out of the way, hopes of a peaceful summer recess were dashed on 27 June when another letterbomb posted in Glasgow was intercepted at the House of Commons. The bulky nine-inch-by-four-inch brown envelope was addressed to the Home Secretary, Leon Brittan, and bore a white adhesive label addressed in ballpoint pen. It was safely defused by police experts. A letter had also been sent to the Fleet Street office of the Press Association from the SNLA claiming attacks on 28 and 29 June were protests against the Royal family's visit to Scotland. The second attack never came – or did the SNLA letter refer to projected attacks since the letterbomb had arrived at its destination on 27 June?

The head of Scotland Yard's anti-terrorist squad, Commander William Hucklesby, ordered a redoubling of security at the Royal family's engagements. The Queen had two engagements in Edinburgh, one at the Garden Party in Holyroodhouse, while Princess Anne was visiting Jedburgh and Lanark. Buckingham Palace security staff and Special Branch officers conducted extensive searches of premises to be visited. There was an official denial that security was being intensified, although anyone on the route of the Royal visits could see that it plainly was. The bombing campaign had now been in progress for two *years*!

David Dinsmore was charged on 27 July with a second letter-bombing which he also denied. He was released on bail on Thursday, 4 August, having been in Barlinnie prison since 14 May. Almost immediately he joined other members of the SRSP and travelled to Belfast for the anti-internment rally as part of the 50-man kilted colour party from Scotland. Unfortunately, on the way back at the Customs post at Cairnryan he was stopped by officials and, realising that he might be in breach of his bail conditions by leaving the country, told the officials that he was Colin Tennant, the brother of Alistair Tennant, whom he was travelling with. An insurance card with his real name was found in his haversack and he was arrested. He appeared at Stranraer Sheriff Court on 10

August charged with failing to provide necessary information and breaching bail. He was remanded in custody in Dumfries Young Offenders Institute until 16 August for a social inquiry report. Alistair Tennant was held under the same charge. The SRSP hired a minibus for Saturday, 10 September, to demonstrate outside the prison gates. The SRSP also planned to escort Matt Lygate who had at last been given a release date – 19 September – in a minibus from Saughton Prison to a welcoming ceilidh in a Glasgow pub.

On Friday, 19 August, BBC *Reporting Scotland* evening news programme carried the story of another letterbomb from the SNLA. This time the target was the manager of Cardowan Colliery in Stepps, near Glasgow. The bomb did not explode, being detected by an office worker who called the police. The office was evacuated. A letter had been received by the Press Association in Glasgow stating that the attack was in reprisal for the closing down of the mine and redundancies. An NUM official explained that he had received a note from the SNLA months ago warning of the attack – and the date – but had not taken it seriously. He condemned the SNLA as "crazy and totally irresponsible – this is the kind of support we can do without". Production at the pit was interrupted for a short time.

Two more letterbombs were received on 7 September. One exploded – in the offices of Employment Secretary, Mr Norman Tebbit, and although it virtually destroyed itself, the letters "SNLA" could be seen on the remnants. The other, opened by a female member of staff at the Scottish Office was addressed to the Secretary of State for Scotland, Mr George Younger. It did not explode. Although no one was injured in either incident, both the civil servants involved were in shock. The letter to Mr Tebbit had been addressed to him at the House of Commons and redirected to the Department of Employment. The familiar nine-inch-by-four-inch brown envelope had been addressed in ballpoint pen overwritten by a felt-tip pen and bore 12½p and 3½p stamps. It had been posted in Glasgow. It was the familiar *modus operandi* of the SNLA. Again the incidents received considerable publicity. But why had the police so far failed to discover the source of the letterbombs? This was the *twenty-seventh* attack since March 1982.

Three weeks later, on 1 October 1983, another letterbomb was sent to Norman Tebbit. But by now the intensive infiltration of the republican movement had paid off. Three men were arrested on Saturday, 1 October, at 3.20 p.m. Donald Anderson, Benny Goodwin and Thomas Kelly were remanded in custody. A large amount of documents and propaganda material was taken from their homes. Goodwin was released on 6 October and Anderson on 7 October, both without charges, but the police felt confident that Kelly was the letterbomber – or one of the letterbombers. He was charged on 8 October with sending the explosive device to Norman Tebbit, appeared in camera at Glasgow Sheriff Court two days later and was remanded in a unit near Falkirk. He was given very intensive interrogation and his prescribed medicines were denied him. The police were under great pressure to produce a result. Kelly experienced real pain during his time on remand and willingly confessed to the Tebbit bomb . . . to 17 other bombs . . . to *everything*. However, the Special Branch soon realised that he was confessing to *too much*! He began to confess to entirely imaginary incidents which the officers made up. Relatives of Kelly later said that the Special Branch called in a lawyer to *stop* Kelly confessing – in order to defend the credibility of their case! Rather naïvely, Kelly did as he was told. He was moved to Barlinnie.

Meanwhile, another letterbomb was intercepted. This device was addressed to the new Employment Secretary, Mr Tom King. The Press Association received a claim of SNLA responsibility in an identical envelope and this claim was accompanied by a recognised code-word. So, plainly, Kelly was not the letterbomber – or not the only letterbomber – if he *was* involved. However, the police believed they had a good case against him and they had extremely good reasons for believing so.

There appeared to be a sudden and terrifying escalation in SNLA activities. Up to now, these had mostly revolved around crude and rather inept letterbombs – except for some bomb hoaxes and arson attacks – but the bombing of Woolwich Barracks on 10 December shook the entire country and gained massive publicity. The incident was described by Strathclyde Special Branch as "not consistent with their [SNLA] track record". It was much more like the work of the Provisional IRA – but they had not claimed responsibility, as they usually did, and the only claim, in a telephone call to the London News Agency, had come from the SNLA, using the prearranged code-word "Capital". The bomb blast injured four soldiers and a woman civilian but could very easily have killed a larger number.

The SNLA caller had given a warning: "The SNLA will carry out a full-scale bombing campaign in London and other major cities."

Commander William Hucklesby, Scotland Yard's anti-terrorist chief, warned that this could be the beginning of a Christmas bombing campaign and appealed to the public to be on guard. There was some panic in large department stores in London. Barkers of Kensington stated: "We don't want to create panic but we have been inspecting more unattended packages than usual." Up and down the country, defence establishments went on full alert, politicians were given extra attention, large shops and stores were manned by police. Public houses used by forces' personnel were checked, all security staff at Government buildings were briefed on the incident and the House of Commons police were reinforced. A Ministry of Defence spokesman said that facilities for the public would be temporarily withdrawn.

The bomb, constructed of between 15 and 20 lbs of commercial explosive had exploded at 3.45 p.m. at the Royal Artillery Regimental Barracks, just outside the guardroom, and had partially demolished the side wall. It had blown out windows of nearby shops, houses, buses and parked cars. The soldiers were not seriously injured and had miraculously escaped with minor cuts and bruises but were being treated for shock, as was the woman pedestrian. Some children had been hit by flying glass. Three of the injured persons were released from hospital after three days.

The IRA did not claim responsibility for the blast and the police concluded that it had indeed been the work of the SNLA. The facts are that the bomb *was* the work of the IRA but they decided to let the SNLA claim the "credit". The SNLA claim was privately regarded by the IRA as insolence and they ceased active aid forthwith. But the incident had also stirred up the anger of the British public. The Grand Orange Lodge of Scotland demanded that the Lord Advocate order a full-scale investigation into "terrorist links between Scottish and Irish republicans".

Then, three days later, another bomb was discovered outside a restaurant in Kensington. Thousands of shoppers and office workers were evacuated from the area and traffic was diverted for several hours while the bomb, left in a holdall against the wall in Phillimore Gardens was rendered safe through a controlled explosion by army experts. The bomb was similar to the Woolwich Barracks device. Commander Hucklesby now believed that both bombs were the work of the IRA, since the choice of target – a busy street packed with shoppers – the amount of explosive and its type was much more in keeping with previous IRA attacks than with the SNLA's rather inept abilities. "Police intelligence officers" were quoted as now believing that the SNLA had established a link with the IRA or more probably the INLA, and in a *Scotsman* article on 15 December, claimed to have "established a firm link [of the SNLA] with the Irish terrorist group of similar name".

After Kelly's arrest, Scotland became engrossed in the court case of the supergrass and his dupe. Thomas Kelly was an unmarried 28-year-old plate metal worker at Yarrow's Shipyard on the Clyde. Benny Goodwin, 24, was a former police cadet who had been expelled for petty theft and had become a psychiatric nurse. Both had been members of the SNP and then of Siol Nan Gaidheal. Indeed, Goodwin became chairman of the SNG's Drumchapel branch but became alarmed when he heard talk of planned attacks on naval establishments at Ardentinny and Coulport on the Clyde coast, Britoil HQ, Strathclyde Regional Council and even Special Branch HQ in Glasgow. He also heard of other planned activities which included the burning down of the home of a well-known Scottish public figure, an arson attack on an Army Careers office in Maryhill and on the premises of an alleged police informer. Goodwin himself was asked to burn down Sheriff Officers' premises in Dumbarton and invited to participate as an armed paramilitary volunteer in a guard of honour at Matt Lygate's celebration in a Glasgow pub. He managed to get himself so well integrated into the activities of SNG and the SRSP that he had a foot in both camps. But he used his feet instead to walk into Drumchapel police station and offer to "tell all". The police were delighted. The Special Branch decided that Goodwin could be useful to them. Although he had simply wanted to remove himself from the dangerous activities of the republicans, he agreed to become a Special Branch "mole". It was explained to him that he would get no money for the dangerous role he was to undertake, only immunity from prosecution, and that he would not have to give evidence – provided he did exactly what they told him. If he deviated from instructions, he would be disowned and "shopped" to his former comrades. He was assigned the code-name "Trumpet". "Benny's Game" had begun. In the three months which followed, Goodwin participated fully in the republican activities and fed back all the information he gleaned to his Special Branch control.

Goodwin met and befriended Tommy Kelly and within a matter of days was reporting to his control that Kelly was interested in making letterbombs. No one will ever know for sure whether Kelly or Goodwin first suggested the letterbomb idea but Goodwin later testified that Kelly "was in the SNLA" which the SNLA have always denied. Acting on instructions, Goodwin set out to trap the unwitting Kelly. Kelly was having accommodation problems and Goodwin very kindly offered him a room in his flat, having firstly moved his wife and daughter into a boarding house and told Kelly that his marriage had broken up. On the day that Kelly moved in, 29 September 1983, Special Branch men installed electronic listening devices under the floorboards. The trap was set. Kelly, whom the Special Branch had code-named "the Owl" began to plan a letterbomb. The next day, Kelly's mother visited Goodwin's flat and while she made soup in the kitchen, her son was in the bedroom making bombs. Goodwin went out to have a secret meeting with his Special Branch contacts and, as he left the flat, shouted from the front door, for the benefit of the police "bugs": "Okay, Tommy, I'm away. I'll leave you to your own devices!" This caused great hilarity to the agents "listening in" inside a van parked several streets away, but the tapes when finally produced in court proved to be virtually unintelligible.

Special Branch wanted to charge Kelly with conspiracy, an extremely serious charge and notoriously difficult to prove, especially since Kelly's only co-conspirator was a police "mole". They did not want Goodwin to assist in any way with making the bomb or purchasing the materials for it. When Goodwin returned from his secret rendezvous, he saw that Kelly's bomb was complete. He also noticed that two wires were too close together. Kelly disregarded this. "I'm a professional," he boasted. Goodwin quickly got out of the room. The bomb exploded.

When Goodwin looked back into the room he could hardly see Kelly for an intense orange glow. The carpets were burned and Kelly's clothes were singed. Kelly threw the device into a corner. "Don't call the fire brigade," he shouted. He began to make a second device. This was later described by the police as "fairly sophisticated". A flash bulb connected to a battery-operated electrical circuit was arranged on a sheet of cardboard so that it would ignite an explosive substance. Police experts believed it would have caused serious injury if anyone had unwittingly opened it. Once he had finished the bomb he sat down to address a letter to the House of Commons, to Norman Tebbit, Employment Secretary, whom he had selected as the target. He had to ask Goodwin how to spell "bomb"!

The second device was, in Goodwin's opinion, too large, but he agreed to accompany Kelly to post it. The Special Branch watched the two men leave the house but lost them as they deviated into a short-cut across some waste ground. Then Kelly decided they should take a taxi – and by this arbitrary action he destroyed the chances of the Special Branch using "Benny the mole" again, for Goodwin would now have to testify at the trial. If they had taken a bus, other witnesses could have been called instead.

Watched by a highly nervous Goodwin, and disregarding all the dangers to himself, Kelly squeezed and pushed the overlarge package into a post-box in Ingram Street. Then the men went for a drink in the nearby "Press Bar". Goodwin had been instructed to rendezvous with Donald Anderson and others in the hope of entrapping more republicans in the bombing conspiracy. But Anderson was not there and the two men, at Goodwin's suggestion, went to the "Old Barns" pub in London Road. Special Branch had anticipated this and had placed inside the pub an undercover agent wired for sound, with a throat microphone. The Old Barns was a pub favoured by republicans and Anderson and friends were there. Being aware that there was a police agent in the pub, Goodwin strode up to Anderson and said, "Well, we've posted it." He hoped that Anderson would say something incriminating – which he did not. Anderson was actually on a teachers' night out and did not want to be bothered by Goodwin. Then one of the customers recognised a Special Branch man sitting in a car outside the pub. Kelly jumped out of his seat but was unable to escape as policemen crowded into the pub. Kelly and Goodwin were arrested and kept in separate cells. Goodwin was able to tell the officers where the bomb had been placed and took them to the post-box to find it. To keep up his cover, Goodwin was also detained under the Prevention of Terrorism Act. His three months as an undercover agent were over.

Kelly was charged at Glasgow Sheriff Court under the Explosives Substances Act and the Post Office Act and remanded in custody.

The main charge would be conspiracy to send letterbombs but he would also be prosecuted for inducing another person to commit fraud by cashing £68 in National Savings Certificates in the name of David Dinsmore, knowing that Dinsmore was a fugitive from justice.

In the trial, which began under heavy security on 24 January 1984 at Glasgow High Court, Goodwin's evidence was crucial. There was, in fact, no case without it. It was also clear that his evidence could implicate a number of other persons, including perhaps Dinsmore. He claimed that he had uncovered direct links between the SNLA and the INLA and knew of an "escape route" funded by the Irish with safe houses in Dublin. He also said that Dinsmore and a former SNG activist, 36-year-old Adam Busby, claimed to be the "two most successful letterbombers in Scottish history". His evidence was detailed and damning and he was absolutely unshakeable by the defence. Kelly changed his plea on the third day to guilty to the two bombing charges but denied the other charges and the main conspiracy charge. Because of this the trial was curtailed.

Goodwin was accused by the defence of having been a Special Branch officer since his days as a police cadet and of having already "blown" an INLA "cell" in London. He denied this. He had left the police in 1977 and had received only £100 travel expenses and no other payment for his co-operation. He had turned undercover agent because of his hatred of violence and was proud of his part in frustrating the evil tactics of the bombers. He was praised by the prosecution for his courage and Scottish newspapers co-operated with the police request not to print his photograph in their reports of the trial. This was rather pointless for many of the members of the SNG and SRSP were present in the public galleries during the trial, and Goodwin was anyway widely known throughout the republican movement. He claimed he had received death threats and was kept in police protection in a "safe house" during the two days of his testimony. After the trial, Goodwin was taken to a new safe house in Clydebank where his wife and daughter were waiting, with two armed guards. The family stayed in a guest house on the West Coast for three months during which period Goodwin slowly lapsed into alcoholism. Then the family moved to an apartment in England, a caravan in the Borders and finally a council house in a northern English town. His marriage broke up under the strain of his alcohol problem. Today, Goodwin is still in hiding, living under an assumed name and fearful to return to Glasgow.

Kelly was sentenced by Lord Allanbridge to ten years for the bombing charges and one year for contravening the Post Office Act but the fraud charge and the conspiracy charges were dropped. After all, Kelly had conspired with only one man – Benny Goodwin.

Twenty-one-year-old Dinsmore was a fugitive. He had been due to appear for trial at Glasgow on 5 December to face charges of sending a letterbomb to Lord Mansfield. The procurator-fiscal had a warrant out for his arrest and believed that Dinsmore had fled to the Irish Republic. This was soon proved for Dinsmore and Adam Busby were arrested in a branch of Dunns, a large Irish store, on 21 December and charged at Dublin District Court with theft of £14 worth of ham and cheese. The Dublin police did not at first release the identity of "the two Scots" they had arrested who gave false names and a Dublin address and claimed to be unemployed. They were remanded in custody for a week, then rearrested, and due to legal technicalities were to spend the next eight months in Mountjoy jail as the UK Government applied for – and won – an extradition order and Dinsmore and Busby awaited an appeal hearing to attempt to prove that their alleged offences were "political".

Busby's alleged offence was causing damage to a Ministry of Defence truck at Berwick-on-Tweed by painting slogans on it. They finally got bail on 18 August 1984, Dinsmore having to stand surety of £1,600 and Busby £400. Their court case came up at the Irish High Court on 6 October. While Busby attended the hearing and won his fight to stay in Ireland, Dinsmore failed to appear. Busby planned to live in Ireland. "I am afraid to go back to Scotland," he said, "because the authorities will not guarantee that they will not prosecute me on spurious evidence of conspiracy to commit other offences. I am not afraid to stand trial for painting the slogans." In an affidavit he had admitted that he had thrown a smoke-bomb at the platform during an SDP meeing in the McLellan Galleries in Glasgow attended by Roy Jenkins MP. His wife, Joan, had suffered a nervous breakdown and Busby wished to take her and their two children to live in County Dublin where he had obtained a job. He repudiated statements made in Scotland that he was a member of the SRSP and said that he had not sanctioned any political group in Scotland to raise money for himself. The *Daily Record* had referred to Dinsmore and Busby as "both suspected members of the SNLA" and this had been repeated on television programmes.

Warrants for Dinsmore's arrest had been issued in both the UK and the Irish Republic. Dublin police believed that he was in either France or Spain. He had not been seen in fact since the morning of the Brighton bombing. And then, the *News of the World*, on 21 October carried a story that "a terrorist who has confessed to sending letterbombs to the Queen and top politicians was on the run in France last night. After jumping bail in Dublin, the IRA said they had smuggled David Dinsmore out of the country." Whether this story was based on fact or not, it was obvious that Dinsmore was hardly likely to get a fair hearing in any court case.

If the police now believed, with Kelly in jail, Busby in exile in Ireland and Dinsmore on the run from Interpol that the problem of the SNLA had been solved they were wrong. Only three days after Kelly began his jail sentence, the newspapers reported the second arson attack within a month at holiday homes in the Highlands owned by wealthy English families. There had also been threats against absentee landlords in the West Highlands and Skye. The first fire was at Kilphedir Lodge, in the Strath of Kildonan, a favourite holiday retreat of Prince Charles and Princess Diana. The second destroyed nearby Suisgill Lodge on the £1 million Suisgill Estate where the Royal couple had also stayed. In this fire, the estate's manager and his family were lucky to escape by jumping to safety from a first-floor window. A senior detective played down the idea that these were politically motivated attacks. No political group claimed responsibility. Meanwhile the IRA had begun a sustained bombing campaign in England. A large bomb had exploded in Harrods department store and killed several customers. The police mounted a major offensive to track down the terrorists.

On 20 December, at dawn, using information given them by Benny Goodwin, Special Branch raided the homes of a number of SRSP members and others and arrested six persons under the Prevention of Terrorism Act. The detainees were all threatened with lengthy prison sentences unless they co-operated and signed statements incriminating the National Organiser of the SRSP, Donald Anderson, and Creag Browning, a 16-year-old. One of the detainees, a member of the Glasgow Irish Freedom Action

Committee, Sandy Mathers, was charged along with his wife with obstructing the police. He had refused to open his door until the police produced verification of their identity and a search warrant – which they refused to do. They smashed in the door with the aid of a large iron gate-post and gained entry. Only then did they produce their search warrant and their ID cards. Mathers was denied access to his doctor while in custody although he suffered from a chronic illness and all of the detainees were denied access to solicitors.

The police decided to charge Anderson and Browning with conspiracy to aid the SRSP in acts of terrorism in the UK and with possessing explosives. Donald Anderson, 46, was a Modern Studies teacher at John Street Secondary School in Bridgeton. Creag Browning was a 16-year-old Highland youth who had accompanied his father to Siol Nan Gaidheal rallies and meetings as soon as he was able to walk. At school he had written an essay on English oppression and sent a copy of it to the Prime Minister. Then he had moved to Glasgow and joined the SRSP. When the police raided his bedsit in Great Western Road, Kelvinbridge, they found 50 sticks of gelignite inside a cardboard box and 20 sticks inside two plastic bags. Army bomb disposal men were called in to remove the 35 kilograms of explosive.

The explosive had originally been stolen on 15 December from Headless Cross open-cast coal-mine at Shotts by four members of the extreme Protestant group, the Ulster Volunteer Force. One hundred and thirty-two kilograms had been seized in the raid together with detonators. Four UVF men appeared for trial on the charge on 23 December and some of the explosive was recovered in a garage in Blackburn, West Lothian. At that trial, one of the locations of the UVF "conspiracy" was a car scrapyard at Kinnear Road, Parkhead, Glasgow. The owner of the scrapyard was Andrew Wilson who was visited by two UVF men who left some of the explosives with him on 16 December. Wilson later testified that he had thought they might be stolen videos or cigarettes and claimed he tried to get the men to take them away when he noticed they were explosives. The men left and did not return for two days. Meanwhile, Wilson sought refuge in drink and went to the "Old Barns" where he tried to sell the explosives. The publican, who was a friend of his, called Donald Anderson over. Anderson thought it was a joke but Wilson testified that he had paid £40 for a "sample" and offered £200 for a whole case. Wilson then said that Anderson had told Browning to keep the explosives. This cash transaction, according to Wilson, occurred in the lavatory. Unfortunately, his employee testified that it took place outside the pub in the car park! The next day the UVF men returned, Wilson called the police and they were arrested in possession of 250 sticks of gelignite. Wilson was also held for six days under the Prevention of Terrorism Act, which was when he tried to shift the blame on to Anderson and Browning.

When the case came to court, it appeared to be a Special Branch "frame-up" using some of the stolen explosive recovered from the UVF raid. The role played by Andrew Wilson and his associate, Andrews, was called into question. Wilson was a known associate of the UVF and both he and Andrews were given immunity from prosecution for supplying information leading to the arrest of the UVF men. They had then apparently agreed to entice others to buy the stolen explosives and had been released from prison with explosives in their possession to do this! Even the judge, when referring to Wilson and Andrews during his address to the jury said: "You may well think that these two men should be facing criminal charges themselves." The charge of conspiracy had been dropped at an earlier hearing at Glasgow Sheriff Court when Browning had dramatically changed his plea to guilty to possession of explosives. Anderson had been pestered on at least two occasions to take possession of the explosive. Finally, knowing that Anderson would not be in the pub, Wilson simply left the rucksack with Browning to give to Anderson. Since Browning was in the habit of receiving packages of leaflets from Anderson he did not look inside the rucksack. When he finally discovered what was inside it, he planned to throw the explosives into the River Kelvin. The police had been watching his flat, hoping that Anderson would visit and when he didn't they were forced to arrest Browning and hope that a circumstantial charge against Anderson could be made. They called a lawyer, believing that a 16-year-old would do everything his lawyer told him to do – and implicate Anderson. But Browning ignored the lawyer's warnings of a lengthy prison sentence and his descriptions of what could befall a young man amongst hardened prison inmates. In fact, he protested strongly until he was allowed to secure a lawyer of his own choosing. Thus, in the High Court, Creag Browning refused to testify against Anderson and wrecked any chance the prosecution may have had to secure a conspiracy conviction against Anderson. The two men had been on remand for almost four months before the case came to trial and the delay was blamed on Browning's change of plea. Since no money had changed hands and Anderson had neither touched nor seen the explosives, it took the jury only 45 minutes to find the charges of resetting and possession of explosives not proven. Browning had pled guilty to those charges and was sentenced on 6 April 1984 to one year's detention in a Young Offenders' Institution.

The *News of the World* carried a large front-page article on 26 August 1984 revealing an apparent confession by David Dinsmore to sending a letterbomb to the Queen which had "got through the Royal security screen and exploded". Dinsmore was also apparently claiming that the Palace had "hushed up" the injuries to the secretary who had handled the bomb – Princess Di's brother-in-law Robert Fellowes. The article claimed that Dinsmore had confessed to being "either involved in or knew of bombs sent to former Defence Secretary John Nott, Social Services Secretary Patrick Jenkin, Employment Secretary Tom King, Home Secretary Leon Brittan, Trade Secretary Norman Tebbit, Scottish Secretary George Younger and Tory ex-chairman Cecil Parkinson". The September newsletter of the SRSP described the article as "totally fabricated . . . sensationalist rubbish". Of course, a fugitive from justice was in no position to sue anyone for libel!

After the horror of the IRA bomb at the Brighton Metropole when four Conservative delegates were killed and several injured, the SNLA attempt to kill Mrs Thatcher at the 1983 Conference in Perth formed a large news feature on *Reporting Scotland* on Monday 15 October. It was also the main headline. The SNLA "contact" was allowed unprecedented time to put forward their views through the reporter. While many were horrified, it did represent an attempt to understand the terrorists' motivations. Four days later, there was an incident at Glasgow Central Station. A suspicious object was discovered in the men's lavatory about 5.35p.m. A member of the public reported it to the police, who sealed off three of the station's four entrances and four platforms. The Army bomb disposal team arrived and, using a controlled explosion, blew up the package. Forensic specialists were called in to examine the evidence. The Assistant Chief Constable of the British Transport Police, Archie MacKenzie, declined to comment on the nature of the device other than to say it was a package.

Commuters had been inconvenienced for several hours. No group claimed responsibility and the SNLA have not listed this incident as one of their attacks. There were many persons now imitating the SNLA attacks and many more participating in bomb scares and hoaxes.

The SNLA did claim responsibility for the attack on Mrs Thatcher on St Andrew's Day, 1984. A letterbomb which the police described as "amateurish and crude" was discovered by a vigilant postman in the Nine Elms Sorting Office in Battersea and disarmed in Cannon Row Police Station. The method and style of the device led the police to believe that it had not been made by the SNLA. They also revealed recent SNLA threats to British military personnel in Scotland and that the organisation regarded the Royal Family as "legitimate targets". The group were also claiming to be much stronger and well-funded, with arms and equipment "for a more vigorous campaign". Security was therefore very tight at the Stone of Remembrance in Edinburgh when the Duke of Kent laid a wreath during the Commemoration Service. All litter bins for hundreds of yards had been taped over and bore signs reading "out of service". Police were taking no chances.

There was only one SNLA attack in 1985, and it was one of their most successful to date. An SNLA active service unit planted a matchbox-sized device containing "a few pence worth of sulphuric acid, sugar and sodium chlorate" in a fifth-floor sub-basement office, 80 feet below ground level, at the Ministry of Defence HQ in London's Whitehall. This attack, right in the heart of the British Imperial war machine, took place in the early hours of the morning. By the time the fire brigade arrived, the fire had a firm hold. Eight fire tenders' crews fought the blaze for six hours to bring it under control. The damage was described by a Ministry of Defence spokesman as "serious" and was well into several hundred thousand pounds. This type of action, and its success, seemed completely at odds with the inept letterbombing campaign, and it was now thoroughly obvious that new and more effective personnel were involved. The "relaunched" SNLA were disparaging about some of the previous attacks which had been attributed by the press to them – for example, a hoax phoned to the *Glasgow Herald* the day before the annual Scotland-England football match, where a group calling themselves "The White Rose" claimed to have infected the Hampden pitch with anthrax-infected soil from Gruinard Island. This was apparently a protest against the switching of the fixture from Wembley on the grounds of English complaints about the Scots fans "running amok" in London, and was simply a hoax.

Another of the allegations made by Goodwin at the Thomas Kelly trial was the alleged plot to burn down the house of Hillhead MP, Roy Jenkins. Although the police had denied that any such attack had taken place, they now revealed that petrol had been poured through the letterbox of the house in Kirklee Terrace on 2 June 1984, and they arrested 23-year-old Stephen Wilson on a charge of attempted murder on 8 May 1985, although the petrol had not been ignited. Wilson was the Secretary of the David Dinsmore Defence Committee and lived in Bearsden. He denied the offence. The SNLA claimed the attack and denied that Wilson was a member. Many journalists were confused. Why did the SNLA claim an inept attack of this sort and why was it that every suspect so far caught had denied being an SNLA member? When were the *real* SNLA men going to be caught?

A year went by, then, on 18 April 1986 – six years after the inception of the SNLA – there were three attacks within a single week. The first was a letterbomb in the now familiar style, which was detected in the House of Commons mail room by the sensitive electronic equipment. The press reports quoted Special Branch as suggesting that the device was linked with the INLA "which attended last month a 'World Revolutionary Council' in Tripoli, sponsored by Colonel Gaddafi". This "Libyan link", an apparent attempt to smear the SNLA as supporters of the Gaddafi regime, the new international "bogey-man", was denounced by the SNLA as "ludicrous". "This attack . . . ," they said, "was carried out by the Willie McRae Commando of the SNLA as a reprisal for the murder of Willie McRae, a veteran SNLA sympathiser and active supporter, by agents of the British State."

Before the speculation of a Libyan link had died down there was a further attack, four days later. On 22 April, another letterbomb was discovered at the HQ of British Steel – a "response," said the SNLA, "to the closure of Gartcosh steel mill".

Two days later there was a devastating explosion at the British Airways office in London's Oxford Street, which hit all the front pages of the next day's newspapers. The device had been placed at the offices in Lumley Street, just off Oxford Street, at approximately

4.45 a.m. By 7 a.m., news bulletins contained reports of an explosion and by 7.30 a.m., after hearing that the SNLA unit had made a successful getaway, the SNLA phoned the Press Association, using the code-word and giving detailed information on the location of the bomb and its type. Despite this, the media at first refused to acknowledge receipt of any claim of responsibility until the next day when the Home Office Minister, Giles Shaw, raised the matter in the Commons. A Conservative MP demanded to know what the Government was doing "to arrest these thugs and get them behind bars". The SNLA described the BA attack as "economic sabotage" and claimed that British tourism had been badly affected and that "in terms of financial damage to the British State this attack has had a devastating effect". The organisation, irritated at being denied the full publicity which they felt they deserved, issued a "communiqué" dated 1 July 1986 which listed their attacks. They claimed that the State's refusal to acknowledge their responsibility claims was "merely inviting cranks and hoaxers to claim responsibility". They also boasted that: "The SNLA's achievements in April – three separate attacks in a single week – not to mention other activities including the production and distribution of the SNLA newspaper *Saorsa* and a postering campaign by sympathisers in Edinburgh and Glasgow – are a positive demonstration of the Army's capabilities. Before the end of July the SNLA will carry out more attacks as a reprisal for the murder of Willie McRae. 1982 – 1986. The War goes on. Victory to the SNLA!"

The only further attack in 1986 came three weeks later, on 16 July – a letterbomb addressed to Home Secretary Douglas Hurd which ignited when it was opened by the Home Office security staff. According to reports, it caused little damage. Again the device was described as "crude and amateur", which seems a little surprising since the bombers had had so much practice!

Three years went by with no further SNLA activity. There had been no attacks, no claims, no arrests. Then, on 13 May 1989, on the day that Mrs Thatcher opened the new Torness nuclear power station, there was a massive explosion and fire at the Glensanda Quarry on the remote Morvern Peninsula in Argyll. The SNLA were back in the news.

The emergency services were alerted by the coastguard after local people had observed a black cloud billowing 200 feet above the quarry and heard an explosion from the other side of Loch

163

Linnhe. Firemen had to be brought by boat to the site because of its remote location. The SNLA claim was telephoned to the Press Association at 2 a.m. on Sunday 14 May, two hours before the blaze had been brought under control and four hours before the first news bulletins broadcast details of the incident. The quarry, owned by the Foster Yeoman company, produces large quantities (60,000 tonnes per day) of crushed granite for use in projects such as the Channel Tunnel but it had been the subject of speculation and rumour. Groups such as Greenpeace had queried the vetting of quarry workers by the MOD police and why several Government agencies were involved, why the total cost of the quarry was in excess of £150 million and why so much secrecy surrounded the plant. The SNLA claimed to possess evidence that the site was being prepared as a deep burial site for civil and military nuclear waste. They alleged that the company involved was Strachan and Henshaw in association with the British Nuclear Association and that "the project is funded indirectly by the English Ministry of Defence through loans obtained through the Euro Investment Bank".

Throughout the day, media reports quoted this detailed SNLA claim and their statement that the fire had been caused by commercial explosive placed in a store containing cyanide-based chemicals. Some reports also mentioned the presence of a bomb disposal squad at the site and the explosion heard by local people. By the next day, however, all reports were downplaying the incident. Instead of being referred to as a terrorist attack it now was an accidental fire – there was no mention of the explosion at all and, in most reports, no mention of the SNLA claim. The *Glasgow Herald* stated that "an industrial rubber conveyor had caught fire". Work at the plant was disrupted for a fortnight and the damage was assessed at almost a quarter of a million pounds.

What conclusions can be drawn from the activities of the SNLA? While about half of the attacks were letterbombs – possibly the work of one or two men – the sheer scale and duration of their "military campaign" and the variety of their methods and targets suggests an organisation capable of inflicting considerable damage at will. Clearly the SNLA is an organisation which does consist of a number of individuals who have managed to elude arrest for ten years, who have carried out some successful terrorist acts and caused considerable damage and inconvenience to the public and to the Government. Only minor injuries have resulted from their attacks. Clearly, however, several of their attacks could easily have killed. It seems unlikely that the SNLA will fade away. Having once experienced massive publicity they are quite likely to strike again in the future. What is also likely is that others, hitherto uninvolved, will be tempted to emulate their activities, making the unmasking of the perpetrators of the attacks described in this chapter even harder for the police. The SNLA clearly regards itself in a war with the British State, and until its members are caught, the war will continue.

12   DEATH OF AN ACTIVIST

To my mind it is abundantly clear that Willie McRae was a well-established, dangerous and deadly enemy of a state which will go to apparently any lengths to sustain and protect itself.

Alan Clayton, Scotsman *letters page, 9 April 1988*

THE A87 road from Invergarry to Kyle of Lochalsh outwith the tourist season is a lonely road. It curves steeply up from Invergarry village on its 54 miles to the Skye ferry at Kyle. At the spur of Mullach Coire Ardachaidh (3,130 feet) just before the road turns due north, away from Loch Garry, there is a viewpoint and a lay-by at the height of 1,100 feet. The view is dramatic. Then the road plunges down to the south-eastern side of Loch Loyne, facing Meall Odhar (2,677 feet), a square buttressed monster. The road crosses two cattle grids but it is possible, knowing the road, to accelerate to a considerable speed. The road descends, winding around the mountain. Just about 100 yards after the sign "Inverness-shire" there is a rather sharp bend which has a lay-by on its lochside at the flattened-out top of a spur which careers down to the loch, and then the road straightens out at about 920 feet above sea-level. One hundred yards further downhill, there is another lay-by at another spur, about half a mile short of the dam at the north-eastern end of the loch. It is in this lay-by that a cairn has been built, and a flagpole erected, to commemorate the mysterious death of Scottish solicitor, Willie McRae, in April 1985.

McRae's importance to the nationalist movement dated from the 1940s. He was involved with other nationalist groups and his name has been mentioned in previous chapters of this book. His links with David Dinsmore had led to his being the subject of close police scrutiny and he was the subject of 24-hour surveillance by officers of Strathclyde Special Branch.

His crashed car was discovered on the hillside, about 100 yards below the road, at 10 a.m. on Saturday, 6 April, but the cause of death was later found to be due to a bullet lodged in his brain. It took the police *two days* to find a gun. The circumstances, and what happened after the discovery of his body, remain highly suspicious, a complete mystery, yet demands for a fatal accident inquiry have been consistently rejected. Many people have been led to ask: who killed Willie McRae?

William McRae was born in 1923 in Carron, the son of an electrician. His life and career was truly outstanding. At the age of six he could recite the whole of *Tam O' Shanter* and he became a brilliant elocutionist and school debater at Falkirk High School. It was while he was at school that he joined the SNP. In the school holidays Willie and his brother Ferguson spent time in Kintail, the ancestral lands of the McRae's, staying with numerous relations. He retained a love of the area all his life. Outstanding success at school led to a place at Glasgow University studying history. He also edited a local newspaper in Grangemouth. He graduated with first-class honours and received a commission as a lieutenant in the Seaforth Highlanders. He served in India and soon transferred to the Royal Indian Navy, learning Urdu and Hindi quickly. He soon became the youngest captain in the service and had some lucky escapes in sea combat, being for a time in command of a destroyer. His ability ensured a rapid rise through the ranks to Lieutenant-Commander and by the end of the war he was a full Commander. He remained in India, having transferred to Naval Intelligence. There his nationalist sympathies led him into collaboration with the Indian nationalist movement – treason, of course, for a British subject – reputedly assisting a clandestine liberation radio station to keep operating one step ahead of the military police in the New Delhi area. He joined the Congress Party, met Indira Ghandi and helped to prepare the way for Independence in 1948. At the time of his death he was arranging a Scottish visit for Mrs Ghandi who is, of course, now also dead. He took out Pakistani citizenship and for the rest of his life retained dual nationality.

He returned from India and studied for an LLB at Glasgow, winning every single law prize on offer and being regarded as one of the most outstanding law students of his time. He was involved with Glasgow University Nationalist Association and played a part in the "theft" of the Stone of Destiny in 1950, being one of the people who hid the stone. After graduation he became a solicitor in the office of Abraham Levy and developed an interest in the Jews. He lectured for a time in Haifa as Emeritus Professor and assisted the fledgling Israeli state with its mercantile law canon. He was on personal terms with David Ben Gurion and other Israeli leaders and there is a plaque to his memory at Migdal Ha'Emek in Gallilee – "In loving memory of a Scottish Patriot and faithful friend of Israel" – erected in 1986. He travelled widely on business and went to both China and the USSR.

Willie McRae was an outstanding lawyer and when he went into business for himself in 1981, he prospered. He had been able in 1966 to buy the house at Camuslongart in Dornie, Kintail, and used it as a weekend home. He was a decisive man, truthful almost to the point of tactlessness, very forthright. And yet, he was a man with a wicked sense of humour, able to laugh in the midst of the most adverse circumstances – and especially at himself. He was a man of contradictions: extremely modest and yet rather flamboyant, reticent about his own outstanding career, yet he stood for Parliament several times: in 1970 in Glasgow Provan, and in 1974 he came within a few hundred votes of unseating the Conservative Energy Minister in Ross and Cromarty. His naval intelligence background came in handy in 1972 when he represented inshore fishermen against the Ministry of Defence proposal to site a torpedo testing range in the Inner Sound of Raasay. He was also an expert on Highland land use and drafted the SNP's policy on the subject. But his notoriety, as far as the British State was concerned began with the methods he used in the 1980 public inquiry at Mullwharchar.

The first UK public inquiry on the question of burial of nuclear waste commenced in Ayr Town Hall on 19 February 1980. The UK Atomic Energy Authority was appealing against the decision of the local District Council to refuse permission to test-drill into the hill of Mullwharchar in the Galloway Hills, south of Loch Doon, an area of outstanding natural beauty. Mullwharchar was at the centre of a large mass of Caledonian granite, and the application was only the first of several projected sites, nearly all of which were in Scotland. McRae attended the inquiry as legal adviser for the Scottish National Party. The objectors included Friends of the Earth, the Scottish Conservation Society, SCRAM, the NUM and various local councils and two MPs. The inquiry was expected to last several days and instead lasted almost one month. McRae's questioning was aimed at eliciting information from the AEA which they would have preferred to have kept secret, and at one point the refusal of an expert to reveal the source of his information led to a headline "Test Bore Witness Tight-Lipped" in the *Scotsman*. McRae threatened that he would have a parliamentary question asked of the Minister for the Environment – and then he did receive the information on condition that he withdrew the parliamentary question. His readiness to take matters above the heads of the experts direct to Parliament had clearly worried the AEA. He was an expert in discovering loopholes and chinks in the armour, and his participation at the inquiry was authoritative.

After the decision had been taken – to uphold the planning decision and reject the test-drilling – the AEA were forced to reconsider their policy of burial of nuclear waste. The decision was a considerable setback to the nuclear industry and although they have now adopted the idea of vitrifying waste into blocks of glass and storing these at Sellafield for 50 years they have no further plans beyond that point. In effect, the Mullwharchar decision ended the policy of test-drilling in the UK (apart from drilling at a site on land at Altnabreac owned by Liberal peer, Lord Thurso) and the concept of burial of nuclear waste. It is alleged, however, that test-drilling was *not* abandoned but was merely carried out without planning permission. Nationalists were later to claim that electron seismatic testing was conducted in Glen Etive in 1982. Whatever the truth of these allegations, the industry has been prevented from planning publicly for the long-term disposal of its by-product, a situation that has caused them

169

considerable problems in long-term planning. Mullwharchar was a highly significant victory, described in the *Glasgow Herald* as "the most celebrated environmental crusade ever seen in Scotland".

Willie McRae took up the theme of the funding sources of University Geological Departments and the question of the impartiality of higher academic institutions in a series of letters in national newspapers and engaged in a furious correspondence war with leading geologists. He felt he had achieved a partial victory by alerting the public to the fact that the nuclear industry was funding many supposedly independent research bodies. While this battle was going on, there were a large number of "unexplained activities" going on throughout the country and McRae pioneered a very strong SNP line on the issue; the party was committed to direct action and civil disobedience to prevent nuclear dumping.

As has already been seen, McRae was orchestrating the increasingly militant activities of Siol Nan Gaidheal, who held a massive demonstration and march at Ayr at the time of the inquiry and founded the "Oystercatcher" brigade and caravan in Glen Etive to monitor and physically prevent the nuclear industry workers from test-drilling or sampling the rocks and soil. McRae had obtained documents that had been removed from a private meeting of the International Atomic Energy Forum held at Otaniemi near Helsinki in July 1979. One document, titled *The National Policy For The Underground Disposal Of Radioactive Wastes In The United Kingdom* revealed the targeting of Glen Etive and listed a time scale for drilling test-bores *prior* to an application for planning permission! The Glen Etive campaign did serve to draw attention to the secrecy with which the nuclear industry sought to conduct its business and it did delay and ultimately end the geologists' activities.

The SNP were also committed to fighting the nuclear industry's idea for the "European Demonstration Reprocessing Plant" (EDRP), which the Government wanted to site in Scotland to process fast reactor fuel from all of Europe. They thought that by siting it at Dounreay which was already a nuclear installation in a sparsely populated area, where many already depended for their livelihood on the nuclear industry, there would be little or no opposition. They were wrong. McRae was intending to take a full and active part in the public inquiry and his name was already on the list of objectors. The inquiry was scheduled to start in Thurso on 7 April 1986. This was to be, by mysterious coincidence, the anniversary of his death . . ..

At about 6.30 p.m. on Good Friday, 5 April 1985, McRae left his top-floor flat at 6 Balvicar Drive, Glasgow, to drive north to his holiday home at Dornie. He was planning to spend the weekend working on his book about the nuclear industry and he had also made plans to visit some friends in Plockton, about eight miles from his house. He needed to catch up on sleep. He had a busy week ahead of him in Glasgow and his sleep on the night before had been interrupted when, due to his habit of smoking in bed, his bedclothes caught fire in the early hours of the morning.

It had been an unfortunate incident. He had been visiting his godson, Howard Singerman, on the Thursday evening and had come home late and very tired. He had not been drinking, because Singerman did not drink, but had fallen asleep with a lit cigarette in his mouth. He was wakened by a considerable amount of smoke from the smouldering blankets. He jumped out of bed and took the blackened blankets to the bathroom, threw them into the bath and turned on the tap. Unfortunately, he had forgotten that the new bathroom suite was acrylic. It burst into flames and he was overcome with smoke and acrid fumes. Luckily, two tradesmen passing the house on their way to work saw the flames and while one rushed to phone the Fire Brigade, the other ran up the stairs and broke into the flat. He found Willie McRae unconscious on the floor in the hall.

The Fire Brigade arrived and there was chaos while the fire was put out. It was 8 a.m. by this time and Willie's neighbours attempted to console him in his smoke-damaged flat. He was covered in soot and suffering from shock. He had undoubtedly inhaled some of the smoke and acrid fumes but refused to be taken to a doctor. He was embarrassed at the fuss he had caused and annoyed at his own carelessness. He remained in the flat throughout Good Friday and his business partner, Ronnie Welsh, visited him. Gradually his good spirits returned. "I never did like that bathroom suite," he joked.

His next door neighbours, Mr and Mrs Stewart, retired Church missionaries, had been out for most of the day and when they returned about 5 p.m., Willie was alone. They could see him sitting in his lounge. Mr Stewart took him a bowl of soup and they chatted. Willie refused an offer of the use of the Stewarts' bathroom. "No, no, I know where I can get cleaned up," Willie said, indicating that he planned to drive north to Dornie. Mr Stewart returned to his own flat and at approximately 6.30 p.m., as another neighbour arrived at the house, Willie McRae was already in his car and driving away.

The drive from Glasgow to Dornie takes about four hours, depending on the traffic conditions, and McRae's maroon Volvo 244 had made the journey very often before. He used his holiday home as often as he could and knew the route to it very well. He took the A82 round the western side of Loch Lomond and continued through the Black Mountains into Glen Coe, to Fort William, Spean Bridge and by Lagganside to Invergarry where he joined the lonely A87 to Kyle of Lochalsh. It was a dry, moonlit night, ideal for such a drive. We can speculate that, with little traffic on the road, the drive was a soothing and pleasant experience, except that, a few miles past Invergarry, McRae's car developed a puncture and he had to change the wheel in quite dark conditions, at about 9.30 p.m. Once the wheel was changed and he had put the punctured wheel in the car on the back seat, he continued his journey. But it was a journey that was to last for only a couple of miles further. Willie McRae never did reach his beloved "Camusty". The book he was working on, his files and briefcase, have disappeared as if they had never existed.

At about 10 a.m. the next morning, 6 April – by coincidence the 665th anniversary of Scottish Independence and the signing of the Declaration of Arbroath in 1320 – Alan Crowe, aged 43, an Australian airline pilot on holiday with his wife, noticed McRae's car. It was something of a fluke that he had seen the car for it was 100 yards beneath the road on the steep hillside. Crowe was travelling north and drove on for a further three miles discussing with his wife what he thought he had seen, until they decided to turn the car and drive back to look for themselves. They stopped in a lay-by and looked down to the bank of the loch where the Volvo could be seen straddling a small burn. It was upright at an angle of about 45 degrees, facing south, with a dent in the roof; the back screen was partially smashed, the front windscreen was intact and a man was slumped in the driver's seat. He appeared to be dead. The door was jammed against the bank. The window was wound fully down. Crowe ran back up to the road and flagged down the next car that passed. It had just started to rain.

By another of those coincidences that seem to happen more frequently than statistics would allow, the next car to appear was driven by a doctor – Dr Dorothy Messer – and contained her fiancé, George Lochhead, and David Coutts, a Dundee District Councillor and his wife, Alison. The party were on their way to Skye. By an even greater coincidence, Coutts, an SNP activist, actually knew McRae, although only very slightly, and had, only minutes before at the Invergarry Post Office, struck up a conversation with local ex-Councillor Fred McCallum (whom he had not previously met, but who was wearing an SNP badge, leading to their conversation) on the outstanding qualities of McRae as parliamentary candidate for the area.

The first thing that Coutts actually noticed when he scrambled down the steep hillside was the SNP sticker on the window of the car. "My God! It's a nationalist!" he'd remarked to his wife, then he got a shock when he looked into the car and saw that the slumped figure in the driving seat was Willie McRae.

McRae's hands were folded in his lap, on which also lay the car keys. His head was leaning on his right shoulder and there was a considerable amount of blood on his temple, reaching up to the hairline. Everyone assumed McRae had been the victim of a car accident.

Alan Crowe suggested that Dr Messer drive for assistance since neither of the Coutts could drive, and there was a brief discussion over who should go to phone for an ambulance and the police. The problem was solved by another motorist agreeing to drive to the nearest telephone. By this time several cars had stopped and, in fact, several cars went off on this same errand. Meanwhile, introducing herself as a doctor, Dorothy Messer pulled McRae upright and took his pulse. Her initial impression, which she subsequently retracted several days later, was that McRae was already dead. This was the recollection of those other persons present but the doctor now states that she knew that he was still alive, since his chest was moving and he was still breathing. She noticed that one pupil was dilated, the sign of extensive brain damage. She estimated that he had been in that position for about ten hours, placing the time of the "accident" at around midnight.

When an ambulance arrived from Fort Augustus, driven by a one-man freelance ambulance man, the small group of Coutts, Messer, Lochhead, Crowe and the ambulance man, Mr Douglas, began the slow task of extricating Willie McRae from the car – an extremely difficult job. The ambulance driver recalled: "I don't remember whether he had his belt on, but I guess if he hadn't he wouldn't still have been in his seat. He was slumped down on his right-hand side against the door. I do remember the window was open. The car was lying at about 45 degrees and it was a hell of a job getting him out . . . he was a big bloke and I can't see him clambering out through the windscreen." The ambulance driver's testimony differs from that of the other witnesses in several important respects, one of which is his recollection that the front windscreen was missing, though he and all the others agree there were no pieces of glass either in the car or on McRae.

A young policeman, PC McBeth, arrived from Fort William and assisted in lifting McRae into the ambulance. It was now raining very heavily and since everyone was of the opinion that McRae had been the victim of a car accident, there seemed no reason to linger at the scene. The policeman handed Coutts the holdall from the car and asked him to collect up all the personal effects. Coutts obliged, putting his hand into the smashed rear window to collect some papers inside. He looked around to check that he had collected everything and it was then that he saw a small pile of papers "meticulously ripped up" together with a credit card, the bill for a new distributor cap from a garage in Kyle and McRae's watch with smashed face – all in a neat pile about 15 yards north-east of the car, up the hill towards the road. Coutts informed the policeman of this and showed him the bill. PC McBeth finally accepted that the victim *was* McRae because the bill had his name on it. Coutts put all the bits and pieces in the bag; a couple of books, a bible and a half-consumed half-bottle of whisky. There was no sign of a briefcase, nor any cartons of cigarettes in the car. McRae took his briefcase with him everywhere and certainly would have had it on a working weekend at Camuslongart. Likewise, he always had a large carton of packets of his favourite Gold Flake in the car – he was a chain smoker.

Dr Messer travelled in the ambulance with McRae's body to Raigmore Hospital in Inverness. There it was decided that brain surgery was the only hope and he was transferred to Aberdeen Royal Infirmary – standard procedure in cases involving any type of head injury. He was put on a life-support machine and his head X-rayed. The bullet wound was then discovered, and the single bullet was revealed to have macerated his brain, undoubtedly destroying all motor function instantaneously. Willie McRae's brother, Dr Ferguson McRae, and his wife Moira travelled to

Aberdeen and after a discussion with the consultant neurologist and a telephone conversation with Ronnie Welsh, it was decided to switch off the life-support machine. Formal time of death was given as 3.30 p.m. on Sunday, 7 April.

The Pathologist's Nightmare

The body was returned to Raigmore after the formal pronouncement of death and a post-mortem was conducted by consultant pathologist, Dr Henry Richmond. There are very few cases of death by gunshot in Scotland – an average of one per year and even fewer where a handgun is involved. This means that medical staff and pathologists are not experienced in dealing with such injuries and deaths caused by these means are invariably investigated by forensic specialists. Forensic medicine is a highly specialised field and there are few experienced specialists in Scotland. Aberdeen Royal Infirmary had, until his retirement in December 1988, a very experienced forensic pathologist, Dr W. T. Hendry, who would have been very well qualified to carry out an autopsy once the body had been pronounced dead. Dr Hendry had dealt with a number of gunshot cases in his lengthy career. Dr Hendry, however, did not see or hear of the case until he read about it in the newspapers. Instead, the body was returned to Raigmore. Dr Richmond will not comment on whether he was dealing with his first gunshot case, but a check with the Scottish Information Office and the Registrar-General reveals that there has been only one handgun death (McRae's) in the Highland area during the last 20 years. Apparently the procurator-fiscal at Inverness had requested that the body be examined at Inverness. Surely a post-mortem should have been carried out at the earliest opportunity and surely the particular experience of Dr Hendry could have been utilised by having that examination in Aberdeen?

Cases of unexplained sudden death are examined by forensic specialists in terms of the inter-related factors of (a) body, (b) scene, and (c) personal history. By examining these factors closely it is possible to arrive at a conclusion. Often, however, this is merely based on a balance of opinion and a more definitive statement is not possible. In the McRae case the forensic specialists were able only to make a speculative deduction on the manner of death although this has been interpreted by the Lord Advocate as conclusive enough to ride roughshod over all demands from all quarters for a fatal accident inquiry. Clearly, their examination proved that the manner of death was "undetermined" as opposed to being clearly the result of "natural causes", "homicide" or "suicide".

Since the post-mortem report has not been made publicly available – and it should be pointed out that even Dr Fergus McRae did not receive a printed copy of it – several important facts of the case cannot be disputed. The gun which was found, after two days of searching, under an overhang of a narrow, deep burn was McRae's own, a Smith & Wesson 45 revolver (not as rumour suggested a hand-made Afghan gun). Two shots had been fired. The only fingerprints on the revolver were McRae's. The bullet in McRae's head was from his revolver. These factors cannot be disputed. Equally, the fact that the gun's location was more than 20 yards from the site of the car (which had been removed prior to the finding of the gun) is not in dispute either. Indeed, in an off-the-record interview with TV journalist Roger Cook (12 March 1987), Mr Peter Fraser, the then Solicitor-General and now Lord Advocate said: "I don't think the gun was found 40 to 50 feet away, although it was certainly further away than it would have been if it had just fallen from his grasp and it is unlikely, given his head injury, that he could have thrown it . . . I agree that the angle he was lying at and the recoil from the gun is far more likely to have resulted in his arm being found outside the window . . .". Another fact is that McRae's body had no alcohol in the bloodstream. Coutts was told this by the procurator-fiscal and the Solicitor-General later confirmed this, as he also confirmed the existence of the "neat pile" of papers.

In cases of gunshot death, the body should be removed from the scene with as little handling as possible to avoid loss of trace evidence. The hands of those lifting the body should be paper-bagged and the body should be moved in clear plastic sheeting to avoid contamination. None of these precautions had been taken, because McRae was still alive when he was moved. The sheer effort required to move him from his inaccessible place meant that the body had been handled a great deal before his wounds were even examined. Not only that, but his wounds had been washed and dressed at Raigmore and undoubtedly again in Aberdeen Royal Infirmary. So, by the time his body was examined by Dr Richmond at Raigmore, much – if not most – of the vital forensic evidence had already been removed.

Before a post-mortem is carried out, an X-ray is taken, prior to removing clothing, which is examined separately. Residues are recovered from the victim's hands with swabs soaked in dilute nitric acid and the presence or lack of trace evidence; soot and propellant grains is noted. A handgun leaves distinct traces of these in the palms when it is fired, and, in cases of handgun suicide, there are usually traces of blood "spatter" on the index finger and thumb and the back of the hand – particularly if the shot was to the head – and 80 per cent of gun suicides *are* to the head (15 per cent to chest and 5 per cent to abdomen). The wounds are photographed and correlated with the clothing then both are examined minutely with a dissecting microscope. The body is cleaned and photographed, the wounds listed and described, the bullet wounds are traced and the bullet removed. Bullet wounds are three-dimensional. There is the injury mark on the surface of the skin and a "track" inside the body and generally an abrasion "ring" and often "searing" around the wound edge. The length of the gun barrel of the revolver used is directly related to the presence of all these features. Typically, a Smith & Wesson 45 produces considerable amounts of propellant powder and soot on the surface of the skin and inside the "track". If the gun is available at the post-mortem which it wasn't in this case, the muzzle imprint on the head can be compared with the weapon's muzzle. Whenever a bullet enters the body, it displaces the skin around its entry point, causing a crease, the skin being pushed imperceptibly outwards around the entry hole.

The nightmare for the pathologist in this case was that *almost certainly* all traces of soot, propellant powder and blood were already removed. Then there is the peculiar effect known as "tattooing" which is very obvious to the naked eye. This is actually the body's reaction to, or rejection of, the implanting of propellant grains, and it produces a grainy red-brown or orange-red effect like a rash. Tattooing cannot be removed, but this very obvious feature does not appear to have been seen by any of the witnesses, including Dr Messer, and the paramedic, or by the medical staff at Raigmore, raising serious grounds for doubt as to whether any tattooing existed. Tattooing is a definite feature for all close-range shots – which includes shots fired from a few centimetres to one metre from the body – but *may* exist in both contact wounds (where the muzzle is pressed against the body) and in long-range (i.e. over one metre away) wounds. The existence of tattooing would almost certainly be expected in a gunshot suicide. The lack of it, which we must presume and a nurse on duty in ward 40 of Aberdeen Royal Infirmary when McRae was brought in has confirmed that there did not appear to be powder burns. This seriously weakens the presumption of suicide as far as the pathologist is concerned.

Contact wounds are typically, but not always, self-inflicted. The crucial point is that they include hard contact to the body. In such cases, the bullet rarely exits and internal ricochet is common. Generally there is an absence of wound-edge tearing but often several concentric circles of soot and propellant "baked" into the skin and, of course, the tattooing. Soot, propellant, vapourised bullet, primer and cartridge case metals and carbon oxide appear in and along the wound track. It would appear that there were no large rings of soot around the wound when Willie McRae's body was discovered. Certainly, there was no soot by the time the body was examined by Dr Richmond. And if it *had* been present when McRae's body was discovered, surely someone would have seen it and mentioned it. After all, no one at the scene was aware of the fire at his flat or that there might be an "innocent" reason for his being covered in soot – if he was.

The ammunition which went with Willie McRae's Smith & Wesson was of the same age as the revolver itself, dating from 1948, if not earlier: 29 gramme solid or 27 to 29 gramme 0.223-inch hollow point lead bullet, unjacketed, with a standard velocity powder loading. The gun itself was of a low muzzle velocity type – relatively inefficient – and would undoubtedly produce a large quantity of powder and propellant on the skin. So why had this not been remarked by any of the witnesses at the scene?

Clearly, the kind of detailed forensic examination required in the post-mortem conducted by Dr Richmond must have been almost impossible under the circumstances. Apart from the internal injuries and the wound "track" details which he was presumably able to elicit, he must have been entirely unable to decide with any certainty whether the wound was a contact one or caused by a close-range shot. The gun was not available so muzzle imprint – one of the most vital pointers to a contact wound – could not be confirmed. It would appear that there were no visible soot marks, abrasions or tattooing visible on the skin, all features which play a major part in establishing the range of the shot. He would have had to build a case based on generalities: a presumption of suicide based on the statistic that 80 per cent of handgun suicides are caused by shots to the temple, the fact that "test-firing" is common in suicide, that suicide notes are rarely left, that in 80 per cent of suicides the gun is not found in the victim's hand . . . . But perhaps not that last, because the sheer distance of the gun from the position of the victim is the most baffling enigma of the whole case. Nor can an explanation be provided for the presence of the neat pile of papers, watch and credit card found 15 yards from the crashed car, whose driver was unable to get out of the car because of the angle at which it lay, whose driver was brain dead from a shot which had instantly terminated all possibilities of bodily movement . . .

Return to Loch Loyne

At a commemoration ceremony organised by the Willie McRae Society (the Society formed to fight for a fatal accident inquiry) at the cairn, in 1987, there was the start of a remarkable controversy as to where exactly McRae's car had been found! Approximately one hundred people attended this ceremony. The *Scotsman's* Alex Main reported the controversy:

> . . . before the formalities could take place the issue facing those who had braved the cold easterly wind was to establish where the incident had occurred. Mr John Farquhar Munro, an old friend of Mr McRae, had earlier pin-pointed an outcrop overlooking the loch. There, in preparation for the ceremony, he had raised a flagstaff from which the Saltire flew at half-mast.
>
> Mr Munro, a Wester Ross contractor and Alliance chairman of Skye & Lochalsh District Council, had also arranged for one of his lorries to tip a load of rocks as a foundation for a commemorative cairn.
>
> Pointing to where the heather sloped steeply towards the loch, Mr Munro said: "There is no doubt but that it is the spot. I was here the day after it happened and I know this area like the back of my hand."
>
> But Dr [*sic*!] David Coutts, the SNP district councillor who was on holiday with his wife Alison when they were among the first to come across Mr McRae's crashed car, insisted that it had happened at a similar spot more than a mile along the road towards Invergarry.
>
> Mr Coutts led a group of less than a dozen down "his" slope while the remainder of the gathering and a bewildered television crew from

England, debated which location they should attend. The majority decided to join those at Mr Munro's site.

Embarrassment was avoided when Mr Coutts and his friends made a symbolic stone-laying gesture at what they believed was the spot before joining the main group. Mr Coutts conceded: "This is certainly a more convenient spot for the public to visit and pay their respects, even if it isn't where it all actually happened." The site which he believed to be the locus is 1.4 miles further south – in Lochaber District.

The dispute over the precise site was undoubtedly a factor in the postponing, indefinitely, of a TV documentary programme on McRae's death. David Coutts also found himself at the receiving end of a considerable amount of criticism by his refusal to accept Mr Munro's site. He subsequently wrote to the procurator-fiscal at Inverness: ". . . as there is dubiety, unfounded in my opinion, as to the exact location of the accident, could you please give me exact details of this and specifically with regard to how far the car was off the main road at the time it came to rest. Could you tell me if a reconstruction did take place and if that was the case, was it in the correct place?"

Coutts's theory was that a reconstruction had led, by some error, to the adoption of the wrong location and had created its own car debris in a different locus. The fiscal did not reply. Instead, Coutts received a lecture from the Solicitor-General, Peter Fraser, on the advantages of the Scottish legal system over the English system, and the support which various SNP figures had given it over the years. There was no reference whatsoever to the subjects of Coutts's inquiry. The tone of the letter is hectoring and aggressive. "I am only surprised," it ends, "that you are not prepared to accept the views of your own chairman."

Coutts claimed that he had been told by the fiscal that a reconstruction was to take place. Chief Superintendent Andrew Lester, Northern Counties Commander CID, denies this. "There was no need to do a reconstruction as far as we were concerned." Chief Superintendent Lester took over the investigation personally after the discovery of the bullet wound. Coutts was later shown a large number of photographs by the police, and found it impossible to confirm that they had been taken at the spot where he had found the car. These photographs clearly showed the car in its correct position relative to the ground; upright, slightly on its side, door jammed into the earth, etc, and had been taken early on the Sunday prior to the removal of the car about midday. On some of the photographs there was a cross marked to reveal the position of the gun which had been found subsequent to the car's removal. The new Northern Counties Commander, Chief Constable Hugh C. MacMillan has refused access to the photographs, on the grounds that they are "confidential to the Crown and the police", thus direct and definitive evidence as to which site the police and the fiscal regard as the correct locus cannot be obtained.

It was claimed that marks on the soft verge between the two lay-bys revealed that the car had left the road at an approximate angle of 30 degrees. Two persons who had been fishing in the loch on the Easter Monday (or the Tuesday) came up to the road and substantiated the marks on the soft verge and glass on the road approximately 50 yards south of the marks. One of the men was Councillor John Farquhar Munro. This is odd, since the car was recovered up the section of hillside to the north of the locus for its journey to Inverness. The glass was, in fact, according to the allegation, at the lay-by.

One of Willie McRae's friends, Donnie Blair, was at the scene on the Sunday about 3 p.m. and took photographs of the site and later of the car in the garage in Inverness. He was able to substantiate the tyre tracks on the verge and marks where the car had "ploughed" over the grass as if, he felt, the brakes were being applied as it went over.

As to how the car's final positioning could be explained, it has been assumed that the car's speed was in excess of 50 mph. McRae was a fast driver and knew the road very well. The stretch prior to the corner allows for build-up of considerable speed. The car may have left the road and careered down the steep bank. What may be a tiny fragment of rusty undersill has been found. The car's progress was altered by the presence of a line of stones and heathery bushes, and possibly by the brakes of the vehicle itself. Quantities of windscreen glass are still visible in the roots of the heather which grows around the rocks. Interestingly, while the ambulance driver claims the windscreen was completely removed, and Coutts recalls that it was intact, all the witnesses agree there was no glass either inside the car or on McRae. There is also the statement of John Munro and his friend of the large amount of glass on the road 50 yards south of the locus, at the lay-by, which implies a windscreen shattered in the course of the incident, but not the crash.

Blair's photographs reveal some crumpling of the roof but relatively low levels of damage to the car and do not clearly imply a somersault. Surprisingly, none of the small rocks show any signs of being scraped. Such violent action would cause considerable damage to the car, yet there is the testimony of the witnesses that there was not much damage. "Not much damage," was also the verdict of Donnie Blair. The photographs which he took apparently also show bloodstained marks on the bulkhead above the driver's door. He had not been able to test these marks and feels that they may possibly have been rust. There was a "clean" new wheel on the rear offside. The amount of damage is inconsistent with somersaulting or violent collision, yet the car had come to rest in an upright position, facing back the way it had come . . . logistically, it is difficult to explain.

Surely Coutts and his wife Alison must be wrong! Why would the police turn the matter over to the Inverness procurator if the death had occurred within Lochaber? The Fort Augustus police "beat" spans both Inverness-shire and Lochaber and they deal with investigations on behalf of both procurator-fiscals at Inverness and at Fort William, and they are aware of the boundaries.

Both the fiscals, Mr Aitchison (now retired) at Inverness and Mr McGillveray at Fort William knew McRae slightly, both having worked at Dingwall Sheriff Court when McRae was a prospective parliamentary candidate at two general elections. But this was a professional acquaintance and they were hardly close. The local rumour that the investigation was handled by Mr Aitchison who was a "friend" so as to give the impression of a fair and rigorous investigation while a cover-up was being perpetrated is a slur on the integrity of both fiscals and, of course, utter nonsense. If the investigation was handled out of jurisdiction this was because of some error or mistake over the site. It had nothing to do with either fiscal. But what would be the motivation for the Coutts's refusal to accept the other site if not a simple belief that it was wrong and "their" site was right? They had no reason to lie. It would have been easier for them to have gone along with the crowd – after all they are only witnesses and are not interested in trying to prove anything. It is hardly fair that Coutts should have been blamed for causing discord when, in fact, the cairn which everyone else seems to have accepted so readily was erected without consultation! One wonders what could have prompted Mr Munro to take such a precipitate action one year after the incident, and why he did not consult with the eye-witnesses with regard to the site. He was one of the fishermen who came up from the Loch on the Easter Monday (or the Tuesday – he cannot recall) and confirmed the glass on the road and the marks on the verge, but he did not see the car itself at all. He was not present, as he claimed, "the day after it happened" because the car was found on the Saturday, removed on the Sunday and he didn't arrive on the scene until Monday or perhaps even Tuesday.

An examination of both sites is clearly necessary for the purposes of this book. One of the first impressions obtained after such an examination is the *similarity* of both sites in all essential features. The hillside above Loch Loyne is rugged and steep and, really, for someone who did not know the area well, one place could be confused with another. The only way to orientate yourself in such a place is to judge your position relative to prominent natural features. Clearly, the loch with its two small islands was the most prominent feature in view from the hillside. There is, however, one essential difference between the sites. At Coutts's site you see the loch – but at the other site you see the dam. Standing beneath Mr Munro's cairn you cannot fail to notice that you are near the end of the loch. You also see an island directly opposite you and another about halfway to the dam. At Coutts's site, 1.4 miles south-east, all you notice is the loch, the end of which you cannot see, and neither of the small islands are visible. None of the witnesses present on that day mentioned the dam, and Dr Messer (now Lochhead) and her husband, when specifically questioned on this point, remembered that the site was "about the middle of the loch". The most auspicious feature of the "Munro site" itself is the concrete culvert, which no one could fail to notice. Yet no one present at the locus of the crashed car seems to have remembered it! The compelling feature of the "Lochaber site" is its distance from the road. It will be remembered that the initial statements of the witnesses, of the mechanic and the police was that the car was at least 100 yards from the road. The problem of the "Munro site" is that the locus of the car is only 35 yards from the road.

It is difficult to prove something without evidence. The "Munro site" has a large amount of evidence in its favour. Mr Michael Strathern and his son, Lachlan, friends of Mr McRae, have a large amount of parts of a car, or cars, which they collected from this site one full year after the incident. We are asked to believe that the police investigation was conducted in such a sloppy manner that a large amount of important physical evidence remained at the site unexamined, despite the clamour of the press, despite the pressure on the authorities to produce results. Clearly, the car parts collected by Mr Strathern must be from several cars, though what person or persons would add such "evidence" to the site is a matter for psychiatrists. There have been several such incidents. A car-load of persons disembarked for a photo-session at the site. Prior to taking the photos they carefully placed a Volvo hub-cap on the verge; a hub-cap they had brought with them! Of course, if the car parts collected by the Stratherns *are* from McRae's car, then questions need to be asked about the thoroughness of the police investigation.

It might be supposed that the garage mechanic could assist with the question of the site. Unfortunately, the evidence which he has supplied seems so contradictory as to support neither case, and creates an enigma all of its own!

The mechanic recalls "very vividly" the operation to retrieve McRae's vehicle on Sunday, 7 April 1985. This is partly because of the practical difficulties which he had to overcome. He remembers that the car was "at least 100 yards off the road" near the head *of Loch Cluanie*! The mechanic, who lives in Inverness and is not very well acquainted with the area, could have made such an error. However, he recalls that he had to reverse very slowly down *a side road* past *rocks the size of cars*, and attach a winch. He then pulled the Volvo on to this old road. He did this because he did not want his operation to block the main road. Unfortunately, there are only two side roads on the hillside above Loch Loyne; one is just above the bridge and runs back to the dam, used only by Hydro-Electric engineers and is nowhere near either site, and the other, with a steel boom gate, is at the other end, about 35 yards south of Coutts's lay-by, but offers no access to the slope for that site. A check of the area around the head of Loch Cluanie reveals one side road to a house just beneath the dam, but no rocks of the size which he describes, and not even a slope . . .. What are we to make of his testimony? Is it simply all wrong, the product of a faulty memory? What are we to make of Mr Douglas, the one-man ambulance service who initially claimed that the distance was 100 *feet*, which might seem to favour the "Munro site", then became converted under questioning to 100 yards, which favours the "Coutts site". He too, remembered a very rocky environment, which simply isn't the case at either site.

Despite the fact that the "Coutts site" is logistically more favourable, the corroboration by Donnie Blair of John Munro's testimony, and the finding of material evidence at the other site must mean that David Coutts and his wife are mistaken. The large amount of car parts left at the site cannot be a deliberate attempt to confuse, nor could the car possibly have been moved from one site to the other for any reason by the police. That calls for a very high degree of collusion throughout the police force to ordinary constable level – and that is plainly nonsense. We still regard the explanation as to how the car achieved its final position at the "Munro site" as unsatisfactory. Since the car had been found there, there must be a way to explain its positioning. And, simply, we believe that the speed of the car was much less than proposed. The testimony concerning what could be seen at the locus – the loch, dam, islands, culvert – was collected five years after the initial questioning. These questions were not asked at the time and, while interesting, can in no way be considered conclusive evidence. The material evidence of the marks on the verges and the glass and car parts cannot be over-ruled. The police photographs, when finally revealed in the course of a public inquiry, will show that the incident occurred beneath the cairn, about half a mile from the end of the loch.

Quite apart from the debate over the site, there is an extraordinary amount of disagreement over the extent of the damage to the car. The garage mechanic recalls that the car was "a write-off". Chief Superintendent Lester refers to "considerable damage", "definitely consistent" with the car rolling over, though he concedes that this occurred largely on moss. Both David Coutts, Mr Gillespie (the McRae & Dick garage manager) and Donnie Blair, who took photographs of the car in the garage on the Tuesday, testify that there was relatively little damage. "Simply not enough evidence of roof damage to suggest the car somersaulted," said one. "The pictures made that quite clear." Blair felt that the damage was not extensive enough to conclude that the car had been travelling very fast, although he felt that it had probably rolled as it came off the road.

And what about that half bottle of whisky in the glove compartment that didn't smash? The holdall and the wheel with the puncture which remained on the back seat until the car was found? McRae had remained in the driving seat despite his safety belt being unfastened. Or had he unfastened it later, after the car had come to a halt?

The discovery that McRae's car had had a puncture during the fatal drive, only a couple of miles from where he met his death, at such a late stage gives grounds for serious doubt about the extent and thoroughness of the original investigation. What, for example, had caused the puncture in the first place? Why had McRae put the punctured wheel in the back seat instead of in the voluminous boot? The new wheel, which *was* brand new, on the rear offside, had been changed only a mile or two before the crash and was still extremely clean when seen in the garage on the Tuesday. The fact that he had had to change the wheel and had done so, in very dark conditions, says important things about his mental state. If, as some have suggested, a puncture was "the last straw" and had triggered violent anger in an admittedly irascible man, why calmly change the wheel, drive on for a couple of miles and then shoot oneself?

The Australian tourist/airline pilot, Alan Crowe, first on the scene of death on 6 April, is not now contactable. There is no Crowe listed in Bracknell, Berks., and mail addressed to him at his address has been returned marked "not known here – return to sender". It may be that Crowe's holiday simply ended and he left the country entirely naturally – after all, investigations were complete and no one had requested he stay for official reasons. He collaborated entirely freely with the fiscal's investigations although he had little contact with press reporters, and neither of the other principal witnesses spoke to him after 6 April. He seems to have left behind two separate addresses where he could be contacted; 8 Birch Grove, Bracknell, Berks., and, jotted on a postcard at the scene and handed to David Coutts, another address, 8 Church Way, Aldgrove. Here is a further mystery. There is no "Aldgrove" anywhere in the UK. The nearest to it is "Aldergrove" – which is of course an airport, near Belfast. None of the pilots there – and it is a relatively small airport – had ever heard of him and the British Airline Pilots Association has no record of his ever having worked in the UK.

It is little satisfaction to know that the police photographs – definite proof which still exists – could solve the dispute over the site and the amount of damage to McRae's car. And, with Mr Crowe summoned as a witness in a public inquiry, there would be no room for dispute on such crucial factors.

Some Kind of a Breakthrough?

Several times in the weeks before his death Willie McRae had confided to close friends including Ian Watt, a retired educationalist whom he had known since his days at University, in a tone of elation, "I've got them! I've got them!", though he did not specify what this meant. Why did he feel the need to have his revolver with him on all occasions? He was certainly under surveillance by Strathclyde Special Branch. This was originally confirmed several months after his death but is now denied. A list of number plates of cars allegedly involved in "tailing" Willie McRae was checked on the police network computer and while one belongs to a car that apparently doesn't exist – a small light-blue car BGS 4255 – another, a Triumph with a black vinyl top and registration PSJ 136X, is a "blocked vehicle" (making it either a Special Branch or MI5 vehicle) and the third, XSJ 432T, belonged to a man from Telford, Shropshire. This third car, brown in colour, was following McRae *at least* up to and including the day before his trip to Dornie. The list was originally supplied to a BBC Scotland journalist by David Dinsmore. McRae's links with Dinsmore and other members of the nationalist fringe groups have been covered in previous chapters and it is clear that he was a thorn in the flesh of Special Branch. He had had more than one angry altercation with Special Branch officers in Glasgow concerning the release of SNG activists and in one episode had nearly come to blows with one senior officer. Yet McRae does not appear to have been interviewed or arrested in connection with their investigations. McRae himself was certainly aware of the recent Special Branch interest in him and aware also that he had been "tailed" on a previous trip to his holiday home, as he confided to several friends.

There are several other peculiar circumstances which should be mentioned. His house was "attacked and heavily vandalised" in mid-August 1984 – four months before his death and five months after the "burglary" of Hilda Murrell's Shropshire home. Nothing was stolen but his papers had been quite systematically rifled. Secondly, there was the story which came to light in the *Oban Times* as a front-page article after a police "leak". Less than one hour before the discovery of Willie McRae's body a group of hikers at Creag Bhan on the shores of Loch Eilt, 20 miles to the south of Loch Loyne, reported an incident which had startled them. They had watched a red Ford Escort estate car pull up on the road, a man had got out and began shooting a high velocity rifle up the hillside almost directly at the hikers, who were clearly visible. The police were at first disinterested in this story but later became very interested, so much so that they tracked the hikers around all the pubs in Fort William that evening to get further information. The crucial point is that this proves the police did not entirely believe the "suicide theory", even although they had been pointed in that direction by Dr Ferguson McRae. Another coincidence might be the red Ford Escort car. A car of this type was seen seven times in the vicinity of Hilda Murrell's house prior to her murdered body being found in nearby woods. This fact was highlighted by Graham Swift in his book *Death of a Rose-Grower* (1985). He also mentions the existence of Section A1A, the MI5, "burglars" and their assumption that they may disregard all laws with impunity. Swift believes that Murrell was murdered by the secret police and, before his book was in print, his house and his publishers' houses were broken into, and though nothing was stolen his papers had clearly been disturbed.

The second, and most important, police "leak" was made to Joe Donnelly of the *Sunday Mail*. A police officer involved in the investigation – whose identity was withheld – claimed to Donnelly that the gun had been fired twice, but not from point-blank range and that the rear window had been shattered by a bullet. This leak may not be entirely unconnected to a second, internal, inquiry that was conducted within the police force itself relative to the conduct of the McRae case. This internal inquiry was kept highly secret and has never been publicly admitted.

There have been persistent allegations that there is a "witness" to the events of 5 or 6 April at Loch Loyne and local residents, former estates managers, persons acquainted with the poaching fraternity and the Freemasons (very prevalent in the area) have been consulted in an effort to get to the truth of these allegations. They remain allegations and unsubstantiated rumours, similar to allegations that Willie McRae had homosexual tendencies. Several close friends, relatives and women who knew him – at least one of whom he proposed marriage to – deny that he ever exhibited such tendencies.

A Glaring Anomaly

The extraordinary conduct of the Solicitor-General must be re-marked. While frankly admitting in private that the case remains a mystery, in public he continued to deny requests for information on this highly mysterious death of a senior politician and public figure. Then, in an extraordinary about-turn, on 13 April 1990, he "reluctantly" revealed that the post-mortem had proved that the single gunshot wound to the head had been a contact wound – and that the revolver had been found directly beneath where the car door had been. This completely contradicts his earlier private statement. The Scottish National Party made an official request to Mr Fraser, now Lord Carmyllie, in which Mrs Winifred Ewing, a personal friend of Willie McRae, and also a solicitor, could have confidential access to the case papers in return for an oath that she would not reveal the contents of the file. This was refused – on the grounds of Dr Ferguson McRae's wish not to have a public inquiry! It is extremely hard to see how Mrs Ewing's request for private and confidential scrutiny of the papers could have been construed as being contrary to Dr McRae's wishes. Other members of the McRae family have indicated their disquiet over the situation and have suggested that Dr McRae's motives are almost purely in the interests of keeping the story quiet, of letting the matter rest, which is of course entirely understandable.

The statement by Peter Fraser that he did not wish to "capitalise from the sad death in questionable circumstances of a political opponent" by holding a fatal accident inquiry must also be deplored. While this may seem, on the surface, laudable, Peter Fraser has been hard at work behind the scenes suggesting a range of lurid possibilities for McRae's death: Archie Kirkwood MP was told that McRae had had "his own sexual preferences", a history of drunkenness, treatment for drying-out, an extensive debt problem, was seeing a psychotherapist, facing a major bust-up of his business, facing the prospect of a jail sentence for a drink-driving offence. Mr Fraser also consulted SNP leader Gordon Wilson, who apparently accepted that there was no need for an FAI in the case. It is inaccurate to suggest that it was Wilson who decided that an inquiry be not held. He had no power in the matter. To Roger Cook, TV journalist, Fraser suggested that McRae was depressed, a "dissipated old drunk" and "a dissipated and disillusioned man inclined to fantasise ...". Such disgraceful slanders, peddled in such a way that they cannot be refuted, have undoubtedly damaged Willie McRae far more than any public inquiry ever could. Nor does the "reluctant" revealing of details of the case improve the situation. The case, and its handling, has been described by the Scottish Council For Civil Liberties as a "glaring anomaly" and "very disturbing", revealing the lack of accountability to the public of Scotland's highly political senior judges.

Too Many Clues?

If Willie McRae was under surveillance, and it is almost certain that he was, and if he had already been "tailed" to his holiday home in Dornie, probably under the belief that he might lead them to Dinsmore – and he had given Dinsmore the keys previously to his holiday home – then it is probable that he was not alone on the A87 road to Kyle. It would be unlikely for surveillance to stop simply because McRae left Glasgow.

We can only speculate at the circumstances of 5 April 1985 at Loch Loyne which led to the death of Willie McRae, but it would seem from an examination of such evidence that is available that not only is the death highly suspicious, but that there are clear grounds for the belief that McRae did not die willingly, or as a result of his own actions.

While people die in car crashes and people do shoot themselves in cars in remote places, it is not even remotely credible that a man involved in an accidental car crash would then decide to commit suicide – unless, of course, the car crash was a deliberate suicide attempt. And, if it *had* been, why, knowing the road well, had he not chosen a steeper place where a clean death was more likely? "If I was going to do away with myself I'd have found a better spot. Along that road there are lots of gullies where you could put the car over and vanish for days," concluded the local ambulance driver.

The problem with the case is not the *lack* of clues but that there are simply *too many clues*: the car crash that didn't kill him; the gunshot which didn't kill cleanly; the gun itself being at least 20 yards from the car and yet McRae's hands being on his lap; the "neat pile" of papers where they could not have been put if the driver was unable to leave the car; the half-consumed half-bottle of whisky which had not smashed; no trace of alcohol – so often a feature of suicides – in McRae's bloodstream; the missing briefcase and the missing cigarettes – all clues pointing in different directions, all inconsistent with any one theory. It is the very combination of all these clues which points inescapably to the conclusion that his death was planned – at least in part. The planners, however, not being intelligent enough to see that the clues were inconsistent with each other. It was a tableau left to be found by the *paparazzi* who would seize on the gory details and create ever wilder speculative theories. But it is the evidence of McRae's lengthy involvement with the Scottish nationalist movement and particularly with the fringe groups documented in this book which confirm that he was regarded as "a subversive" and therefore likely to be a target of surveillance. A consideration of Willie McRae's activities and significance in this context provides the most telling evidence against the "secret police" – or the Special Branch.

Only after Invergarry would it have become obvious to McRae that he was being tailed. The headlights of the pursuing car would have become monotonous and McRae was driving fast on a road he knew well, which the other driver almost certainly wouldn't have been so sure of. Most drivers experience irritation when a car follows closely but refuses to pass and McRae was an especially irascible man. He might well have stopped to "have it out" with them. After all, he was tired and his threshold of anger would be lower. Or perhaps he *had* to stop when his tyre punctured? What would they do in that circumstance? They could have passed by. They may have stopped short. McRae and the officers became embroiled in an embarrassing confrontation, which wasn't meant to happen – and would be embarrassing in their reports. During the altercation, McRae may have produced his revolver, may even have fired a shot before he was disarmed. He would be more easily disarmed if the altercation took place with McRae out of his car. The men whom McRae was facing were certainly of a breed which regards itself as above and beyond the reach of the criminal law – essentially violent men. What happened next resulted in the near death of McRae. Most likely they rolled him in the car down the hill to make it seem like an accident then decided to make it look like a gunshot suicide.

The investigating police would quickly have identified Special Branch interest in McRae and were told that this interest had lapsed several days before his death. While the policemen had their suspicions, and evidently they did, McRae's death was almost certainly not officially sanctioned – it was more likely to have been the result of an unexpected confrontation, entirely unpremeditated, thus no one was "covering up" anything. The only person(s) who knew the truth were the perpetrators – for whom the incident was an embarrassment. Thus, they "sharpened up" the suicide motive, hastily and rather clumsily, by setting up the cache of torn papers (entirely inconsequential, and of no importance whatsoever – why was McRae supposed to have wasted time shredding them?), putting his smashed watch on top of the pile. They had already taken the briefcase and could not resist purloining the large carton of cigarettes and the hundred pound Bank of Scotland note – McRae's first fee as a lawyer — the personal memento which went with him everywhere. They possibly also emptied half of the bottle of whisky.

The suggestion has been made – the "leak" from the Northern Counties policeman – that Fiscal Aitchison conducted a second investigation – into the misconduct of two police officers involved in the case. Aitchison made two remarks on 16 June 1985 when he agreed to conduct this second investigation: he said that there were no suspicious circumstances, but that was "before other matters were raised", and also that "all sorts of factors were coming into this". These remarks were made more than two months *after* he had declared to the press (9 April) that "the death has been fully investigated. There is no suspicious circumstance in this case." The statement made by the Lord Advocate on 31 July that "no grounds had been found to warrant *criminal procedures*" almost certainly related to this second investigation. Something was going on behind the scenes. A senior police officer involved in the investigation has made a vague hint to the authors that "it would all come out in an inquiry", without saying *what* would come out.

Dinsmore is still a fugitive, so whether or not Willie McRae was questioned about his whereabouts in the lay-by at Loch Loyne on Friday, 5 April 1985, he did not reveal, if he knew, Dinsmore's hiding place. Surely this is a far more compelling motive for his death than any theory of sudden suicidal depression? Disputation of these deductions, or any of the facts on which they are based, from the authorities concerned is to be welcomed.

In a sense, Willie McRae lives on, in the memories of his friends and comrades, and he continues to assist the SNP through his Memorial Trust Fund which donates over £580 each year to party campaigns.

13 CONSPIRACIES OF *AGENTS PROVOCATEURS*, INFORMERS AND DUPES?

ALTHOUGH some of the groups and organisations in "Britain's Secret War" have been linked, caution must be exercised in analysing the phenomenon. While "tartan terrorism" is a convenient umbrella term for the purposes of this book, it is not correct to assume that the causes and origins of each group is similar. The manifestation of each new phase of terrorist activity has been varied and the reaction of the secret police to each has been different. Professor Wilkinson and others have outlined general theories of terrorism and it is clear that, although terrorism is an extremely general concept, the incidents involving Scottish groups could be described as "spasm terrorism", defined by Wilkinson as "a series of attacks of relatively low intensity and brief duration". They have occurred against a pattern of "waves" of international terrorism but have been almost entirely indigenous, with relatively few foreign links.

There are broadly four categories of "tartan terrorism", each arising from different conditions and circumstances. The origins of Scottish nationalist extremism in the 1940s and 1950s clearly arose from political frustration and this element is common to all the groups and phases of "tartan terrorism". But it is not simply frustration that is the motivating factor and that is demonstrated by the emergence of episodes when political nationalism was highly successful and likely to succeed by the ballot box. Clearly, the motivating factor at such a period is more complex. Wilkinson outlines seven classifications of politically motivated violence and four of these classifications could be considered to apply in a Scottish context. The APG could perhaps be defined in the "Inter-communal" classification, since the group attempted to set up a national defensive force. The Tartan Army were "Remonstrative", seeking to punish the British State for its actions such as the "theft" of "Scottish" oil. The "Workers' Party of Scotland" and Peter Wardlaw's "Army of the Scottish People" were clearly "Revolutionary" in intent, seeking to provoke a repression which might result in a political backlash beneficial to them. The SNLA fit into Wilkinson's "Terroristic" category due to the longevity and persistence of their activities and their variety of methods.

The origins of violent terrorist activity in Scotland began in 1968 with the founding of the Army of the Provisional Government by Major Frederick Boothby after an initial period of propagandising on behalf of the almost entirely mythical "Scottish Liberation Army". Boothby, who made himself known to nationalists through his journal *Sgian Dubh*, acted as a focus for numerous individuals who went on to create other groups. He clearly acted in an inflammatory manner and attempted almost single-handedly to provoke Scottish nationalists into violent action. His attempts to entrap the Chairman of the Scottish National Party in his conspiracy failed but Boothby's activities resulted in 11 persons being jailed. It is highly likely, considering the scope and nature of his activities, that Boothby was an *agent provocateur*. He was always an unlikely Scottish nationalist and his sudden appearance on the Scottish scene after a military background and a life full of adventure is simply too much of a coincidence, as is the fact that he took a cottage virtually next door to Hugh MacDairmid, a man of well-known revolutionary principles. The most telling factor against him is that he emerged from obscurity and perpetrated his conspiracies at just the moment when the SNP were expecting ultimate success – in other words, at just such a time as it was likely that *agents provocateurs* were infiltrating the nationalist movement. While there may have been scores of *agents provocateurs*, it is highly likely that Boothby was one. He was a man who revelled in clandestinity and conspiracy and his appearance in Scotland closely followed a period when he was seeking more excitement from his life.

But if Boothby was, as Hugh MacDairmid and Ronald Mac-Donald Douglas suspected, a "double agent" then the movement which he started was virtually a creation of the secret police. It had been conceived by the 1320 Club nationalists as a contingency preparation, a defensive force to be utilised only if Independence was achieved and denied by the English, but it became simply a group of persons entrapped into a bank raid that never was perpetrated, and since Boothby had remained undiscovered, he did exactly the same again. He initiated a second bank raid, four years later, and again the raiders were easily mopped up. This role of an agent acting as a "focus" for potential terrorists then involving them in conspiracies leading to their arrest has proved to be a recurrent theme; in nearly every phase of terrorist activity there has been a figure playing the "Boothby" role. And of course, there have been numerous other lesser figures within each group acting as informants. When the groups have been arrested, many of the participants too have been quite willing to incriminate their fellows to save their own skins.

There are then three levels of infiltration within the groups, the first being the active infiltration by police agents or *agents provocateurs*. These were installed as part of a systematic campaign by the Special Branch and their remit was not merely to provide information leading to arrests. These persons were to actively promote conspiracies and criminal activities amongst persons who might not otherwise have wished to do so. The pre-emptive formation of "bogus" terrorist groups by the Intelligence services to entrap potential terrorists has been outlined by Gavin Kennedy, a former Lecturer in Economics at the University of Strathclyde, in *Anti-Terrorism and People Control* (1979). In other words, the agents were to *create* tartan terrorism. Frederick Boothby has already been suggested as one such *agent provocateur*. But there were others whom it is possible to name. Steven Niven was the police agent within the "Workers' Party of Scotland". He did not appear at the trial, although his name was mentioned in passing, and was not called upon to give evidence. Benny Goodwin, the failed police cadet and erstwhile nationalist, became a willing agent within the republican movement although

his cover was "blown" when his evidence was required to convict
Thomas Kelly. And Kelly was convicted only of one letter-bombing
offence – a clear indication that he made only two letter bombs, the
first exploding in Goodwin's flat and the second posted by him and
Goodwin. Clearly, Kelly was not the *real* SNLA letter-bomber –
quite apart from the fact that the bombing continued when Kelly
was in jail – because his sheer inexperience contradicted the fact of the
considerable experience at making the devices which the *real* bomber
undoubtedly had. Goodwin's crude attempts to involve others in
their conspiracy failed. There was at least one police agent within the
ranks of Siol Nan Gaidheal and Arm Nan Gaidheal who participated
in the Glen Etive campaign. This could hardly have been Goodwin
in view of the dates involved. Colin Boyd's role within the Army
of the Provisional Government comes close to that of the *agent
provocateur* but he was merely a willing informant who participated
in a conspiracy and reported back at each stage to his Special Branch
"control".

There have been a large number of informants within each group
of terrorists. Every new group which emerged had its informant
almost before the group was formed. Some have been more willing
to co-operate with the police than others. Some informed for money
and some from fear of being pointed out to their comrades as a
"grass". Several have co-operated to obtain remission of sentences
which had already been passed on them for other offences. Others
seemed to have become involved almost by accident in activities
that frightened them and informed from a sense of duty. The result
has been that most groups have operated against a background of
mutual suspicion. But this has not led to terrorists being more
aware of agents and informers in their midst. On the contrary,
the groups seem to have been at all times naïvely open to such
infiltration. The Army of the Provisional Government in both its
manifestations contained a large number of informants. The first
was from the Glasgow underworld who tipped off the police after
William Murray's attempts to purchase weapons in Glasgow. And
then Boyd volunteered his assistance and a massive Special Branch
entrapment game began, with the aim of discrediting the SNP by
involving some of its senior members. The attempt failed and 16
months of surveillance, almost 13,000 man-hours involving a large
number of personnel, at numerous locations, resulted in only a
handful of arrests. William Murray was under surveillance by the

entire establishment of 12 men from the Glasgow Crime Squad plus six from the Lanarkshire unit for three and a half months, 18 hours per day, during which time he did not commit one unlawful act. Yet this large-scale operation may have been merely routine. Tax-payers may well question whether their money is being spent wisely. The mysterious William MacKenzie, the "Big Fiddler" who had played his violin at meetings of the APG conspirators, co-operated fully with the police and was released. Ex-soldier Alastair Smith and ex-policeman John Carlyle also probably supplied useful information and were released without charges. The informant in the "Tartan Army" trial was David Sharkey, a man serving a sentence for culpable homicide, who supplied the police with a detailed 16-page statement on the activities of the accused terrorists in events in which he admitted to playing perhaps the leading role. Yet he was not charged with any additional offence. Similarly, in the "Scottish Citizens' Army of the Republic" trial, Anthony Currie, serving a sentence for armed robbery, was the main source of evidence against Stan Green, although his evidence failed to convict Donald Anderson and Peter Wardlaw. An unknown young female volunteered the names of Raymond Lester, Robert Maldar and the 15-year-old Alistair Crawford which led to their conviction for the bombs on Dumbarton railway line and the Clyde Tunnel. Ian Paton, a member of Arm Nan Gaidheal supplied information regarded as vital in the conviction of several persons in two trials and was rewarded by a non-custodial sentence of community service. The role of scrap-merchant Andrew Wilson and his employee Andrews in attempting to entrap republicans at the behest of the Special Branch was remarked upon by the trial judge. The Special Branch had also attempted to coerce the members of the UVF whom they had arrested, to give testimony at the trial, acting perhaps on the belief that such persons would be politically motivated to do so. Wilson and Andrews acted almost as *agents provocateurs* since they were allowed out of custody with a package of gelignite and instructions to entrap the accused, Anderson and Browning.

The extensive powers of the Prevention of Terrorism (Temporary Provisions) Act, 1974, and its revised provisions in 1976 and 1979 have been widely used in Scotland and have allowed the police and Special Branch to probe deep into legal political movements by frequent "trawls" of activists. Large numbers of ordinary law-abiding members of political parties in Scotland have been detained and questioned at length. No evidence of criminal activity is required – merely suspicion – and approximately 89 per cent are never charged with any offence. The powers of detention under the PTA are 48 hours without charge, extended to an extra five days with the agreement of the Home Secretary – an agreement which, in practice, is never withheld. For the first 48 hours, the suspect can be denied access to a solicitor. The authorities are under no legal obligation to disclose the whereabouts of their prisoner, the nature of their suspicions or the sources of their information. A suspect can be forcibly fingerprinted and photographed. His or her home can be searched – and everyone in it – without a warrant. They are denied the right to silence. Interrogation can take place on a 24-hour basis for several days on end and can involve stressful confrontations, use of vicious language and implied violence, an atmosphere of fatigue, tensions, isolation and uncertainty.

In a BBC TV programme in February 1990, *Taking Liberties*, reporter David Jessel estimated that upwards of *one million* people a year are questioned in the UK under the PTA – mostly however at ports of entry. In the first six years of the PTA well over 20 per cent of UK mainland detentions were in Scotland, the majority in Dumfries and Galloway, due to the proximity of the ferry crossing to Ulster, though many of these were detentions for short periods only. Apart from this, many PTA suspects are detained after arrests involving violence. Many have had their doors battered down in the early hours of the morning. Some have been denied vital medicines, others claimed to suffer physical beatings in police custody, mental cruelty and various kinds of sensory deprivation. Some persons, such as Donald Anderson, have spent up to five months in custody awaiting trial, only to have charges dropped at the last moment. Under such circumstances, of course, "suspects" can and have lost their jobs and suffered humiliation and suspicion. In at least one case a suspect developed severe mental illness as a result of continued interrogation. Of the large numbers of persons detained under the PTA only a tiny minority – about 6.8 per cent – have ever been charged. If terrorism is defined as the use of violence for political ends, then this term can also be used to describe the activities of Britain's secret police. The powers of the PTA allow the police and Special Branch to perpetrate legalised terror campaigns against political activists. The PTA contravenes Articles 5, 6, 8, 10, 11 and

14 of the European Convention of Human Rights. It is a draconian measure described by one journalist as "The Suspension of Human Rights Act" and is, of course, entirely ineffective in stopping the terrorist bombings. It merely intensifies and entrenches resistance and anger among those closest to the terrorists who have useful information to give. It is effective, however, in creating a climate of fear and mistrust in which everyone is prepared to inform on everyone else.

Apart from the police agents and informants, the largest number of persons whose evidence has contributed to arrests and convictions can be termed "dupes". This includes many persons who have been called as Crown witnesses and who have subsequently been tarnished as "grassers". These fall into many categories; those who incriminated only themselves, such as Thomas Kelly. Matt Lygate's defiant but inept political speech from the dock convicted himself and his associates, who had pled not guilty. William Bell, the kilted Inverness supporter of the APG, showed a defiance which did nothing to assist the other accused. The three Perth APG men, Fairlie, Berwick and Coventry, were all involved in mutual informing on each other and others. A large number of persons peripheral to the activities of the "Tartan Army" gave evidence for the prosecution, such as Alec Swan, Kenneth Taylor, Gerald Sweeney, Iain Paterson, Catherine Alston, Gloria Monaghan, Jeannette Mackie and Lyla Cathie. In the event, however, such evidence was contradictory, vague and of little practical use. In general, these were hapless persons caught up in very serious situations in which they had little involvement, a situation which was at odds with their own motives and they had no option but to tell everything they knew. For each of these "dupes" there was a much larger number still of others whose names may never be known, who contributed to the general mood of suspicion and self-incrimination. The term "dupe" also refers to their initial involvement in the criminal activities, many being unwilling participants and unwilling also to be involved in the court proceedings.

Through the use of agents and informants and the skilful treatment of "dupes" the State has thoroughly infiltrated and controlled the outbreaks of terrorism in Scotland. Indeed, so extensive is the network that it is suprising that so many terrorist incidents ever occurred at all. Especially when the links between the groups themselves are considered.

The events of this book have not been as unco-ordinated as they might appear. There have been clear links between virtually all the tartan terror groups. It is these links which justify the use of the term "war" rather than sporadic, isolated incidents to describe the events of this book. The Army of the Provisional Government was, in itself, to be a co-ordinated "defence force" involving other groups and in August 1974 the APG sought to build a Scottish Army Council at a meeting attended by members of the "Scottish Liberation Army", "Scottish Republican Army", "Scottish Citizens' Army of the Republic" and some potential deserters from the Royal Highland Fusiliers. Attempts were made to recruit members from the various factions associated with the "Tartan Army" and "Border Clans", the "1916 Club", the "100 Club", "Scottish Activists" and the "Patriots" which failed. There were, however, considerable links of continuity of individuals from the APG periods, the Tartan Army, the SCAR, Peter Wardlaw's "Army of the Scottish People" through to "Arm Nan Gaidheal" and the SNLA. There may even have been links with the "Scottish Civilian Army" which perpetrated "Operation Dark Harvest". The youngsters associated with the mythical "Army for Freeing Scotland" are unique in that their group had no links with any other group whatsoever. All the other groups have been linked in some way. Jeanette Carpenter, previously the girlfriend of convicted "Workers' Party of Scotland" terrorist, Bill McPherson, married Alistair Smith, implicated in both the APG trial and the "Scottish Citizens' Army of the Republic" trial. Tony Tunilla's sister, Bernadette, was the girlfriend of "Army of the Scottish Peoples" leader, Peter Wardlaw. In prison, Wardlaw associated for a time with Matt Lygate. Lygate shared a cell with William Murray, an APG leader. Many of the tartan terrorists' accomplices were recruited in prison and this may be partly to do with the status which "political" inmates enjoyed as the prison's "heroes". Some even involved themselves in electioneering within the prison at General Elections, spreading political propaganda, agitating for the right to receive subscriptions to political journals, organising hunger strikes and even "dirty protests" in Scottish jails. The jail "cadre" included Tunilla, Alexander Ramsay, Ian Doran, Anthony Currie – none of whom had been interested in politics until they met convicted tartan terrorists in prison.

There have been approximately 79 bombing incidents, 40 armed "political" bank raids and numerous hoaxes and bomb-scares since 1968. Judges at 18 trials, involving 1,095 witnesses, have handed out sentences to 52 Scottish terrorists, a total of 286 years in jail. The cost to the State in terms of damage has been several million pounds. The cost of the police and Special Branch activities to track down the terrorists has been incalculable. Add to this the undoubtedly massive investment of the various agencies of the "Anglo-American security and intelligence services" in their programme of ensuring Scotland's political climate remains stable and it can be seen that the "war" has cost millions – some admittedly not borne by the British tax-payer.

And the secret war continues. The mysterious death of Willie McRae has provided extremists with what they clearly regard as a "martyr". Whatever the truth of this claim, it seems unlikely that tartan terrorism will disappear overnight. It is considered that the SNLA now exists in name only but that some members in Scotland have reformed the organisation, under new leadership, whose new name and aims are presently unknown but which is intent on attacking "military targets" and the symbols of "English rule" at some time in the future. These claims, if proved accurate, will be treated with great attention by the authorities. Clearly, the threat is always present in modern society. It is in fact already endemic in Scotland, symptomatic perhaps of the powerlessness of a nation which remains stateless against the wishes of the majority of her population. Continued failure to respond to legitimate Scottish demands for self-government could cause a greater and more widespread sense of alienation. Until democracy in Scotland can be clearly seen to fulfil the needs of the Scots, the threat of new outbreaks of tartan terrorism will continue to exist and some Scots will regard themselves at war with British rule.

14   INSIDE THE ANGLO-AMERICAN
STATE

THE events of this book prove that the forces involved in combating the tartan terrorists are not merely the Scottish Police and Special Branch. Nor has the State merely been reacting to the incidents as they occur. The State has been involved in pre-emptive action in all phases of "tartan terrorism". The events themselves have had wider implications within the Cold War scenario of the 1970s and early 1980s and Scotland's role as a key part of the Anglo-American State means that her domestic politics have come under considerable scrutiny from external forces.

The decision to authorise a 15-month, 24-hour surveillance of several suspected members of the "Tartan Army" in 1975 was taken at Cabinet level – undoubtedly upon the advice of senior intelligence officers. The attempt to implicate William Wolfe, Chairman of the SNP, with the activities of the APG clearly also came from instructions from similar quarters. The surveillance of Willie McRae and his mysterious death seems also to show the hand of the Security and Intelligence Services. McRae's death was referred through the Special Branch Regional Co-ordinator to the SIS/Police liaison officer who is an Under-Secretary of State at the

Home Office. These matters show the involvement of the SIS in what might normally be regarded as purely police business. Clearly, there was SIS involvement, but how far did it extend and what part did the CIA play in Scottish politics?

When the CIA arrived in force in Scotland, with the Polaris missiles, in 1961 – the high point of their interference in European affairs and worldwide – their Head of Counter-Intelligence was James Angleton. He wanted to set up a separate CIA operation in the UK and had feelings of grave mistrust about the SIS, based on his belief that it was riddled with enemy spies. Angleton had a paranoia about intelligence information coming into the hands of politicians and believed that the Prime Minister, Harold Wilson, the political master of the SIS, was a KGB agent! There was some evidence, obtained from Czeckoslovakian defectors, of Soviet penetration into the Labour Party, CND, trade unions and even MI5. Although a very close relationship was forged between the CIA and SIS – "a core element" in the special military partnership of the UK and USA – the CIA were extremely wary of sharing all their information. Many battles were fought out at the top levels of both agencies. One of the most vicious concerned the CIA's campaign to destabilise Harold Wilson, in which the SIS participated half-heartedly. The operation, codenamed "Oatsheaf" in the MI5 files, aimed to prove Wilson's Soviet links through his friendship with industrialist Joseph Kagan and through his own visits to Russia. CIA officers put pressure on their SIS counterparts to adopt the campaign and a powerful section within SIS did back it. Meanwhile, the CIA persevered with its own independent covert approach and began low-level operations within CND and the Labour Party. Peter Wright, in *Spycatcher*, has reported on further American pressure on SIS to adopt a more pro-American direction. It was nothing less than a naked bid by the Americans to control the British agencies.

The CIA routinely monitors all "subversive" groups and their foreign links. They were involved in Scotland especially because of the potential threat to the oil installations and to American investment such as in "Silicon Glen". Many US Corporations established themselves in Scotland, particularly in the early 1970s, and tartan terrorism and industrial unrest would put at risk further investment and could create economic instability. Then, of course, there is an enormous US military presence in Scotland. "Scotland is very much the forward base in the UK, the front line of Western Defence Strategy," according to Air Vice-Marshall Sir David Brook. The US Services in Scotland worked very hard at their image, creating the myth of polite, generous and friendly "all-American boys" while allowing little hard information about their activities or the sheer scale of their presence to filter out. A leading US Admiral has gone on record expressing his shame at the secretive manner in which the indigenous population have been treated. Even major disasters have been effectively "hushed up". Major leaks of radioactive material were not notified to the British Government, and certainly not the British public. Many collisions of nuclear submarines with fishing boats have occurred, nets have been fouled, pollutants and radioactive material almost routinely dumped close in to shore without warnings being given. In bases "remotely located" (the US Navy's own description of its bases in Scotland) housing was permitted as close as 100 yards from nuclear installations – although in the USA they are not permitted within three miles. Nor has the American presence led to as much employment as is often postulated. The US Services bring their own supplies and their own staff. Scotland is still foreign territory to them, a land which they expect to have the use of for only 60 days in the event of a nuclear war – expendable along with everything and everyone in it. But there have been even more serious incidents; when a MIRV Poseidon warhead charged with unstable LX09 explosive was "dropped" against the mother ship, USS *Holland*, in the Holy Loch in 1981, there was an alpha alert. Had this warhead been triggered, it would have obliterated the city of Glasgow and most of the conurbations of the lower Clyde, yet the British Government, far less the public, were never officially informed. Nor were they informed in 1973 when the US nuclear forces were put on to Def Con 2 readiness at the time of the Yom Kippur War or in 1980 when the Iran hostages' rescue attempt failed. In 1983 when the USA invaded Grenada, unilateral American action was taken from bases on British soil without prior consultation with the UK Government, which repeated itself in 1986 when US aircraft from British bases were used in the raid on Libya. US nuclear submarines from Scottish bases in Holy Loch make constant incursions into Soviet waters, once even entering Vladivostock harbour. Similarly, long-range reconnaissance planes daily fly over Soviet airspace from British bases, typically Lossiemouth. All this clearly shows that, despite the close partnership, the "special relationship", it is the USA who are very much the masters and capable of independent action.

Other incidents too have been "hushed up". A US serviceman killed a mother and baby in Dunoon – and was eventually fined the equivalent of £35. US servicemen are, of course, entirely outwith prosecution by British Courts under the United States (Visiting Forces) Act. Yet all of these embarrassing incidents and events have been whitewashed by the powerful US Military publicity machine which operates (like the CIA) from the US Embassy in Grosvenor Square. This operation has been extraordinarily successful in diverting attention from the US presence and its side-effects. Obviously, they were hard at work countering possible political opposition and this too has been highly successful.

CIA operations in Scotland face a problem similar to their operational difficulties in Northern Ireland, where, because of their own domestic political situation with both Republicans and Democrats influenced by a large ethnic Irish population, the CIA cannot be seen to be collaborating with the British in counter-insurgency. So in Scotland too the CIA must tread carefully and in both arenas they do not have a large number of agents on the ground. Instead they have operated through liaison with the Special Branch and SIS and their own low-level network of informants within Scottish political groups and the Scottish Police. This is not the manner in which they operated in many other countries, but in Scotland they needed to create a much more sensitive and covert operation so as not to embarrass their host government. They did seek at first to establish their own independent operation but this was soon abandoned due to upheavals within the service consequent to the Watergate revelations.

The CIA is very much aware of the operations of the SIS within both Northern Ireland and Scotland. The extraordinary testimony of Colin Wallace has exposed the nature of the counter-insurgency methods adopted by SIS: the routine spreading of disinformation, the attempts to discredit nationalist and Labour politicians which included the forging of documents, the spreading of slanderous rumours and black propaganda, the creation of spurious political organisations – which on at least one occasion led to the death of an entirely innocent man – and not least the claimed "framing" of Wallace himself on a murder charge after he leaked the story of the Kincora Boys' Home scandal. The SIS were turning a blind eye to the sexual abuse of orphan boys because the abusers were supplying useful information to them. Yet Wallace was a hardworking member of the SIS whose zeal and skill at his trade was attested to by many colleagues. If the SIS could do this to one of their own, why should we doubt that they attempt similar activities against perceived enemies of the State? How can we doubt that they were involved in similar activities against the Labour Party and the SNP, not to mention the alleged sympathisers of the tartan terrorists in mainland Britain?

The situation in Northern Ireland has been useful as a training ground for a wide range of military tactics such as those espoused by Frank Kitson and has also afforded a pretext for the introduction of authoritarian legislation within the UK mainland, such as the Prevention of Terrorism Acts, 1974 and 1976. The PTA is now widely used in Scotland to deal with non-Irish related events and groups. Under the guise of dealing with "imported" terrorism from Northern Ireland, political fringe groups within Scotland have been investigated in depth. Indeed, partly because of the availability of their "training-ground" in Northern Ireland, the British Army and the SIS have acquired an unrivalled expertise in counter-insurgency. They have shared their information from a position of considerable authority with other countries at numerous anti-terrorist summits.

The Scottish Police and even their Special Branch sections may have remained largely unaware of the wider context of their day-to-day activities to combat terrorism within Scotland but they were at the sharp end of a very wide-ranging operation. Information gathered was passed to the very highest levels of the Special Branch where there were indivisible links with the SIS and CIA – at levels where there is a complete lack of public accountability. Once the information was gathered it was often shared around these separate agencies – but not always, for there has always been a rivalry between them. Their response to the potential threats has not always been unified. There was often a marked lack of co-operation. Another reason for this was that the command structure of each agency was never entirely stable. Like the terrorist groups, the leadership of each agency has been subject to faction-fighting, endemic rivalry, backstabbing and empire-building. Right-wing groups battled with more moderate elements for complete control. Some of these factions would stop at nothing to achieve their aims. Even Prime Ministers, as has been already noted, were not immune from their plotting.

In the mid-1970s, Scottish politics was "on the boil" and there was great political mobility. It was a time of considerable risk for both the US Military Services Overseas – facing a political challenge – and for the UK Government – facing considerable industrial unrest. Many "right-thinking" individuals in Government or in the apparatus of the Anglo-American State were prepared to take risks to combat the dual menace. Links were forged between security and intelligence services and international businessmen of the N.M. Rothschild group who were "working to prevent the return of a Labour Government" which they felt "would spell the end of all the freedoms we know and cherish". MI5 were aware of the group but took no steps to undermine it; many of their chiefs were secretly in favour of the setting up of such organisations. The "conspiracy" was not publicly revealed – it would have caused a scandal and possibly a backlash against the right wing – but its implications were very wide-ranging. The CIA and SIS would provide damaging information on politicians to be leaked to sympathetic press barons, such as Lord Cecil King of the *Daily Mirror* group. The businessmen would raise funds and the military leaders would plan a coup to save the country. The groups involved in this conspiracy were united in their belief that the country was on the brink of social and economic breakdown. It can be speculated that the Rothschild group had connections with individuals and companies who wished to secure political stability in Scotland. Some of these companies contributed to the setting up and founding of right-wing organisations such as the Economic League which has headquarters in Glasgow which monitored and collected information on known "subversives" such as political and trade union activists and provided the information, for a fee, to their friends in industry. The Economic League has a blacklist containing over 25,000 "subversives" which is subscribed to by over 2,000 UK companies. It claims its services are "essential in identifying revolutionary activists and their supporters". In May 1990 the first ever public investigation, by a House of Commons Select Committee, was held into the sinister activities of the League. The far right also jointly set up *ad hoc* political groups such as the "Scotland Is British" campaign which was very well funded to fight against Scottish devolution. Funds were channelled to the "Scotland Says No" campaign for the same purpose. Then too, other organisations such as the Freedom Association and Aims of Industry were set up. The Confederation of British Industry in Scotland also assumed a highly political role in combating devolution, and leading industrialists such as Lord Weir frequently issue statements suggesting that if Scots vote for home rule, thousands of jobs will be lost (a less than subtle form of industrial blackmail).

Military leaders like General William Walker and Colonel David Stirling believed (like the APG!) in "contingency planning" and began training paramilitary forces for when they would have to "restore order" in the event of imminent civil breakdown. For them, tartan terrorism was a convenient smokescreen and provided a good pretext for legitimising their authoritarian ideas. In a sense, it was because of Scotland's mobile political climate and tartan terrorism that Scotland became virtually a university for the far right. "Scotland is where the action is . . . those who will make the decisions are here or are arriving," said Richard Funkhauser, the US Consul to Scotland, in 1976 and what he was really getting at was the situation developing in Scotland where threatening levels of popular support for the SNP, cross-party support for anti-nuclear, anti-NATO attitudes and worsening incidents of tartan terrorism coupled with significant industrial unrest genuinely seemed to indicate a crisis for the Western Alliance.

Funkhauser's own role has been described as "inordinately political". He had previously been Ambassador to the African oil-producing nation of Gabon, where the CIA had been less concerned with the sensitive feelings of the host country. His appointment to Scotland indicates the USA's preoccupation with Scotland for Funkhauser was a much higher grade of consular official than might have been expected as consul of a friendly country. Soon after his arrival in Scotland he began to take a course of action described as "a gung-ho approach", in which he showed his willingness to use all sorts of methods to cause embarrassment to those he regarded as potential enemies. Chief among the potential enemies were the SNP, whom he was prepared to go out of his way to discredit and regarded as a serious threat. He held a series of dinners, private meetings and secret briefings and soon expanded his influence within all of Scotland's political groups. He offered money, favours, the prospect of power and influence – and his "stick" was the denial of all of these. He "leaked" official information and US State Department telexes in such a blatantly political way that he soon went too far for President Carter's sensitivities and was ignominiously ordered to return to Washington. He refused to do so and instead joined an oil company as its Head of Security, and was soon recruiting ex-serving US officers into positions in Scotland where they might be useful in preserving the stability of the Anglo-American State. Funkhauser also participated in numerous military anti-terrorist exercises and international seminars by right-wing sponsored academic institutions. The setting-up of the Centre for Strategic Studies and the Institute for the Study of Conflict, both at Edinburgh University, allowed regular get-togethers of top NATO military with SIS and CIA and Police Chiefs for regular briefings on the developing Scottish situation and other areas of mutual concern. Scotland had become the strategic centre of NATO activity on the front line of the Cold War scenario. It was bristling with international "experts" on counter-insurgency and defence specialists and academics with theories on the control of terrorism. Professor Paul Wilkinson, for example, has played a part in the specialist anti-terrorist training of 22 SAS Para and has led the field, from Scotland, in outlining general theories on terrorism.

The right-wing's activities extended far into academia and it is probable that some supposedly independent tertiary education institutions are indirectly funded by NATO.

St Andrews' University, where, coincidentally, only about one third of the students and staff were Scots, generated a right-wing think-tank of students and academics which became associated with the Adam Smith Institute which now has a direct and influential input to Conservative Government policy. Many of the key policy directions emanating from Mrs Thatcher's Government originated within Scottish right-wing politics. The influence of this hot-bed of radical reaction upon those who were involved, particularly those members of the Federation of Conservative Students at St Andrews, has been wide-ranging and has influenced a generation of Tory thinking and led to a basic shift in the Conservative Party towards a more pro-American policy direction.

The serious attempts by the Rothschild group and their associates to take over the State were abandoned by the CIA. But, of course, by then the "conspiracy" had petered out. It was simply not needed any more for the views and values which they shared had achieved a new legitimacy at the heart of Conservative Party power. This had been achieved by a coup against Ted Heath engineered by Airey Neave in 1975 which brought Margaret Thatcher into the leadership. Thatcher was more than susceptible to the influence of the far right. It was now only a question of getting her into Number 10 and this was done by concerted action behind the scenes alongside a parliamentary strategy to create a crisis of confidence in Prime Minister Callaghan and prevent him from carrying out his priorities, including the Scotland Act. This enraged the 11 Scottish nationalist MPs. It was then a simple matter to provoke the SNP Parliamentary group – and pressures were brought to bear – into a vote to topple Callaghan, and Thatcher was in. The strategy had been wildly successful and thus the destabilising of the SNP by the manipulation of tartan terrorism was discontinued and replaced by agitation of anti-Labour bias within the SNP through legitimate political channels and the press. The idea was to split the party irrevocably and the move very nearly succeeded in the bitter aftermath of 1979. Then, "nationalist" terrorism virtually disappeared and all that remained was the ideological terrorism springing from the republican socialist tradition.

There are a number of unexplained events in recent British and Scottish politics which hint at foreign or external influence. The parliamentary toppling of the Callaghan Government and the advent of Mrs Thatcher to power is clearly one such. Another is the way in which, during the Devolution Referendum, the pro-devolution side were never able to unite effectively, were sluggish, poorly funded and inconsistent while the anti-devolutionists were united, successful and well funded. The sudden dropping of the highly successful oil campaign of the SNP is another intriguing mystery. The campaign had three phases, all under the general slogan, "It's Scotland's Oil". The initial phase in 1972/3 was a leaflet *To London With Love: Scotland's Oil*. The second phase, in 1973, was *England Expects: Scotland's Oil* and the third phase, in the General Election of February 1974 defined the potential benefits which the oil could bring to Scotland: *It's his oil, It's her oil . . ..* Sales of the purple and black stickers outsold all previous SNP publicity material and were in evidence on every piece of public property in the land. Opinion polls confirmed the tremendous potency of the campaign. An Opinion Research Centre poll in April 1974 found that 66 per cent agreed that Scotland would get little benefit from the oil and 59 per cent agreed that the oil belonged to Scotland and should be used to benefit the Scottish people. Less than a third felt that the oil did not belong to the Scots. Yet this successful campaign never reached its fourth phase, despite the fact that most political campaigns generally take 18 months to begin to make an impact! For whatever reason, the policy was dropped and the SNP's OPEC-style position softened into acquiescence of the Labour-Tory line of acceptance of the right of international oil companies to derive maximum profit without the need for any guarantees on employment for the Scots, or any drastic change in licence fees or Government royalties.

Professor Roger Levy in *Nationalism at the Crossroads* (1990) has suggested that "internal and external restraints exercised an enormous influence on party [SNP] strategy." The élite, whose subjective analyses formed party policy were "very influenced" by these factors. "Pressure came from a new source to modify the party's OPEC-style policy – requests from MPs of *other* parties and some SNP members . . .". According to SNP Convener Gordon Wilson, elements within the National Executive grew bored with the campaign and the idea of a single issue strategy and after several attempts succeeded in getting the policy dropped. The challenge to American oil company investment, like the earlier challenges to the US/NATO bases, had been derailed. Oil was the most important single factor in Scottish politics in the 1970s and developed a crucial significance after the Yom Kippur War in October 1973 and the resultant OPEC crisis. Had the SNP succeeded at that time, as indeed looked likely, then the threat to the supply of crude oil to the American domestic market was as obvious as the possibility of destabilisation of the Western Defence Alliance.

Such was the excitement in Scotland that for the first time the wave of outward migration from Scotland was halted and reversed. All kinds of strange people came to Scotland, floating in with the tide, and some soon became involved in Scottish politics. The motivations of these persons can only be guessed at, but by the end of the 1970s, Scotland was much more politically stable – and governed by a right-wing Conservative Government at Westminster whose commitment to the security of the Anglo-American State was total and unquestioning.

BIBLIOGRAPHY

We have consulted a large number of political journals including material from clandestine sources, not publicly available. The list of periodicals consulted included various issues of: *Alba Free Press*, *Carn*, *Catalyst* (1967–74), *Crann-Tara*, *Firinn Albannach* (nos 1–6), *Lochaber Free Press*, *National Liberation* (published by the SNLA Media Group), *New Left Review*, *Nevis Quarterly*, *Pendern*, *Radical Scotland*, *7 Days*, *79 Group News*, *Saorsa* (journal of the SNLA), *Scots Independent*, *Scottish Breakway* (newsletter of the SRSC), *Scottish Marxist*, *Scottish Prisoner* (newsletter of the Scottish Prisoners' Support Committee), *Scottish Republic*, *Scottish Vanguard*, *Scottish Workers' Republic*, *Sgian Dubh*, *Socialist Scotland*, *The Patriot*, *Time Out*, *Wee Red Rampant Lion*, *Welsh Republic*, *Wildcat*, *Y Faner Gogh*.

ACKROYD, Margolis, Rosenhead & Shallice; *The Technology of Political Control*, Pluto Press, 1980

AGEE, Philip; *Inside the Company: CIA Diary*, Stonehill Publishing, 1975

AUBREY, Crispin; *Who's Watching You?*, Penguin, 1981

BAYLIS, John; *Anglo-American Defence Relations, 1939–84*, Macmillan, 1984

BOLD, Alan; *The Letters of Hugh MacDairmid*, Hamish Hamilton, 1984

BRAND, Jack; *The National Movement In Scotland*, Routledge & Kegan Paul, 1978

BROWN, Gordon, Ed.; *The Red Paper on Scotland*, EUSPB, 1975

BRUCE, Steve; *No Pope of Rome*, Mainstream, 1985

BUNYAN, Tony; *The Political Police In Britain*, Quartet, 1977

CAMPBELL, Duncan; *War Plan UK*, Paladin, 1983 and *The Unsinkable Aircraft Carrier*, Michael Joseph, 1984 (plus many articles in *New Statesman*)

CAMPBELL, James; Editor, *Alternative Edinburgh*, EUSPB, 1979

CLEWS, Roy; *To Dream Of Freedom*, Y Lolfa, 1980

COOGAN, Tim Pat; *The IRA*, Fontana Books, 1980

CUTLER, James, and Rob Edwards; *Britain's Nuclear Nightmare*, Sphere, 1988

DALYELL, Tam; *Devolution: The End of Britain*, Cape, 1977

DONALDSON, Arthur; *Ways of Scottish Nationalism*, SNP Publications, 1976

DONN, Gari, Ed.; *Missiles, Reactors and Civil Liberties*, SCCL, 1983

DRUCKER, Henry; *Breakaway: The Scottish Labour Party*, EUSPB, 1976

DUKE, Simon; *US Defence Bases in the United Kingdom*, Macmillan, 1987

ELLIS, Peter Beresford, and Seamus Mac A'Ghobhainn; *Scottish Insurrection of 1820*, Gollancz, 1970

FAIRBAIRN, Zoe; *Study War No More*, CND, 1974

FERGUSON, Sir James; *The Declaration of Arbroath*, Edinburgh University Press, 1970

FREEDMAN, Lawrence; *US Intelligence and the Soviet Strategic Threat*, Princeton University Press, 1986

GREENBERG, William; *The Flags of the Forgotten*, Clifton Books, 1969

HARVIE, Christopher; *No Gods and Precious Few Heroes*, Arnold, 1981; *Scotland and Nationalism*, Allen and Unwin, 1977

HOOPER, David; *Official Secrets*, Coronet, 1988

HURD, Douglas, and Andrew Osmond; *Scotch on the Rocks*, Fontana, 1971

KITSON, Frank; *Low Intensity Operations*, Faber, 1971

LAMONT, Archie; *How Scots Opposed The Peacetime Call-Up*, Scots Secretariat booklet, 1964

LEVY, Roger; *Nationalism at the Crossroads*, Scottish Academic Press, 1990

MACDIARMID, Hugh; *A Political Speech*, Reprographia, 1972

MACLEAN, Colin, Ed.; *The Crown and the Thistle*, Scottish Academic Press, 1979

McKAY, Ron, and Brian Barr; *The Story of the Scottish Daily News*, Canongate, 1976

MULHOLLAND, Robert; *Scotland's Freedom Struggle*, Crann-Tara, 1978

NAIRN, Tom; *The Break-up of Britain*, Verso, 1981

SCORER, Catherine, and Patricia Hewitt; *The Prevention of Terrorism Act – The Case for Repeal*, NCCL, 1981

SWIFT, Graham; *Death of a Rose-Grower*; *Who Killed Hilda Murrell?* Cecil Woolf, 1985

THOMPSON, E. P.; *The State Versus Its Enemies*, Merlin Press, 1979

TRANTER, Nigel; *Nigel Tranter's Scotland, A Very Personal Review*, Richard Drew, 1981

WEBB, Keith; *The Growth of Nationalism in Scotland*, Molendinar Press, 1977

WILKINSON, Paul, Ed.; *British Perspectives on Terrorism*, Allen & Unwin, 1981; and *Terrorism and the Liberal State*, Macmillan, 1977

WILLIAMS, Rhodri, Ed.; *John Jenkins' Prison Letters*, Y Lolfa, 1981

WOLFE, William; *Scotland Lives*, Reprographia, 1973

WOOD, Wendy; *Yours Sincerely For Scotland*, Arthur Bowyer, 1970

WRIGHT, Gordon; *MacDiarmid: An Illustrated Biography*, Gordon Wright Publishing, 1977

WRIGHT, Peter; *Spycatcher*, Heineman (Australia) 1987

BRITAIN'S SECRET WAR

Also the following publications:

Operation Fire, Welsh Campaign for Civil and Political Liberties, 1980

Poison In Our Hills: The First Inquiry on Atomic Waste Burial, SCRAM, 1980

Interception of Telecommunications Act 1985; Chapter 56; Report of the Commissioner for 1988, HMSO, 1989

Chief Constables' *Annual Reports* for Central, Dumfries & Galloway, Fife, Grampian, Lothian & Borders, Northern, Strathclyde and Tayside Police Forces, 1988/89

Tapping The Telephone, POEU Guide, 1980

INDEX

INDEX